TEACHING TRANSLATION FROM SPANISH TO ENGLISH

DIDACTICS OF TRANSLATION SERIES

Catering to the needs of students in schools of translation and interpretation, the textbooks published in this series are also very helpful to professional translators and interpreters who wish to improve their technique. The series' titles cover various fields in the discipline such as general translation and specialized translation as well as editing, writing, and lexicology for translators. Works that analyse the discipline from a more theoretical or practical point of view can be found in the "Perspectives on Translation" series. Both series welcome manuscripts written in either English or French.

Advisory committee

Jean Delisle, Series Director, University of Ottawa
Marie-Christine Aubin, Collège universitaire de Saint-Boniface
Annie Brisset, University of Ottawa
Luise von Flotow, University of Ottawa
Daniel Simeoni, McMaster University
Paul St Pierre, Université de Montréal
Lawrence Venuti, Temple University (Philadelphia)
Agnès Whitfield, York University

In the same series

Jean Delisle, *La traduction raisonnée: Manuel d'initiation à la traduction professionnelle de l'anglais vers le français*, 1993
Jean Delisle, *La traduction raisonnée: Livre du maître*, 1993

Allison Beeby LONSDALE

TEACHING TRANSLATION FROM SPANISH TO ENGLISH

WORLDS BEYOND WORDS

"Didactics of Translation Series, No. 3"
University of Ottawa Press

University of Ottawa Press gratefully acknowledges the support extended to its publishing program by the Canada Council, the Department of Canadian Heritage, and the University of Ottawa.

CANADIAN CATALOGUING IN PUBLICATION DATA

Beeby Lonsdale, Allison, 1948–
    Teaching Translation from Spanish to English: Worlds beyond Words

(Didactics of Translation; 3)

Includes bibliographical references.
ISBN 0-7766-0399-X

1. Spanish language—Translating into English—Study and teaching (Higher).
2. Translating and interpreting—Study and teaching (Higher).   I. Title.   II. Series

PC4498.B43 1996   428'.0261   C96-900322-6

Cover design: Robert Dolbec
Typesetting: Infographie G.L.

Excerpt from *Conversations with Socrates* by Xenophon on pp. 222–223, edited by Robin Waterfield (Penguin Classics, 1990). Introduction © Robin Waterfield, 1990. Page 1 reproduced by permission of Penguin Books Ltd.

Excerpt from *Estructura económica internacional* on pp. 150–152 © Ramón Tamames, reproduced by his permission

"Un hombre providencial" (1991) on p. 82, "Fallece Kim Philby" (1989) on pp. 127–128, and excerpts from "La amenaza del 'frente' sur" (1991) on pp. 50–51, "*Triunfo*, el eslabón perdido" (1992) on p. 85, "Llueve sobre mojado" (1992) on p. 194, and "Preguntitas" (1991) on pp. 217–218 © El País International, S.A.

"Cabeza rapada" on pp. 157–158 © Antonia Gala

The five comic strips by Quino on pp. 145–147 are reproduced by permission of Editorial Lumen, S.A.

Excerpt from *A Brief History of Time* by Stephen Hawking on pp. 227–228 reproduced by permission of Al Zuckerman at Writers House Inc.

© University of Ottawa Press, 1996
ISBN 0-7766-0399-X
Printed in Canada

TABLE OF CONTENTS

PART 3
METHODOLOGICAL FRAMEWORK

PART 4
UNDERSTANDING PRINCIPLES AND LEARNING SKILLS

FOREWORD

Now that the twentieth century, the era of translation, is coming to a close, there is no doubt that Translation Studies is fully established as a discipline of its own. Recent theoretical research has shown that translation is not only a textual operation, but also an act of communication and a cognitive process. Therefore, translation research should start from this triple perspective and, fortunately, can now count on a minimum theoretical foundation based on discourse analysis of comparative texts, the translator's cognitive processes, and the factors that intervene in translation as an act of communication. These approaches are often taken in isolation or as mutually exclusive; however, in my opinion, only by integrating them can our discipline advance. *Teaching Translation from Spanish to English: Worlds beyond Words* is situated within this integrating line of research, taking into account not only the internal relationships between original text and translated text, but also the relationships between text and context, and the cognitive processes involved.

James Holmes' 1972 classification of Translation Studies[1] is beginning to be a reality. At that time the three separate branches described by Holmes—theoretical, descriptive, and applied—were only just emerging. To a certain extent, Holmes was a prophet, who foresaw the future of our discipline. Both theoretical and descriptive translation studies have multiplied in recent years, but perhaps the advances have been fewer in applied translation studies (translation teaching, translation in language teaching, and translation criticism and evaluation).

Given the worldwide importance of translation and translator training, and the rise of Translation Studies, translation teaching has not developed as fast as one might expect. Most of the publications in translation teaching have been either contrastive (which identify learning problems in translation training with problems of a contrastive nature), or theoretical with a few practical exercises (which

---

1. "The Name and Nature of Translation Studies," in *Translated: Papers on Literary Translation and Translation Studies* (Amsterdam: Rodopi, 1988). This article has been published on several occasions: 1972, 1975, 1987.

confuse learning problems in translation training with problems of translation theory). Thus, translation teaching still lacks clearly defined learning objectives and a specific methodological framework. Jean Delisle has been a pioneer in developing translation-teaching methods based on learning objectives which go beyond contrastive linguistics.[2] He proposes a heuristic methodology with one main objective for the student—to discover the principles necessary for a correct development of the translation process.

I believe that the most important challenge facing translation-teaching research is defining general and specific learner objectives for direct and inverse translation, and for each branch of specialized translation (technical and scientific translation; economic, legal, and administrative translation; audiovisual translation; and literary translation). At the same time we have to develop appropriate methodologies and learning activities aimed at achieving these objectives. Of course, we still have a long way to go and we need empirical research into the acquisition of translator competence at different levels that will help us to define learner objectives and methodologies more clearly. This research will help us to distinguish between problems of translation (i.e. the problems of a professional translator) and the problems of learning to translate (i.e. the problems of an apprentice translator). It will also help us to separate the learning objectives in the beginner stages of translation training from the different branches of specialized translation and from inverse translation.

Allison Beeby's book should be seen as an advance in this field, defining specific learner objectives and a methodological framework. It fills an urgent need for teaching methodologies that avoid the pitfalls outlined above, teaching proposals for translation between Spanish and English, and, above all, specific teaching methodologies for translation into the foreign language. Translation theorists have concentrated on translation into the mother tongue (considered the only "real" translation) and have ignored translation into the foreign language despite its importance in the work market and the fact that it is taught in most translator and interpreter training centres. The specific nature of the inverse translation process, which implies greater difficulties in the reformulation stage, is reflected in the specific nature of the work market that tends to be confined to standardized or static text types, such as commercial or legal texts, and conversation interpreting. Thus, teaching inverse translation should be distinguished from teaching direct translation by giving full importance to the specific nature of the process and the market.

Teaching Translation from Spanish to English: Worlds beyond Words is important because it fulfils a real need in translation-teaching methodology, due to the absence of research into inverse translation. This book demonstrates the specificity of translating into the foreign language and proposes interesting and varied teaching

---

2. See *L'analyse du discours comme méthode de traduction* (Ottawa: University of Ottawa Press, 1980) and *La traduction raisonnée* (Ottawa: University of Ottawa Press, 1993).

strategies. It has the further merit of proposing a theoretical framework that integrates process and product, and a teaching methodology that is designed to achieve learner objectives. I am sure that the proposals made here will be of great use to translator trainers and trainees.

Amparo Hurtado Albir
Barcelona, March 1996

PREFACE

This book is the result of conclusions drawn from two differing but complementary perspectives. The first is the practical perspective gained from exposure to the problems of translating and teaching translating. The second is the theoretical perspective gained from exposure to representatives of many different schools of translation studies. Through my job at the Faculty of Translators and Interpreters of the Universidad Autónoma de Barcelona, I have had the privilege of attending seminars with and talking to E. Coseriu, J. Delisle, E. Etkind, V. García Yebra, B. Hatim, J.R. Ladmiral, M. Lederer, I. Mason, G. Mounin, P. Newmark, E. Nida, S. Nirenburg, K. Reiss, and D. Seleskovitch.

My personal interest in some of the central issues discussed in this book began at a very early age. Born in Amoy, China, and brought up in Taiwan, speaking Taiwanese and English, I learned to appreciate misunderstandings due to "translation" errors. One of the ongoing discussions in my home was the question of deverbalization: my father maintained that there was no thought without words and my mother argued for the possibility of thought without words. I have taught in England, France, Germany, and Spain; my husband is Spanish, but his father was French; and my children are trilingual in Catalan, Spanish, and English; so linguistic debates continue in my home today.

I started reading translation theory under the guidance of Victor Raskin, who taught me linguistics at Purdue in 1980. When I started to teach translation in Barcelona, I found that what I had read was not of much use in the classroom. My guide was a colleague from the French department, Amparo Hurtado, who introduced me to the Paris School and, in particular, to Jean Delisle at the University of Ottawa. I am also greatly indebted to Basil Hatim and Ian Mason.

I am grateful for the help I have received from the Faculty of Translators and Interpreters and the Department of Translation and Interpreting of the Universidad Autónoma de Barcelona. I have probably learned the most from my students, who continue to amaze me with their ability to learn the difficult skill of translating into a foreign language and to have fun in the process.

GLOSSARY

Boldface indicates terms defined elsewhere in the glossary.

Adequacy. Term by which a given translation procedure can be judged in terms of the purpose of the translation. (Preferred to **Equivalence**.)

AL. "A" language (native language).

Anaphoric. Back reference.

Appropriateness. The suitability of language use to its context.

Bilingualism. True bilingualism; native-language competence and performance in more than one language is very rare.

BL. "B" language (active foreign language).

Bottom-up. Processing a text on the basis of surface textual evidence. *See also* **Top-down**.

Cataphoric. Forward reference.

Cognitive environment. The set of assumptions, beliefs, knowledge, and so on shared and referred to by language users.

Coherence. The network of semantic relations that organize and create a text by establishing continuity of sense.

Cohesion. The surface network of lexical, grammatical, and other relations that provide formal links between various parts of a text.

Collocation. The tendency of certain words to co-occur regularly in a given language.

Comment. The part of a sentence that has most communicative importance or provides new information. *See also* **Topic**.

Comprehension. First stage in the translation process, when the translator makes sense of a sequence of sounds or graphic symbols. *See also* **Deverbalization; Reformulation; Verification**.

Conjunction. A word or phrase that links together two clauses, groups, or words. In this work it is also used to refer to the process by which **cohesion** is formed.

Connotation. Additional meanings that a lexical item acquires beyond the primary, denotational meaning. *See also* **Denotation.**

Consecutive interpreting. Oral translation following a speech or segment of a speech.

Context. The extratextual environment that exerts a determining influence on the language used.

Context of situation. All aspects of the situation in which a language event takes place that are relevant to the interpreting of that event.

Co-operative principle. The assumption that interlocutors co-operate with each other by observing certain conversational maxims.

Cultural codes. Conceptual systems that allow denotative meanings to take on extra connotative meanings.

Deixis. Formal features of language (demonstratives, personal pronouns, tense, and so on) that relate the concepts and entities evoked to the time and place of utterance.

Denotation. The primary meaning of a lexical item, involving its relation to the nonlinguistic entities that it represents. *See also* **Connotation.**

Deverbalization. Second stage in the translation process, stage of language-free semantic representation. *See also* **Comprehension; Reformulation; Verification.**

Dialect (geographical/temporal/social/standard). Variation in language performance depending on the characteristics of the user.

Directionality. Refers to whether the translator is working from **BL** to **AL**, **AL** to **BL**, or any other possible combination.

Equivalence. Equivalence not only of content but also of form between **SLT** and **TLT.**

Explicature. The making explicit of an implied meaning. *See also* **Implicature.**

Field. Aspect of **register**, variation in language according to the use to which it is put in various professional and social settings, such as scientific or legal discourse. *See also* **Mode; Tenor.**

Genre. Conventional forms of texts associated with particular types of social occasion (sonnet, cooking recipe, and so on).

Hyponym. A specific word in a **semantic field.** *See also* **Superordinate.**

Idiolect. Features of language-use characteristic of an individual language user.

Illocutionary. Having to do with the intentions of the speaker of an utterance.

Implicature. An implied meaning derived from an utterance on the basis of a shared cultural code. *See also* **Explicature.**

Initiator. The part of a **sign** that serves to identify it. *See also* **Interpretant; Object.**

Interpretant. The effect that a **sign** is meant to convey. *See also* **Initiator; Object.**

Intersemiotic translation. Translating from one semiotic code to another.

Intertextuality. A precondition for the intelligibility of texts, involving the dependence of one text on another.

Inverse translation. Translation from the translator's **AL** to his or her **BL**.

Lexical set. (a) Words and expressions within a **semantic field**. (b) Items that collocate with a specific word or expression.

Locutionary. Having to do with the act of uttering.

Macrostructural processing. Another term for **top-down** processing.

Marked. *See* **Unmarked.**

Metalanguage. The use of language to comment on language.

Microstructural processing. Another term for **bottom-up** processing.

Mode. Aspect of **register**, the medium selected for language activity: speech, writing, and so on. *See also* **Field; Tenor.**

Object. The part of a **sign** that serves as a vehicle of the sign itself. *See also* **Initiator; Interpretant.**

Perlocutionary. Having to do with the effect intended in uttering a sentence.

Pragmatic dimension. A dimension of context that controls intention.

Prose translation. Translation from the translator's **AL** to his or her **BL**.

Reformulation. Third stage in the translation process, when the translator expresses what he or she has understood in the first and second stages. *See also* **Comprehension; Deverbalization; Verification.**

Register. The tendency to pattern language behaviour in relation to a particular type of activity. *See also* **Field; Mode; Tenor.**

Reiteration. The recurrence or repetition of an item or phrase in a text.

Relevance. One of the aspects of the co-operative principle whereby interlocutors seek to relate their utterances to the current situation.

Restricted code (register). Any variety of language that is characterized by a restricted range of formal properties (phonology, lexis, and grammar).

Rheme. The part of a sentence that occurs last and usually has most communicative importance. *See also* **Theme.**

Semantic field. Conceptual field that reflects the divisions and subdivisions imposed by a linguistic community on the continuum of experience.

Semiotic dimension. A dimension of **context** that regulates the relationship of texts to each other as **signs**.

Service translation. Newmark's term for translation from **AL** to **BL**.

Sign. A unit of signifier plus signified in which the linguistic form (signifier) stands for a concrete object or concept (signified).

Simultaneous interpreting. Oral and simultaneous translation of a speech.

Skopos. Term used by a German school of translation theorists to denote the purpose for which a text is translated.

SL. Source language.

SLT. Source-language text.

Speech act. The action that is intended in the utterance of a sentence.

Style. Variation in language-use achieved by choosing from the range of phonological, lexical, and grammatical resources of a language in order to produce some effect.

Superordinate. A general word in a **semantic field**. The meaning of a superordinate includes the meaning of all its **hyponyms**.

Tenor. Aspect of **register** that reflects the relationship between addresser and addressee, such as level of formality, distance. *See also* **Field; Mode**.

Text. A set of mutually relevant communicative functions, structured in such a way as to achieve an over-all rhetorical purpose.

Text linguistics. The branch of linguistics that analyzes spoken and written texts above the level of individual sentences.

Text type. Classification of texts according to the parameters of **register: field, mode, tenor**.

Text-type focus. The aspect of **context** that is seen to be the dominant function of a text and that determines **text type**.

Theme. The part of a sentence that occurs first and usually has less communicative importance. *See also* **Rheme**.

Thème. French term for translation from **AL** to **BL**.

TL. Target language.

TLT. Target-language text.

Top-down. Predicting the meaning of a text on the basis of information gathered from contextual and preliminary textual evidence. *See also* **Bottom-up**.

Topic. The part of a sentence that has less communicative importance or carries known information. *See also* **Comment**.

Traducción directa. Spanish term for translation from **BL** to **AL**.

Traducción inversa. Spanish term for translation from **AL** to **BL**.

Unmarked. Certain lexical or grammatical items or structures that are considered to be more common than other structures that are marked for a particular effect.

Usage. The meaning of a linguistic item in terms of its **denotation** within the linguistic system.

Use. Aspect of language variation relating to what a user is doing with language.

Verification. Fourth stage in the translation process, when the translator returns to the **SLT** to check if the sense expressed in the **TLT** is the same. *See also* **Comprehension; Deverbalization; Reformulation.**

Version. French term for translation from **BL** to **AL**.

Vouloir dire. Preverbal intention behind an utterance.

World knowledge. Whatever extralinguistic or real-world factors are brought into text-processing activity.

PART I

INTRODUCTION

The greatest pest of speech is frequency of translation.
(Samuel Johnson, "Preface," *A Dictionary*, 1755: xii)

CHAPTER 1

THE IMPORTANCE OF TRANSLATION

Professional translators have been around for nearly five thousand years, and yet, like members of another of the "oldest professions," they are often forgotten, underrated, and misunderstood by the general public. However, the importance of translation should not be underestimated, particularly in a world that has to learn to husband its resources as one world or perish in the attempt. Without translators, commerce, trade, international relations, politics, law, science, and art would be severely limited, and in some cases would wither away. "Shoot first and talk later" would be the order of the day.

The tremendous expansion of international relations in the twentieth century has led to an exponential growth in the number of texts translated every year and in the number of professional translators. However, recognition of the importance of this profession has been slow. In Spain, for example, translation and interpreting were not recognized as an independent area of research until 1991.

Today, translators are joining together in professional organizations to assure better working conditions and professional standards. Nevertheless, there is still a long way to go. Even public entities like Televisión Española do not pay sufficient attention to the quality of translation and interpreting. During the 1992 American election campaign, the face-to-face debates between George Bush, Bill Clinton, and Ross Perot were transmitted live on TV2 with simultaneous interpreting. The interpreters were obviously not professionals, and at several points in the debate they failed entirely to get the message across in Spanish. For example, Clinton said that Europe would have to take more responsibility for its own security, but the interpreter said, "Tendremos que ocuparnos de la seguridad de Europa" (We shall have to assure the security of Europe).

Mistakes of this kind can have serious consequences. Basil Hatim (1992) suggested that many of the events leading up to the Gulf War could have been avoided if both George Bush and Saddam Hussein had had better translators.

The Barcelona Olympic Committee prepared its team of translators and interpreters with care. All the same, those responsible for linguistic control often had their work sabotaged by other Olympic officials who did not understand anything about translation quality. The 1992 Olympic Games would not have been possible without the team of translators and interpreters, whose work began many years before the event and is not yet completed. Nevertheless, this letter appeared in *El País Semanal* (16 Aug. 1992, emphasis added):

> **Traductores olímpicos.** Me apena comprobar que en el artículo sobre "Personajes olímpicos" (*El País Semanal*, 19 de julio), que agrupa a 197 personas representantes de los colectivos que han hecho posibles los Juegos Olímpicos, hayan omitido a los traductores e intérpretes; *sin nosotros, Barcelona hubiera sido una inconexa babel en la que la gran idea no se hubiera hecho realidad.*
>
> JOSEP PEÑARROJA
>
> *Vicepresidente de la Asociación Profesional Española de Traductores e Intérpretes, Barcelona.*

The Tower of Babel was so called "because the Lord did there confound the language of all the earth; and from thence did the Lord scatter them abroad upon the face of all the earth" (Genesis 11:8). Fortunately, after Babel there were a few translators around to assure communication among the different language groups.

CHAPTER 2

THE IMPORTANCE OF PROSE TRANSLATION

Translating from the mother tongue into a second language (*traducción inversa, thème*) has become the Cinderella of translating among translators, translation theorists, and teachers of "real" translation (*traducción directa, version*). It is so consistently ignored that it is difficult to know what to call it in English. The traditional English expression "prose translation" is not well known or often used. The 1964 edition of *The Shorter Oxford English Dictionary* defines prose as "expressing or translating in a foreign language, 1805."

Most British and American translation exchange students and Spanish graduates in English philology have never heard of this definition. If they attempt a definition of prose translation, they assume that it means translating ordinary written language, as opposed to poetry. *The Collins Cobuild Dictionary* distinguishes between "prose (uncountable)—ordinary written language in contrast to poetry" and "a prose (countable)—a piece of writing in a foreign language done by a student in a language class; used mainly in British English." There is no reference to prose translation. There are few references to translating into a foreign language in recent literature on translation, and no agreement as to terminology: prose translation, translation from the mother tongue, inverse translation, service translation, translation AL → BL. "Prose translation" is the expression that has been chosen in this book.

According to the Code of Professional Conduct of the Institute of Translating and Interpreting, "a member shall translate only into a language in which he has mother-tongue or equivalent competence." In international organizations such as the United Nations and the European Community, translators are expected to translate into their A language, or mother tongue. This attitude is a natural reaction to the non-texts, or nonsense texts, that are sometimes produced as prose translation. This sign was found in the window of a Majorcan shop: "English well talking. Here speeching American." This one was in a Paris hotel: "Please leave your values at the front desk." The following was posted at the entrance to a camping site in Germany's Black Forest: "It is strictly forbidden on our black forest camping that people of different sex, for instance, men and women, live together in one tent unless they are married with each other for that purpose." However, the shopkeeper in Majorca, the manager of the Paris hotel, and the owner of the camping site in the Black Forest do not have easy access to international "high fliers" with English as their A language. There is no reason that local translators cannot be trained to transfer this kind of message from their AL to their BL: "English spoken. Americans welcome"; "Please leave your valuables with the receptionist"; "Unmarried couples are not allowed to share a tent."[1]

The general public makes no distinction between translating from BL to AL and from AL to BL, and assumes that a translator will have no problem translating in both directions. In popular belief, linguistic competence is symmetrical. In 1989, candidates for a translation post with TVE 2 (San Cugat) were tested not only on their translation from English into Spanish and Catalan, but also from these languages into English. Those in charge were unaware of the problems involved in translating into the foreign language and expected a level similar to that reached in Spanish and Catalan. They assumed that anyone who "knows" Spanish and English should be able to translate in both directions. Translators know that linguistic competence is rarely symmetrical. True bilingualism (in which both languages are equally developed) is a rare phenomenon. Catalonia is a bilingual society, and most people speak both Catalan and Spanish. However, in individual speakers one language is always more developed than the other.

Very few authors have written about prose translation. Ladmiral wrote about it only to deny its existence—"Le thème n'existe pas." He recognized it as a pedagogical exercise to test performance, but as a professional aim it was "une espérance démesurée et de plus une exigence absurde" (1979: 40–50). In fact, in France, a metaphor for a brilliant student used to be "un élève fort en thème."

No one would deny the difficulties involved in translating into a foreign language, and yet it is a possibility. Newmark admitted that "brief translations from native to foreign language are useful for the consolidation and testing of spoken and written utterances" (1981: 184). Later, he introduced the term "service translation, i.e. translation from one's language of habitual use into another language. The term is not widely used, but as the practice is necessary in most countries, a term is required"(1988: 52).

The practice is necessary in most countries. This has always been the case, and it is a growing trend in most parts of the world, particularly with the predominance of English as an international trade language. Translators of "exotic" languages often have to work into their B language. This is true of the Japanese and Chinese translators in Barcelona, because there are too few native Spanish speakers with high enough levels of Japanese and Chinese. (All of Mishima's novels have been

---

1. These examples were suggested by second-year Spanish students.

translated into Spanish from English translations.) It is a common practice in the Scandinavian countries, where English standards are very high and there are few native English speakers with adequate competence in, for instance, Finnish or Swedish.

The importance of English as an international trade language means that many Spanish translators sometimes have to work into English. English is so widespread that translation clients are likely to have passive competence in English and expect their linguistic experts to offer active competence. Many businesspeople, technicians, scientists, and politicians know enough English to be able to read and understand texts in their own fields. However, they need professional help to write a text in English, whether it is a letter, a speech, an article, an advertisement, the presentation of a research project or new technology, or instructions on how to use a new product. In 1985, teachers at the School of Translators in Mons, Belgium, said that market conditions had forced them to insist on near-native performance in English.

Furthermore, rapid changes in international relations and technological development require flexibility on all levels, and rigid labour markets are doomed to failure. Translator trainers have an obligation to improve their students' performance in prose translation in the areas where they are most likely to be working. These include many oral situations,[2] such as customer relations, public relations, conversation interpreting, and non-intensive conference interpreting, where less-than-perfect pronunciation and syntax are acceptable if they do not interfere with the communicative situation. Written translations usually include work in restricted registers—business letters, contracts, and so on.

Translating for a local or central government is another area of work. Whereas the translation of legal documents, laws, and legal texts from Spanish to English presents considerable difficulties and should not be attempted in the prose class, interpreting for the police and the courts does not involve the same difficulties. The language has to be accessible to the woman who is reporting the theft of her handbag and to the witness in the courtroom. Because a large number of tourists visit some parts of Spain every year, many police stations and courts have interpreters and translators on the payroll. For example, the police chief of Rosas, the popular Costa Brava resort town, hired a translator with English and German to solve the daily communication problems involving tourists. The translator is expected to work as translator and conversation interpreter in both directions: English ↔ Spanish and German ↔ Spanish. Court interpreters are also expected to do work toward both languages, and at present in Spain there are no specific exams or qualifications required of court interpreters. Work in this field will probably increase as mobility within the European Community and immigration pressures from outside Europe grow.

---

2. Pym (1991) refers to these situations as non-100% situations.

Traductores jurados (official translators who have passed a state exam) are also often expected to translate in both directions. The kinds of texts they translate include those related to foreign trade (such as exportation documents, business letters, business reports, accounts, bills, banking and insurance correspondence, telegrams, and faxes) and to the government (such as birth, marriage, and death certificates, changes of nationality, academic certificates, social-security documents, and tax returns).

In a questionnaire answered by seventeen *traductores e interpretes jurados* in Barcelona in 1991, twelve offered multidirectional translations.[3] Here are the language combinations offered by three of these translators:

a) From: Italian, Romanian, Spanish, Catalan
   To: Italian, Romanian, Spanish, Catalan

b) From: French, English, Italian, Portuguese, Catalan, Spanish
   To: French, English, Spanish

c) From: English, German, Spanish
   To: English, German, Spanish

The work market obviously exists. The question remains whether translators are born (spring fully armed from the *Collins Bilingual Dictionary*), mature on their own over a very long period of time, like a good Rioja, or can be taught.

---

3. Faculty of Translators and Interpreters, Universidad Autónoma de Barcelona.

CHAPTER 3

CAN TRANSLATION BE TAUGHT?

Translation, unfortunately, is something you learn only by doing.
(William Weaver, translator of *The Name of the Rose*)

Much as I admire the work of William Weaver,[4] my own experience denies his statement. Many professional translators, like Weaver, suggest that translating is an art that requires aptitude, practice, and general knowledge, and that the ability to translate is a gift that you either do or do not have. Lanna Castellano doubts whether a translator can be useful before the age of thirty and concludes that maturity is not reached until fifty (1988: 133). I was not trained as a translator, but my reading and research on translation and translation theory have made me a better translator. However, it has taken a very long time. If I had had a teacher to guide me and show how insights from communication theory, discourse analysis, pragmatics, and semiotics can illuminate the translation process, I might have matured as a translator more quickly. Granted that the linguistic competence and encyclopedic knowledge of undergraduate trainee translators is limited by their youth, translation programs can help to speed up their maturing process by providing them with mental maps so that they can recognize the priorities of any translation situation.

In Europe, at least half of the classes at most schools of translation and interpreting are "practical" translation classes. However, these classes should enrich translation competence in the wide sense. According to Cristianna Nord, of the Heidelburg School of Translators,

> The translation exercises develop and enrich not only translation competence in the narrow sense, i.e. transfer competence, but also, wherever necessary, other translation relevant competences, such as (a) linguistic competence in the native language (L1) and in the foreign language (L2) with regard to formal and semantic aspects of vocabulary and grammar, language varieties,

---

4. See also his translations of Italo Calvino and Primo Levi.

register and style, text-type conventions, etc., (b) cultural competence (e.g. studies about the target culture ranging from everyday life to social and political institutions), (c) factual competence in sometimes highly specialised fields (e.g. knowledge of matrimonial law, economic policies, balance of trade, information technology, etc.), and (d) technical competence for documentation and research (use of dictionaries, bibliographic methods, storage of information, etc.). (Nord, 1991: 146)

Translation programs can help students to improve their translating skills. The foundation of schools of translation around the world suggests that this principle is accepted by a wide body of opinion. However, the effectiveness of many translation programs may be questioned: "Existe, pues, a mi juicio, una insuficiencia de planteamientos pedagógicos, ya que, excepto algunos casos aislados . . . no existe una propuesta clara de los objetivos de aprendizaje, sus contenidos, los medios, la progresión, la evaluación" (Hurtado Albir, 1995: 53).

There is a need to define teaching objectives as a framework to structure and systematize translation programs more clearly. Too many translation classes rely on sight translation of a text in class (*traducción a la vista*), which is hardly more efficient as a learning process than is gaining experience through a work placement.

TRADITIONAL TRANSLATION EXERCISES AND LANGUAGE TEACHING

The traditional translation exercise as a part of secondary-school language classes has given teaching translation a bad reputation. The translating of fragments of non-authentic texts out of context to test foreign-language competence is both boring and unenlightening. Some of these fragments have become the basis of popular jokes. In English, *"La plume de ma tante"* is sometimes used to refer to something that is totally irrelevant. Los toreros muertos, a contemporary Spanish rock group, have composed a song made up of these fragments from Spanish textbooks that have passed into folklore, with lyrics such as "My tailor's rich and my mother's in the kitchen." The song might be considered a non-text because it seems to have no semantic coherence, and yet, as a semiotic entity, it expresses the frustrations of young people who have to go through an incomprehensible educational system that fills them with useless facts.

For hundreds of years, translation was the basis of language learning, and even the basis of most other fields of knowledge, because many medieval universities developed out of what were originally schools of translation. Right up to the first part of this century, "the Greats" (Greek, Latin, and philosophy) was considered the best degree for the brightest students at Oxford and Cambridge. "However, over the centuries translation became fossilized. It became less and less associated with the excitement of new discoveries, more and more with the tedium of book learning. What should have been a vital and challenging discipline had degenerated into a pointless routine exercise, a chore, a punishment" (Duff, 1989: 5).

In his classic *The Practical Study of Languages*, Sweet recommended a judicious use of translation into the native language and maintained that translation into the foreign language should be undertaken only if and when a thorough knowledge of the foreign language is already guaranteed—"translating into a partially known language being an impossible task . . . that can be accomplished only under restrictions which make it either an evasion or a failure" (Sweet, 1964: 3).

Developments in language teaching in the mid-twentieth century eliminated translation from the syllabus. The Direct Method was developed out of the American Army Specialized Training Program used in the Second World War. This method, based on Bloomfield's (1933) structuralism and Skinner's (1957) behaviourism, banned the native language from the classroom and proclaimed the predominance of oral language. Language laboratories were given a prominent role in the language class, and students were drilled using stimulus and response.

Cognitive-code language-learning methods began to appear at the beginning of the 1970s. These methods are based on transformational and generative grammar and gestalt and cognitive psychology. The cognitive trend in language learning replaced mechanical pattern drills with exercises that develop a conscious understanding and control of the structures of the foreign language. The learner is encouraged to use linguistic structures actively and creatively in a situation. Some cognitive methods have allowed the carefully dosed use of translation at advanced levels. The exception is the community language-learning method, which is based on oral translation and the learner's own communicative needs right from the beginning of the learning process (La Forge, 1979).

Functionalist language-learning methods developed out of the work of linguists such as M.A.K. Halliday (1973). Educators soon saw the advantages of teaching language in context and for a purpose. The functional-language teaching proposals made by Widdowson (1974) include translation, in particular for teaching English for special purposes, such as scientific English for university students.

Rivers and Temperley (1978) compiled a guide for teaching English using exercises based on different theoretical approaches. Translation exercises were included. Rivers (1972) called translation "the contrastive technique par excellence," but at the same time she suggested translation exercises that were contextualized in such a way as to motivate the students.

The ideal of the Direct Method was never to put learners in a situation in which they were likely to make mistakes, because behaviourist psychology indicated that making mistakes only reinforced bad habits. From a cognitive point of view, mistakes are no longer considered to be always negative; rather, they are seen as a necessary part of the learning process:

> On ne saurait l'éviter parce qu'elle fait partie du processus normal d'apprentissage. En outre, elle constitue un facteur du progrès non négligeable et une excellente filière de formation pédagogique puisqu'elle permet à l'apprenant

> de vérifier la résistance des hypothèses qu'il forme sur le système de la langue
> et d'en avancer d'autres. (Galisson, 1980: 56)

The Direct Method never really took hold in Spain, partly because there were not enough language teachers who could conduct a class in English without resorting to Spanish. In the last two decades or more, however, the predominance of communicative, functionalist language-teaching textbooks in Spain has, on the whole, driven old-style translation exercises out of the modern language class. Nevertheless, some teachers in Spain must still be using them, because traditional translation manuals are still being published.

A recent example of this approach is the *Manual de traducción inversa español-inglés* by José Merino and Patrick Sheerin (1989). The first seventy-five pages of exercises are dedicated to *palabras básicas*, mostly prepositions and adverbs (*a, al, algo [de], algún, alguno, aún, todavía, ya,* and so on). The words are presented in short sentences, with the Spanish on one page and the English on the other—for example,

> 1. Cuesta *a* cien pesetas la pieza.
> 1. It costs a hundred pesetas apiece.
> 3. ¿Te parece que vayamos *a* Roma de vacaciones?
> 3. What do you think of us going to Rome for holidays?

The next sixty pages are dedicated to *puntos gramaticales: adjetivos, adverbios, artículos, condicional, estilo directo, indirecto, futuro,* and so on—for example,

> 618. *Si él tiene razón,* ella está equivocada.
> 618. If he is right, she is wrong.
> 953. ¡Ojalá no *sufras* todo lo que yo he sufrido!
> 953. May you not suffer all [that] I have suffered!

It is hard to imagine how these exercises are going to help students to translate better or to communicate in English, either orally or by translating. Yet the manual then "progresses" to translating *fragmentos literarios,* including poems by such authors as Juan Ramón Jimenez. These texts have a dominant expressive function that would be difficult even for a native English speaker to translate. The only guide given to the student is *"lea y traduzca."*

In Spanish secondary schools, Latin is still a compulsory subject in which fifteen-year-olds have to translate sentences out of context such as: *Acies planitiem ocupat.* → *The army in formation occupies the plain.* (Which army? Where was the plain? When? Who cares?)

A NEW APPROACH TO TRANSLATION IN THE LANGUAGE CLASS

Recently, some communicative, functionalist language teachers (Duff, 1989; Galisson and Costa, 1976; Grellet, 1991; Lavault, 1985) have reconsidered using translation as an important resource for language learning, introducing translation by imaginative and communicative preparatory exercises. Translating authentic texts for a purpose is a communicative activity. Indeed, it is more natural and necessary than are many of the activities invented for language learners. The pragmatic dimension of translation invites all kinds of discussions: there is no such thing as a perfect translation. It is not necessary for all of the work in class to be done alone and in writing; oral exercises can be prepared for pair, group, and class work. Depending on the students' needs and the particular contrasts between language pairs, the teacher can select material to illustrate aspects of language and structure with which the students have difficulties. By working through these difficulties in the A language, students learn to see the difference between rules and usage.

Alan Duff's *Translation* (1989) is a resource book for teachers who wish to use translation as a language-learning activity. It is aimed at students with a wide range of A languages, and the source material is all in English. The final step of most of the exercises is translation from B language to A language, but the main purpose of most of the work is to improve the foreign language—in this case, English.

The Third Language, also by Duff (1981), investigated the problems of all trans-lators when translating into English (even when it is their A language). It is a very useful reference book, defining three qualities that are essential to translating: accu-racy, clarity, and flexibility. Duff believes that these qualities are also essential in any language learning, and this is one of the reasons that he advocates the use of trans-lation in the language class: "It trains the learner to search (flexibility) for the most appropriate words (accuracy) to convey what is meant (clarity). This combination of freedom and constraint allows the students to contribute their thoughts to a dis-cussion which has a clear focus: the text" (Duff, 1989: 7). Duff's pre-translation exercises in English provide an interesting approach to improving the B language: expanding knowledge of vocabulary, register, word order, reference, linking, tense, mood and aspect, idioms, and varieties of language. The translation focus of these exercises makes them ideal material for language classes in a translator training program.

TEACHING PROFESSIONAL TRANSLATION

A clear distinction must be made between teaching translation as part of a training course for professional translators and teaching translation to improve B-language performance. The aim of professional translation teachers is to have their students learn to translate (translation is an end in itself). The object of pedagogical transla-tion is to use translation as a way to improve linguistic skills (translation is the means to an end). In theory, this distinction is widely accepted in most translation faculties in the West, although, in practice, many prose-translation classes do not go beyond the aims of pedagogical translation.

A further confusion seems to have arisen in recent years between teaching translation theory (theories about translation and related disciplines), teaching methodology (understood as translation "strategies" such as transposition, modulation, and compensation, which are in fact a taxonomy of results rather than processes), and teaching translating (criteria for selecting texts, how to approach a text, progression, class techniques, and organization of a teaching module so that students understand the *why* as well as the *how*) (Hurtado Albir, 1994a). This confusion about aims and a real concern to provide a structure for the translation class mean that translation teachers may end up either teaching translation theory or lists of taxonomical translation strategies.

The translation-teaching methodology proposed in this book is based on learner-centred objectives defined as a function of the skills needed by translators: ideal translator communicative competence. Translation theory (the study of the process [translating] and the product [translations]) is used to define translator communicative competence: extralinguistic (pragmatic) knowledge and documentation skills; linguistic competence in both languages; reading skills in the SL and writing skills in the TL; skill in switching codes, registers, and languages; and awareness of interference at all levels.

The task of the translator trainer is to organize, structure, and present the content of the course so as to achieve the learner-centred objectives. Ideal translator competence is, of course, an ideal and cannot be reached in a four-year degree program. The organization, structuring, and presentation of each teacher's program will depend on the levels of student-translator competence, the general socio-historical context, and the goals of the class. Directionality is certainly an important parameter that should be taken into account when preparing a translation program. If the goal is not BL $\rightarrow$ AL but AL $\rightarrow$ BL—that is, if the direction has been changed—this should affect the teaching methodology. So far, however, little attention has been paid to this question. The two most common reactions in the professional prose-translation class have been either to teach pedagogical translation, or to present the students with tasks that are completely beyond their capabilities.

CHAPTER 4

TEACHING PROFESSIONAL PROSE TRANSLATION

Despite the importance of prose translation, it has generally been ignored by translation theory. Nor has much attention been paid to developing a specific teaching methodology, although prose translation is included in all of the European schools of translation. Contemporary theories give the impression that directionality is not important—and perhaps it is not, from a strictly theoretical point of view. A professional translation into the B language should meet the requirements of the client as well as does a translation into the A language (the client being a real person who wants a specific job done—for example, an English-language menu for a restaurateur in Spain); thus, the translator will have to work within the same parameters—semiotic, pragmatic, semantic, syntactic, and lexical—and the translation process will have to pass through the same stages.

The theoretical model may be the same, but putting it into practice will be different. Some stages in the process will be easier for one translator than for the other, and vice versa. Experience has shown that native speakers of English with no training or experience in translation are unlikely to produce better Spanish-English translations than are well-trained Spanish translation graduates, for they make different mistakes and do not necessarily better preserve the function of the translation.

One goal of the European Community has been to encourage student exchanges between European countries. The Erasmus Programme, which includes grants for undergraduate exchanges within the Community, has made it possible for a great number of students to study abroad for a year. The development of student exchanges between schools of translation has meant that students in a Spanish-English translation class in Spain are often not homogeneously Spanish AL speakers; there may be quite a high percentage of English AL speakers. Therefore, the class may be *inversa* for some and *directa* for others. This situation allows teachers to analyze more clearly the effect of directionality, the practical differences, and the "mistakes" made by the different groups.

During the academic year 1991–92, one of the second-year (introductory) prose classes at the School of Translators in Barcelona included a large group of exchange students (most of them British). Depending on the function of the text, the English AL students' difficulties in understanding the SLT were not compensated for by their greater skill in writing in the TL. A full understanding of the SLT is essential in translation. Eugene Nida (1992) insists that most mistakes in translation are due to misunderstanding the SLT rather than to limited linguistic competence in the TL. The Spanish AL students did not expect to find the comprehension of SLTs as difficult as they did; they had assumed that this first part of the translation process would be easy in the prose translation class. The exchange students had such serious problems understanding SLTs that their misunderstanding often interfered with the functionality of the translation.

For example, before translating a newspaper article entitled "Un hombre providencial," by Haro Tecglen (*El País*, 24 Nov. 1991), all of the students in this second-year class were given a discourse-analysis questionnaire as a pre-translation exercise. The text was about Butros Ghali, the newly elected Secretary General of the United Nations. In fact, the text was heavily ironic and its purpose was to identify Butros Ghali as providential for the United States and no one else. *None* of the exchange students recognized the irony, and they were convinced that Tecglen thought that Butros Ghali was the best man for the United Nations. As the English AL students did not recognize the irony, they were not able to transmit this function. In some cases, their translations were in danger of becoming non-texts, as they tried to fit the words of the text to their concept of what the text was about. (The specific difficulties of this text will be discussed in chapter 7.)

The results of the questionnaire were so unexpected that the same exercise was given to other students from the centre (see table 4.1).

Table 4.1
"Un hombre providencial": Questionnaire Results

	Aware of irony		Unaware of irony	
	Spanish AL	Exchange	Spanish AL	Exchange
First-year English B class	12	0	11	0
Second-year English B class	17	0	7	15
Third-year English B class	13	0	8	5
Third-year French B class	7	0	15	4
Total	49	0	41	24

The experience of having such a high percentage of exchange students in the class certainly highlights the practical differences. *Directa* teachers have had similar experiences. In my opinion, although these heterogeneous classes present difficulties and force teachers to adapt their teaching methodology to this new situation, there are advantages to be gained. The presence of English-language and -culture experts other than the teacher is a valuable resource. Activities should be organized to facilitate the interchange of knowledge and experience between the locals and the visitors within the classroom, as well as in their leisure time. The presence of English students also redresses the imbalance between *inversa* (artificial) and *directa* (real) translation classes.

The aim of this book is to establish the theoretical and methodological basis for structuring a professional prose-translation class. The students are learning to develop translator-transfer competence between Spanish and English. If all of the students possessed ideal linguistic and cultural competence in both languages, there would be no need to establish different programs for *directa* and *inversa*. The reality is, of course, different. Any teacher, like any translator, has to start with "Who does what when where why how for whom what for with what effect?" (quoted in Nord, 1991: 36).[5]

To answer these questions, the translation teacher has to work from a theoretical and methodological framework to delimit difficulties and establish progression for a particular context (place, time, students, work market). This is the order followed in the next three parts of this book: theoretical framework, methodological framework, and understanding principles and learning skills.

THEORETICAL FRAMEWORK

The theoretical framework (part 2) is divided into three chapters based on the different uses of the word *translation*: translation (the theory or abstract notion), translating (the process), and a translation (the text) (Bell, 1991).

TRANSLATION (THEORY)

The theoretical approach is based on the principle that there is no perfect theory and that all theories, like all grammars, "leak" (Sapir, 1921). The aim is not to argue linguistic theory but to present tools that will aid in the development of translation skills, bearing in mind that the value of the tools depends on the validity of the theory. The section begins with a brief summary of the historical development from prescriptive to descriptive theories of translation and the relationship between the old rules about what made a "good" translation and recent descriptions of text functions. Taking into consideration the functions of prose translation, a communicative model of translation theory is considered the most adequate for teaching purposes. Recent publications that have expanded the concept of communicative

---

5. The New Rhetoric developed the "Wh- questions" in the twentieth century, but they can be traced back to the second century B.C., when the Stoic Hermagoras of Temnos coined the formula "Quis quid quando ubi cur ad modem quibus adminiculis," which was framed in a hexameter verse by Matthew of Vendome in 1170 ("Quis quid ubi quibus auxilii cur quomodo quando?").

translation make it possible to claim that the model chosen fulfils the four basic requirements of a theory: empiricism, determinism, parsimony, and generality.

TRANSLATING (PROCESS)

Insights from consecutive and simultaneous interpreting and the cognitive sciences provide the basis for the description of the translation process. The École Supérieure d'Interprètes et de Traducteurs de Paris's three-stage model (comprehension → deverbalization → reformulation) is adapted to include discourse analysis categories, the creative role of the reader, and the importance of the *skopos*, or purpose of the translation. The stages are shown to be cascaded, a continual movement of top-down ↔ bottom-up, macrostructures ↔ microstructures.

A TRANSLATION (TEXT)

A Spanish text is analyzed to show the interdependence, text in context, of macro-structures and microstructures: pragmatic, semantic, syntactic, lexical, and formal. The consequences of this analysis for translating the text into English are then described, emphasizing the difference between standardized and nonstandardized language. Finally, the same text is judged from the semiotic (intertextual) dimension of translation.

METHODOLOGICAL FRAMEWORK

The methodological framework (part 3) is explored to define the contents and objectives of the prose-translation class. The methodology described is based on the definition of learner-centred objectives. Part 3 is divided into four chapters and begins with the goal of teaching translating: ideal translator communicative competence. The starting point, student-translator communicative competence and the teaching context, is then described. When general and specific objectives have been defined, the question of achieving objectives is discussed.

IDEAL TRANSLATOR COMMUNICATIVE COMPETENCE

The theoretical framework—in particular, the knowledge and skills needed at each stage of the translation process—provides the information needed to define ideal translator communicative competence. From this, we can deduce the general objectives of any translation program.

STUDENT TRANSLATOR COMMUNICATIVE COMPETENCE

Teaching translation into the foreign language is constrained by the limits of the students' translator competence. The description of this competence gives the starting point of the learning process and makes it possible to define the objectives of the prose-translation class.

THE TEACHING CONTEXT

The demands of the market and professional opportunities have to be taken into consideration in limiting the objectives. Students' motivation and expectations are another decisive factor.

ACHIEVING OBJECTIVES

General learning principles have to be defined: inductive and deductive learning, the cycle of inquiry, and the dynamics of the classroom. Translation strategies are defined as putting into practice the theoretical principles that allow correct development of the translation process. These principles are used to delimit translation difficulties and establish an ordered and rational learning progression. The students learn to use these strategies through a variety of activities, in a range of discourse fields. Wherever possible, the activities and fields chosen are directly related to the employment opportunities available to prose translators.

UNDERSTANDING PRINCIPLES AND LEARNING SKILLS

Part 4 of this book applies the theoretical, methodological, and contextual conclusions reached in parts 2 and 3 to selecting and organizing the content of teaching translation from Spanish to English. The content is divided into five chapters: "Words in Context," "Sentences in Context," "Deverbalization," "Restricted Codes and Transcoding," and "Cohesion and Coherence." The twenty-nine teaching units in these chapters are prefaced by objectives, tasks, and commentaries for the teacher and include forty-eight task sheets that show how the material is presented to students.

PART 2

THEORETICAL FRAMEWORK

Translation teachers are obliged to work within three different frameworks: the theoretical framework of the "subject" they are teaching; the methodological framework related to education in general and to how people learn; and the classroom framework, which includes the constraints of one particular pair of languages, and of one particular set of students within a certain geographical and historical context. Teachers have to decide how to use the guidelines provided by theory and methodology in order to teach a content and a skill in a particular context (in this case, translating from Spanish to English in the 1990s). Thus, teachers make theoretical and methodological choices in the context of their teaching situation.

In this book, translation theory is approached from the perspective of searching for guidelines that will provide the tools needed by the teacher to help students to learn the skill of translating from their own language to a foreign language. The starting point is similar to that adopted by Mildred Larsen: "The aim of the book is not to argue linguistic theory but to present tools which help translators" (1984: 26).

However, this does not mean any theory will do if it serves our purposes. If the theory is not reliable, the tools will be unreliable. Ernst-August Gutt argues that even if our concerns are eminently practical, "theoretical assumptions are important in that the value of the tools suggested depends on the validity of the framework in which they are developed" (1991: 82).

CHAPTER 5

TRANSLATION (THEORY)

It is easy for teachers to get lost in the maze of literature on the subject of translation.[6] Translation dates back almost as far as does writing itself, and translation has played an essential role in the spread of government, culture, and science. Bilingual inscriptions have been found in Mesopotamia that date from 3000 B.C. The bureaucratic apparatus of the Roman Empire could not have functioned without translators. The Toledo School of translators provided the basis for the development of science in the West by translating the Arabic versions of Greek scientific and philosophical classics. The influence of the King James Version of the Bible on the English language and culture cannot be measured.

FROM LAWS TO FUNCTIONS

From a very early date, translators began to think about what they were doing. Cicero was already concerned with maintaining a balance between "faithful" and "free" texts: "If I render word for word, the result will sound uncouth, and if compelled by necessity I alter anything in the order or the wording, I shall have seemed to have departed from the function of a translator" (Cicero, 1959: 43). He obviously felt that the function of the translator was to be faithful to the SL text.

King Alfred (871–899 A.D.), known as Alfred the Great, seems to have solved the problem by concentrating on the function of the translation. When he translated a Latin handbook for parish priests, the *Cura Pastoralis,* into English, his purpose was to help the English people recover from the havoc caused by the Danish invasions. Therefore, he was most concerned with getting the message of the SLT across to a group of simple parish priests who did not know Latin, in the hope that they would put into practice the suggestions for restoring law and order in their villages. In the preface to his translation, Brook (1955) claimed that Alfred had followed the teachings of his bishop and priests and had translated "whilum word be

---

6. A useful guide can be found in Delisle and Woodsworth (1995).

worde, whilum andgiet of andgiete" (sometimes word by word, sometimes sense by sense).

Alfred was pragmatic, a man of action as well as a scholar. However, most writers on the subject saw their task as laying down the law, making rules and regulations. Louis Kelly (1979), in a well-documented history of translation theory and practice in the West, divides the different theories into three categories.

1. The *prelinguistic theories,* which were concerned with the conflict between free and literal translations and the inherent impossibility but absolute necessity of translating.

2. *Linguistic theories* that take communication to be the main role of language. Eugene Nida, who dominates the literature in this field, has suggested a variety of strategies for approaching translation through linguistic analysis, but always within the context of communication theory. For Nida, whose main work has been based on translation of the Bible, "Translating consists in reproducing in the receptor language the closest natural equivalent of the source language message, first in terms of meaning and secondly in terms of style. But this relatively simple statement requires careful evaluation of several seemingly contradictory elements" (Nida and Taber, 1969: 13).

3. *Hermeneutic theories,* which allow the word (*logos*) its own creative entity. For George Steiner, "Language is the true and only verifiable a priori framework of cognition" (1975: 82). Steiner's main concern is whether justice is being done to the original text.

Kelly himself suggests a *functional approach.* Language use varies according to its function in a specific context, and translation is language use (communication) within a social context. Translation theorists who take discourse as the basis of analysis for translation studies are concerned with establishing the different functions of the SLT and the TLT within their different contexts (Delisle, 1980; Hatim and Mason, 1990). Recent studies concerned with constructing a theoretical framework to deal with practical translation problems have opted for a variational approach, based on the functions of the translation.[7] This approach accounts for the complexity of the translation process and seems to be very productive.

This approach frees translation theory from the normative, prescriptive approach adopted by Alexander Fraser Tytler (1907 [1791]): "It is no exaggeration to say that the programme followed by most translation theorists in the English-speaking world at least (with a small number of exceptions; Nida and Catford in the

---

7. See Hewson and Martin (1991), for teaching translation from French to English, and Patrick Zabaleascoa (1993), for a theoretical basis for dubbing TV comedies from English to Catalan.

mid 1960s in particular), has been, and still is, dominated by the thinking put forward in an essay written two centuries ago in 1791" (Bell, 1991: 10).

Tytler began by defining a *good* translation, which provided the basis for his three main "laws" of translation: (1) that the translation should give a complete transcript of the ideas of the original work (content); (2) that the style and manner of writing should be of the same character as that of the original (form); and (3) that the translation should have all the ease of original composition (receptor). Obviously, very few translations (if any) can follow all of these "laws," and this has led to sterile discussions about the impossibility of translating. Recently, interest has been concentrated on which law should have priority in which text, depending on the different functions of a SLT and the purpose (*skopos*) of the TLT. These are the parameters that oblige a translator to adopt a certain methodology. Thus, there are no laws that apply to all translations; rather, translators adopt a variational approach that is defined for each translation according to the functions of the SLT and the purpose of the TLT.

It is interesting to compare Tytler's laws with Katerina Reiss's first "text typology," which was also broken down into three main sections. She divided texts according to their main function, and these functions partially coincide with Tytler's laws. The first is *Inhaltsbetonte Texte*, in which the predominant function of the language is representative, to transmit the *content* of the text. The second is *Formbetonte Texte*, in which the predominant function of the language is expressive, to transmit the *form* of the text. The third is *Appelbetonte Texte*, in which the predominant function of the language is to provoke a reaction in the reader, or *receptor* (Reiss, 1971: 31).

The parallels are quite clear: Tytler refers to ideas, Reiss to content; Tytler to style of writing, Reiss to form; Tytler to ease of original composition, Reiss to the effect on the reader or the receptor. Reiss later changed her terminology and called the three text types *informative, expressive,* and *operative* (Reiss, 1976).

However, in 1981, Reiss stressed the multifunctionality of most texts. The variational approach is needed even within a single translation, because different functions may be dominant at different times. Nevertheless, the definition of text types is one of the most useful directions in translation theory today, and it has direct implications on teaching methodology.

A MULTIDISCIPLINARY, INTERDISCIPLINARY FIELD OF STUDY

Although the history of translation dates back almost as far as writing itself, the practice of translation and the demand for translations and translators have been far greater in the twentieth century than at any other time. In fact, the twentieth century has been called the "Age of Translation." The Nuremburg Trials were seen as the event that established the need for professionally trained translators and interpreters in the twentieth century (Bowen, 1985). After the end of the Second World War, the number of translations increased as the number of international organizations, multinationals, and worldwide communication systems increased. Expanded translation activities and the creation by universities all over the world of centres to train translators and interpreters are two reasons for the growth in translation theory in the last twenty years.

The growth in translation theory is also due to developments in related disciplines. Any translator who tries to get up to date on the latest theories will be faced with a wide range of possibilities. There are three main reasons for this. First, the complexity of the translation process makes it very difficult to fit it into one theory. Second, this is an area in which there is considerable divergence in the ways the subject has developed in different countries. Third, translation theory is a multidisciplinary study and has itself been studied by many different disciplines from their own special points of view and with their own priorities.

There is a tendency among some translation theorists to make simplified claims of the type "Translation is comparative linguistics/ethnography/pragmatics/ semiotics," and so on. Translation theory can learn from the multidisciplinary approach taken by discourse analysis, which was developed to try to deal with problems that could not be solved at the level of word or sentence. Most translation problems can be solved only at the level of discourse. Like discourse analysis, translation theory has drawn on work from many other disciplines. Going back in time, there is much to be learned from classical grammar, rhetoric, and logic. The painstaking research of the nineteenth-century philologists provided invaluable historical, geographical, and comparative data. Modern linguistics now seems to be moving toward functionalist text linguistics, which may be the most useful approach for translation theory, but there is also much to be learned from the structuralist, formalist approaches.

In fact, one of the most fascinating aspects of translation is that it is a multidisciplinary, interdisciplinary activity, and many of the disciplines involved have been developing very rapidly in recent years. Multidisciplinary cognitive science emerged in the late 1970s, drawing on fields such as psychology (psycholinguistics, cognitive psychology), computer science (artificial intelligence), sociology (sociolinguistics and social psychology), and anthropology. This new integrated science provides valuable tools for the study of language, discourse, and translation as communicative modes of action.

> Si algo hay de cierto en el panorama de los estudios lingüísticos de hoy en día es que constituyen un territorio en el que confluyen tradiciones académicas de muy diversa procedencia. Tanto la lingüística estrictamente considerada como la psicología, la lógica, la filosofía, las ciencias de la computación, las matemáticas o la sociología tienen cosas que decir sobre el lenguaje y van configurando cada vez más un dominio de saber que se nutre de todas ellas aunque al no especialista pueda parecerle que su naturaleza es híbrida. . . .

> Pasó la época estructuralista en que nos esforzábamos por separar el lenguaje de cualquier otra institución. Hoy hemos vuelto a aprender que el lenguaje, más que un objeto científico, constituye un problema, uno de los problemas, sin duda, más apasionantes a los que cualquier persona curiosa puede enfrentarse. (Vide, Martí, and Serrano, 1992: 25)

There is increasing interest in interdisciplinary studies[8] and in the search for a general science of man. Translation is a perfect field in which to study all these different disciplines in interaction.

The process of translation is a linguistic operation, and therefore our knowledge of it is as limited as our knowledge of language, its relation to thought, and how the human brain works. Studies of the human mind are being carried out on two levels: biological and cognitive, the study of the organism and the functions that depend on it. The debate over whether thought is possible without language has been a long one. Advances in neurosurgery and the cognitive sciences seem to have established that, in effect, the brain stores concepts and linguistic labels separately .

The cognitive sciences are in a state of rapid development, but, as Karl Nager said at the Ciber Foundation Conference on Consciousness in London in July of 1992, a new kind of theory is needed (interview, BBC Radio 4, 15 July 1992). The present situation can be compared to that of physics before the advent of Einstein's theory of relativity and quantum mechanics. Certainly, when a theory is produced that establishes the links between brain and mind, it will inevitably be very complex. Perhaps chaos theory and complexity theory will also be able to contribute to translation theory.

It is to be hoped that future translation theorists will have a more solid basis to work on, but in the meantime, translation teachers cannot ignore the advances that have been made. Roger Bell (1991) makes a valiant attempt to bring all of these developments together in a model that he hopes will be of service to translators, linguists, and translation theory. He makes use of what is known as the computational metaphor, in which the structure of the human mind, the cognitive architecture built on the physical foundations of brain and nervous system, is described in terms of a powerful computer, in the sense that both minds and computers process information (Vide et al., 1992). Bell believes that, despite all the advances in the disciplines related to translation, there is a fundamental misunderstanding by both translation theorists and linguists of what is involved in translation and that "the co-occurrence of exciting advances in cognitive science, artificial intelligence and

---

8. The rich variety and extension of Routledge's Interface series, edited by Ronald Carter, is a sign of this trend: "The aim of the Interface series is to build bridges between the traditionally divided disciplines of language and literary studies." It is hardly surprising that Routledge has also recently published *Redefining Translation,* by Lance Henson and Jacky Martin (1991), and *Thinking Translation,* by Sándor Hervey and Ian Higgins (1992).

text linguistics with the emergence of a genuinely socially and semantically based functional theory of linguistics—systemic linguistics—makes this an ideal moment to attempt to resolve the paradox and develop an adequate theory of translation" (Bell, 1991: 16). Bell's purpose is to stimulate translation theorists and linguists to work together, drawing on each other's fields. However, translation theory still has not found its Einstein, and when an "adequate theory of translation" does emerge, it will have to account for innumerable variations and new forms of translation that emerge as technology develops (for example, TV dubbing).

Some translation theorists feel that the task of developing an adequate theory of translation is so far beyond our grasp that translation theory would be better occupied dealing with concrete problems. This is Peter Newmark's position, which is completely opposed to Bell's:

> From the point of view of the translator, any scientific investigation, both sta-
> tistical and diagrammatic (some linguists and translation theorists make a
> fetish of diagrams, schemas and models), of what goes on in the brain (mind?
> nerves? cells?) during the process of translation is remote and at present
> speculative. Translation theory broadly consists of, and can be defined as, a
> large number of generalisations of translation problems. (Newmark, 1988: 21)

Newmark is always thought-provoking, he is an excellent teacher, and his books are full of useful suggestions and insights. For a long time, he was the only well-known scholar in Britain writing about translation. Nevertheless, he mistrusts attempts to make a "science" of translation. The debate over whether translation is a science, an art, or a craft is an old one. In fact, translation is a hybrid, and there is an element of "science" involved. A model can help us to gain an over-all view of the subject. The process of developing a translation theory is like the process of analyzing discourse. It should be a two-way process, with bottom-up ↔ top-down, microstructural ↔ macrostructural interaction.

The intellectual isolation that affected the United Kingdom and the United States (and Spain) at the beginning of the twentieth century and the anti-theoretical approach to literary criticism also affected translation theory (Bassnet-McGuire, 1980: 60). In the last four or five years, the trend has changed dramatically, as can be seen in the Routledge Interface series[9] and in Longman's Applied Linguistics and Language Study series.

The main interest in translation theory in this book is to define a methodology to help students to learn a skill: translating. However, translating is not like riding a bike, in which it makes no difference whether the cyclist knows how the appropriate muscles function (although perhaps Miguel Indurain needed to know quite a bit about physiology and psychology to win the Tour de France five years in

---

9. This series was established in the 1970s, but it has only recently turned its attention to translation studies.

succession). Translating is such a complex skill that if translators know more about the process, they will perform better. How much they need to know about the process depends on a number of factors. Translation teachers have to define how much translation theory their students need. Bell uses the term "threshold of termination" to describe how much time should be spent at each point of the transla-tion process. It is "the point at which the writer feels that the text is adequate to ... e reader has got enough out of the the text and/ ...s little point in continuing" (Bell, 1991: 213). ...ised to describe just how much translation the- ...ght as a framework to improve their translation ...slation class into a translation theory class.

...gmentation in translation studies, and this can ...in which many languages are taught. Many of ...within different national schools of theory: the ...iental, the English, the American, the Spanish, ...that students may have to cope with three or ...iich can be an enriching, but confusing, expe-

...simplified by the constraints of teaching trans- ...ore a translator begins to translate any text, he ...Who wrote the text, when, why, where, how, ...he translation, when, why, where, how? Trans- ...questions about their class—that is, put their ...ng which theoretical approach to use. In the ...of the educational and professional utility of ...Spanish and Catalan students. Obviously, these ..."acred" texts, texts where the form, or Reiss's ...ey will not be translating Clarín or Borges into

TEACHING PROSE TRANSLATION

...ng distinction between semantic and commu- ...imunicative translation as an attempt to pro- duce the same effect on the reader of the translation as that made on the reader of the original (Tytler's third law). Semantic translation attempts to render the exact contextual meaning of the original, within the limits allowed by the semantic and syntactic structures of the second language (Tytler's first law).

A semantic translation may require more effort on the part of the reader. It tends to overtranslate, rather than simplify. Newmark claims that the increasing assumption that all translation problems are communication problems is dangerous: Semantic translation is essential to preserve the quality of literature for certain

Table 5.1
Semantic Translation vs. Communicative Translation

SEMANTIC	COMMUNICATIVE
SOURCE-LANGUAGE BIAS	TARGET-LANGUAGE BIAS
LITERAL	FREE
FAITHFUL	IDIOMATIC
SEMANTIC	COMMUNICATIVE

types of readers. Newmark's point is worth making, and he is supported by writers such as Vladimir Nabokov and Milan Kundera, both of whom have complained about the liberties taken by translators with a strong target-language bias.

This is why Newmark is critical of Seleskovitch and the research group at l'École supérieure d'interprètes et traducteurs (Sorbonne nouvelle, Paris III), although he recognizes the valuable and stimulating contribution they have made. He believes that their approach leads to undertranslation and loss of meaning. Seleskovitch's interpretive theory of translation is based on the sense behind the words. For the Paris School, translation, being a part of a general theory of discourse, has to start with discourse.[10]

Widdowson has defined discourse as "the communicative use of sentences in the performing of social actions" (1973: 69). Therefore, for Widdowson the study of discourse is the study of pragmatics—the purpose for which a sentence is used—of the real-world conditions under which a sentence may appropriately be used as an utterance. The distinction between semantic and pragmatic meaning is behind the theory of speech acts originally developed by Austin (1962) and Searle (1969).

For the purposes of teaching translation into a foreign language, the communicative theories are the most useful. Jean Delisle, who studied with Seleskovitch and teaches translation at the University of Ottawa, led the field in applying theories related to discourse analysis to the teaching of translation:

> Pour être vraiment opératoire, toute stratégie pédagogique appliquée à l'enseignement pratique de la traduction doit reposer sur des fondements théoriques valables. Sans un ensemble cohérent de principes fondamentaux et de règles soumises à l'épreuve de l'expérience, le pédagogue aura du mal à organiser son enseignement. Ne disposant pas d'un cadre général de référence, il risque d'adopter une attitude trop normative ou excessivement laxiste. Pour enseigner à traduire, la connaissance des faits de traduction ne suffit pas. (Delisle, 1981: 135)

---

10. The Paris School uses the word "discourse" to include all of the elements that make up an act of communication, not, as it is sometimes used, to refer to the cohesive elements of a paragraph or text.

The methodology proposed by Delisle (1980, 1993) has proved fruitful for teaching translation from Spanish to English for Spanish students for three main reasons. First, Delisle restricts his method to what he calls pragmatic texts, which excludes texts in which Reiss's expressive function is predominant. Professionally, these students will always be translating texts in which the pragmatic function dominates. Second, Delisle's translation unit is the entire text seen as discourse. In the *inversa* class the students are complete beginners, and their main problem is to get beyond the lexical level. They have to be trained to understand the text as a whole and reach the sense behind the words. Third, the approach is based on communicative theories, and therefore leads to communicative situations in the classroom that encourage motivation.

Delisle is useful because he is concerned primarily with teaching translation, not linguistics; the translation theory is often implicit, rather than explicit; and the learning is inductive rather than deductive. Furthermore, developments in related disciplines in recent years seem to reinforce the idea that translation problems are communication problems.

EXPANDING THE CONCEPT OF A COMMUNICATIVE TRANSLATION

It has been assumed that communicative translations will always be colloquial and easy to read. They have been associated with the image of actors in jeans playing Shakespeare and the idea that depth, quality, and poetry should be sacrificed to "information." However, "information"—facts—makes up a relatively small percentage of all communication. Gutt reinforces the communicative position in translation by expanding the concept of a communicative translation: "The main contribution of this book is a reductionist one on the theoretical level—issues of translation are shown to be at heart issues of communication"(1991: 188).

Gutt is not just a linguist writing about translation in a vacuum. He is a translator who taught translation at the University of Addis Ababa. His book is full of translation examples; it is not the uninterrupted theorizing to which Newmark understandably objects. He did his doctorate with Deirdre Wilson at University College in London, and his dissertation was on the application of Sperber and Wilson's relevance theory to translation theory. The relevance-theory concept of communication that he applies to translation is much wider than that allowed by Newmark, who equates communication with generalization and simplification:

> Meaning is complicated, many levelled, a "network of relations" as devious as the channels of thought in the brain. The more communication, the more generalisation; the more simplification, the less meaning. I am writing against the increasing assumption that all translation is [nothing but] communicating, where the less effort expected of the reader, the better. (Newmark, 1991: 11)

However, on the same page, Newmark also claims that "there is no reason why a basically semantic translation should not also be strongly communicative." This is obviously true if the translation is consistent with the *skopos*[11] of the text—that is, why it is being translated and for whom. Gutt gives an excellent example of how a translation that would have been categorized as "direct versus indirect" (Vinay and Darbelnet, 1958), "formal versus dynamic" (Nida, 1964), "literal versus free" (Catford, 1965), or "semantic versus communicative" (Newmark, 1991) was, in fact, more successful communicatively than one that was ostensibly indirect, dynamic, free, communicative.

In 1982, a draft translation of the New Testament into Guaraní was sent to different Guaraní churches in Brazil to be tested. The draft was communicative in Newmark's sense of the word—that is, generalizing, simplifying, and explicative. After a year's testing, the church decided that virtually everything had to be translated again:

> From the Guaraní point of view, the rationale behind the changes in translation style was that the scriptures in Guaraní should be clearly seen as a faithful translation of the high-prestige Portuguese version. . . . What the Guaranís expect is that the meaning in their translation correspond, in a fairly self-evident way, with what they find in the Portuguese. . . . Much implicit information that had been made explicit in the text was relegated to a footnote, a picture, the glossary or eliminated altogether. (Gutt, 1991: 184)

There was an obvious discrepancy between what the translator thought the Guaraní should have and what they themselves wanted:

> Whereas the translator assumed that a kind of indirect translation would be appropriate, that is, a translation that would communicate implicatures with ease to Guaranís with little knowledge of the original background, the Guaranís themselves seemed to have looked for a translation more along the lines of direct translation, possibly accompanied by resemblances in linguistic properties as well. This mismatch in expectations led to a breakdown in communication. (Gutt, 1991: 184)

A few years ago, I had a similar experience translating a paper for a Spanish academic. I am often asked to translate papers written by Spanish scientists to be read at international conferences. I have always considered that the main purpose of translating these scientific papers is for the scientists to transmit the information related to their research as clearly as possible to an international audience, for the greater glory of science, the advancement of their own careers, and the prestige of their home institutions. As a result, when translating these papers, I follow the discourse model of English-language scientific papers as published in most prestigious international journals. One of the rules of style that Spanish students are taught is

---

11. On *skopos,* see Vermeer, 1983; Reiss and Vermeer, 1984; Nord, 1988.

not to repeat any word in a single paragraph. Therefore, in a Spanish scientific article one may find as many as five synonyms for "test tube" in one paragraph. In the English translation, I shorten sentences and clear up references (for example, doing away with synonyms for "test tube"), bearing in mind that the mode of the TLT is "written to be read aloud" by someone whose English may not be fluent, to an audience composed of native and non-native speakers of English. On the whole, my clients are satisfied. However, when I produced this kind of translation for a social scientist, he was most annoyed. Apparently, in his particular branch of this discipline, there are a group of academics in Spain, France, and Italy who defend the style of the Romance languages against the imperialism of English, even though they are obliged to present their papers in English if they want international recognition. I had to translate the text again, this time making it as literal as possible.

Now, having read the story of the Guaraní New Testament, I feel that my second translation was communicative because it communicated the client's purpose (the author of the SLT was the client). One of his main requirements for the TLT was that it should hold its own against American cultural imperialism, a sort of academic version of breaking the windows of the McDonald's at the top of the Ramblas. This was, perhaps, as important to him as the content of his research.

Gutt explains the Guaranís' objection to the first-draft translation in terms of their familiarity with the high-prestige Portuguese version. There may be another reason. The Portuguese version of the Bible, like the King James Version, is highly poetic. Relevance theory provides a very satisfying explanation of the peculiar strength of poetic language, as opposed to prose: it is often due to what is implied rather than what is explicit. "According to relevance theory, poetic effects arise essentially when the audience is induced and given freedom to open up and consider a wide range of implicatures, none of which are very strongly implicated, but which taken together create an 'impression' rather than communicate a 'message'" (Gutt, 1991: 155).

One of the aims of the first draft of the Guaraní New Testament was to make explicit implicatures that would have been clear to Jews living in the Middle East in the first century A.D., but not to Indians in Brazil in the twentieth century, thereby reducing rather than extending the range of possible interpretations. This reduction of poetic effect can be seen in the *Good News Bible* and *Dios habla al hombre*. In the preface to the Spanish version, the emphasis on message rather than form is made plain: "Los traductores han querido ajustarse al ejemplo de los autores del Nuevo Testamento, cuyo interés principal fue el de narrar los acontecimientos en forma clara y sencilla, dando más importancia al mensaje contenido que a las formas literarias en que el mensaje había de ser expresado."

In prose, the interpretation of the utterance follows the syntactic organization of the utterance. The semantic relations between the different constituents of the sentence are defined by syntax. The precision of the syntactic structure in these two versions allows very little freedom to explore a range of comparatively weak interpretations. Some of the differences can be seen in a brief comparison with two older versions—the King James Version (1611) and the *Biblioteca de Autores Cristianos* (1965). The passage is 1 Corinthians 13:1–2.

KING JAMES (1611)

Though I speak with the tongues of men and angels and have no charity, I am become a sounding brass or a tinkling cymbal. And though I have the gift of prophecy and understand all mysteries, and all knowledge, and though I have all faith, so that I could move mountains, and have not charity, I am nothing.

GOOD NEWS BIBLE (1976)

I may be able to speak the languages of men and even of angels, but if I have no love, my speech is no more than a noisy gong or a clashing bell. I may have the gift of inspired preaching, I may have all knowledge and understand all secrets; I may have all the faith needed to move mountains—but if I have no love, I am nothing.

BIBLIOTECA DE AUTORES CRISTIANOS (1965)

Si hablando lenguas de hombres y de ángeles no tengo caridad, soy como bronce que suena o címbalo que retiñe. Y si teniendo el don de la profecía y conociendo todos los misterios y toda la ciencia, y tanta fe que trasladase los montes si no tengo caridad, no soy nada.

DIOS HABLA AL HOMBRE (1976)

Si yo hablo en lenguas de hombres y de angeles, pero no tengo amor, no soy más que un tambor que resuena o un platillo que hace ruido. Si comunico mensajes recibidos de Dios, y conozco todas las cosas secretas, y tengo toda clase de conocimientos, y tengo toda la fe necesaria para quitar los montes de su lugar, pero no tengo amor, no soy nada.

The most obvious, immediate difference is the length of the four versions. The 1976 versions are more explicit syntactically and lexically. They both make the contrasting second part of each conditional more definite by adding "but"/"pero." The newer English version makes "Though I speak" more explicit by using the auxiliary verb *may*: "I may be able to speak." The Spanish version changes the more vague gerund "Si hablando" for "Si yo hablo." The "yo" is redundant here, so its function is to emphasize reference.

The change from "charity"/"caridad" to "love"/"amor" does not affect the argument. It is a necessary lexical change due to the historical development of the meaning (above all connotative) of "charity"/"caridad." However, there are other lexical changes arising from the translator's search for clarity. "The gift of prophecy" becomes "the gift of inspired preaching," which eliminates some of the possible meanings of prophecy—perhaps, the more awe-inspiring meaning of "predicting the future." "El don de la profecía" becomes "Si comunico mensajes recibidos de Dios," which includes more elements of meaning than the English but sounds incredibly prosaic, as if everyone received two or three letters a day from God. "Mysteries"/"misterios," which are by their nature beyond our understanding, become "secrets"/"secretos," which can be discovered by listening at the door.

Gutt also shows how rhyme and rhythm contribute to the poetic effect by imposing phonological patterns that are independent of syntactic structure and often cut right across it: "These patterns tend to enrich the Interpreting, not only because they give rise to additional groupings, but also because, in contrast to syntactic relations, the relations they suggest are unspecified and so allow greater freedom in Interpreting" (Gutt, 1991: 157).

Translating poetry is not the subject of this book, but Gutt's application of relevance theory to translation is interesting for translation theory as a whole because it takes into account the concern with preserving meaning, content, and style and expands the concept of communicative translation. Although the *inversa* class will be concerned mainly with translating Delisle's "pragmatic" texts, nearly all texts are multifunctional, and even the most pragmatic texts may have "poetic" elements. Whatever their view of translation, translators are communicators addressing the TL audience.

Gutt's theory is less useful when he discusses "translation where all is change" (1991, ch. 3). Relevance theory divides language use as communication into two categories: descriptive use and interpretive use. Gutt categorizes all translations in which the SLT is incidental, rather than crucial, as descriptive uses of language, and comes to the conclusion that they are not really translations and therefore do not need to be taken into consideration in any theory of translation. All "real" translations are examples of interpretive use of language.

Gutt uses an example from Hans Hönig and Paul Kussmaul's *Strategie der Ubersetzung* to illustrate translations in which the SLT is incidental rather than crucial. Hönig and Kussmaul discuss an advertisement for Viyella House from the point of view of the *skopos* of two possible translations. The first is a translation of the advertisement for the purpose of students studying the marketing strategy of Viyella House, so it must be strongly oriented to the SLT, in both form and content. The second is the creation of a corresponding advertisement for Germany. Gutt maintains that the second is not a translation.

There is some truth in what Gutt says, but when discussing translation everywhere else he is very careful to avoid diametrically opposed categories. It is impossible to find a text or translation in which only one function is important. Text categories are always referred to within a spectrum, in which functions are stronger or weaker. Gutt is probably right that the second Viyella House translation was a job for an advertising agency rather than a translation agency, and yet translators are asked to translate texts in which the actual words of the SLT are incidental.

Nord develops a theoretical model intended to cover all kinds of translation situations. Like Reiss and Vermeer, she gives priority to the *skopos* of the translation and subordinates the demand for fidelity to the *skopos* rule. If the *skopos* demands a change of function, the required function of the translation will not be fidelity to the SLT but adequacy with regard to the *skopos*: "The function of the target text is not arrived at automatically from an analysis of the source text, but is pragmatically defined by the purpose of the intercultural communication" (Nord, 1991: 9). Examples of *skopos* may be very varied: a Spanish physicist asks for a translation of an American scientific paper to find out about the latest development in his field; an English businessman wants to open delicate negotiations with a Mexican company; a British publisher aims to publish a Spanish novel as a best-seller; a language teacher wants to find out if his students can tell the difference between the past perfect and the past simple. Nord goes so far as to say, "Functional equivalence between source and target text is not the 'normal' skopos of a translation, but an exceptional case in which the factor 'change of function' is assigned zero" (1991: 23). This is, perhaps, an exaggeration if all institutional and instructional translations are taken into account. However, professional translators do have to provide more than the layperson imagines by a translation. Gutt's quotation from a translation-agency ad, found on the back cover of *Language Monthly* (Aug. 1987) was meant to support his position, but in fact it gives strength to the opposite claim.

More than a translation service . . .

Your translation requirement needs to be managed like any other aspect of your business; it has to dovetail into your overall marketing and publishing plans. We understand your environment and we offer very much more than a translation service.

This is an interesting example: whether the agency offers much more than a translation service is questionable. A professional asked to translate a handbook advertising the master's degree in public administration offered by the politics department of the Universidad Autónoma de Barcelona needs to know that the department's marketing strategy is to send a glossy publication to the most prestigious universities in the United States in the hope of exchanging students, staff, research, and support. The translator needs to understand the environments of the Catalan and American universities. Discussing these factors with the co-ordinator of the program before starting work on the translation is providing a translation service. This is one of the lessons that a trainee translator must learn.

THE SEMIOTIC DIMENSION

If translation is recognized as a communicative act, perhaps translation theory, like discourse analysis, should be defined within a general theory of communication. Semiotics, too, is best defined within a general theory of communication, and the semiotic notion of intertextuality can be usefully applied to translation theory. The individual sign attains its value in relation to other signs. What applies to the individual sign applies all the more to the text in the semiotic, structuralist sense of "a system of signs." The value of a text is attained in relation to other texts—that is, to its intertextuality.

The idea that translation is semiotics is not a new one. In 1980, Bassnett-McGuire suggested that translation can best be explained using semiotics: "The first step towards an examination of the processes of translation must be to accept that although translation has a central core of linguistic activity, it belongs most properly to semiotics, the science that studies sign systems or structures, sign processes and sign functions" (1980: 13). Hatim and Mason describe the translation process in terms of three dimensions:

1. The Communicative Dimension is an aspect of Context (i.e., the extra-contextual environment which exerts a determining influence on the language used) which includes all the variables related to Register (Field, Mode, and Tenor).
2. The Pragmatic Dimension is an aspect of Context which regulates Intentionality (i.e., the feature which determines the appropriateness of a linguistic form to the achievement of a communicative goal).
3. The Semiotic Dimension is an aspect of Context which regulates the relation of texts to each other as Signs. (Hatim and Mason, 1990: 237)

Hatim and Mason's book is based firmly on the assumption that translating is a communicative process that takes place within a social context. While they present convincing evidence of the highly diverse nature of translation, they stress the need for an over-all model of the translation process based on a functional approach as suggested by Kelly: "It is only by recognising a typology of function that a theory of translation will do justice to both Bible and bilingual cereal packet" (1979: 226).

Translators make lexical and syntactic choices that are conditioned by the pragmatic action of a discourse, the purposes of utterances, and real-world conditions. They also have to be aware of the semiotic dimension that controls the interaction between discourse elements as signs within texts, between texts, and between the author of the SLT, the *skopos* of the translation, and the readers of the TLT. Hatim and Mason discuss genre, discourse, and intertextuality within the framework of semiotics and ideology.

Hatim is particularly interested in this dimension because of the vast ideological differences between the Arab and the Western worlds. The differences between Spain and Britain are not so great, and these differences have diminished over the last twenty years, due to economic, political, and cultural changes in Spain and the fact that both countries belong to the European Community. However, recent changes related to the end of the Cold War make it increasingly difficult to capture the ideological position of text producers and to predict their intentions. The old stereotypes are gone: "Nos encontramos así, fuera del confort intelectual de las viejas normas, y tenemos que vivir a la intemperie política, tratando de levantar, poco a poco, los nuevos refugios, practicando el manejo de lo imprevisible" (Fernandez Ordoñez, 1992: 13).

De Saussure assumed that "linguistics would be taken as a model semiotic system and that its basic concepts would be applied to other spheres of social and cultural life" (Hatim and Mason, 1990: 107). However, as later authors (Gumperz, 1982; Stubbs, 1983) have pointed out, semiotics transcends the study of language. Charles Pierce's (1931–58) semiotic analysis started with nonlinguistic signs and then identified the status of language in semiotic systems. This is why Hatim and Mason suggest an approach to the semiotic dimension of translation based on Pierce's categories. This is not a book about semiotics, and his categories have been simplified for pedagogical reasons. Pierce breaks the sign down into three parts: (1) whatever initiates identification of the sign; (2) the object of the sign; (3) the interpretant or the effect the sign is meant to relay.

To illustrate these parts of the sign, we could consider a nonlinguistic sign. In David Lodge's novel *Nice Work*, the characters Robyn Penrose and Vic Wilcox discuss a Silk Cut cigarette advertisement: "A photographic depiction of a rippling expanse of purple silk in which there was a single slit, as if the material had been slashed with a razor. There were no words on the advertisement, except for the Government Health Warning about smoking" (Lodge, 1988: 220). If we analyze this sign in terms of Pierce's three categories, the results could be: (1) The photograph of the slashed purple silk initiates the identification of the sign. (2) The object of the sign is the product being advertised—a packet of cigarettes. (3) The interpretant is the effect the sign is meant to relay, or, in general, the meaning of the sign. According to Robyn Penrose, the brand name "Silk Cut" originally signified a type or "cut" of tobacco that was the opposite of rough and would not give the smoker a sore throat. However, in the Silk Cut advertisement being analyzed, the sign has assumed wider meanings and connotations. These connotations are sexual: "The shimmering silk with its voluptuous curves and sensuous texture, obviously symbolised the female body, and the elliptical slit, foregrounded by a lighter colour showing through, was more obviously a vagina. The advert thus appealed to both sensual and sadistic impulses, the desire to mutilate as well as to penetrate the human body" (Lodge, 1988: 221). The sign, as understood by Pierce and others (Barthes, 1957; Eco, 1973), has an endless capacity to transform and take on other meanings and connotations.

The sign achieves significance through intertextuality. Texts are processed not by empty brains, but by minds already stocked with set ideas, a priori categories, prototypes, and, perhaps most importantly, agenda. In other words, text processing is usually ideologically determined. Each individual brain has its own set of categories, determined by interaction between the dominant discourse of a society and the different systems that make up a culture. Intertextual elements identify a given text as belonging to a particular cultural system. This brings us to Barthes's ideas about signs as generators of myths that may be short-lived, or may span centuries and help to define the value systems of entire cultures.

If translation is seen as transmitting the meaning of different signs from one culture to another, and if part of this meaning is achieved through the interaction between different textual elements, the translator has to be able to recognize and identify the intertextuality in the SLT and transmit it in the TLT. Therefore, the translator has to identify, first, the form of an intertextual reference and, second, its function. Third, the translator has to determine the semiotic status of the reference in order to decide whether to give priority to form or to function. Usually, intentionality takes priority over information content (Hatim and Mason, 1990: 135).

In *Nice Work,* Vic Wilcox finds that some of Robyn's theoretical explanations help him to understand the world around him. Trainee translators can also profit from such explanations. The prose class provides the appropriate conditions in which to consider the semiotic dimension of the text and the syntactic, semantic, and pragmatic properties of the sign. The SLT is in the students' native language, and emphasis can be put on the first stage in the translation process: developing strategies to improve comprehension of the SLT. The students will also be more aware of the intertextuality, ideologies, and assumptions behind the SLT, and therefore will more easily recognize the semiotic dimension. It is a natural contextual situation in which to expand extralinguistic knowledge, an important part of training translators.

CONCLUSION

I have discussed briefly some translation-theory models and recent developments in related fields that can be of use in teaching translation. However, we may also do well to recognize the limitations of theory. As de Beaugrande warns, "It is inappropriate to expect that a theoretical model of translation should solve all the problems a translator encounters. Instead, it should formulate a set of strategies for approaching problems and for coordinating the different aspects entailed" (1978: 135).

Furthermore, the more idealized the theory and the data, the farther away they are from the real world and its "fuzzy" outlines. Translation is an activity anchored in the real world. Teaching translation is a euphemism for helping students learn how to translate, and translation teachers have to integrate insights from the different schools of translation theory. Perhaps Hewson and Martin (1991) are right: rather than one theory, we need a variational approach based on the practice and process of translating. The next section deals with this.

CHAPTER 6

TRANSLATING (PROCESS)

The first part of the theoretical framework was about translation (the abstract concept that includes the process and the product). This second part is about translating (the process, the activity). Teaching prose translating—the activity, the skill—is the subject of this book, so it is essential to understand how people translate and whether the constraints of translating into a foreign language alter the process. This section takes a descriptive approach to the process of translating, because only by understanding the process can a practical teaching methodology be evolved. Indeed, for some writers the whole purpose of translation theory is "to reach an understanding of the processes undertaken in the act of translation and, not, as is so commonly misunderstood, to provide a set of norms for effecting the perfect translation" (Bassnett-McGuire, 1980: 37).

This seems simpler than it is. How can we understand or describe a process that takes place inside the translator's head? Do we have any data that are not the finished translation (i.e., the product)? Few translators can do more than describe the physical process: sit at a desk with paper and pencil or word processor and mouse, read the text; write a first-draft translation; consult a dictionary, data base, or expert; revise. They know that something complicated is going on in their heads, but they find it difficult to verbalize.

Some insights into the process have been gained by observing interpreters at work. Danika Seleskovitch (1968, 1975, 1976, 1982; Seleskovitch and Lederer, 1986) and Marianne Lederer (1973, 1976), at l'École Supérieure d'Interprètes et de Traducteurs de Paris (ESIT), developed *la théorie du sens*, which is based on what goes on in the process of simultaneous and consecutive interpreting. Jean Delisle (1980), at the University of Ottawa, went further and applied this theory to teaching translation of pragmatic texts (defined as those in which the informative function outweighs the expressive function). Amparo Hurtado Albir (1990b) has clarified and developed the description of the translation process based on *la théorie du sens*.

The ESIT approach fulfils three of the four basic requirements of any theoretical model: empiricism, determinism, and parsimony. Whether or not it fulfils the requirement of generality has been questioned. Delisle applies the theory only to pragmatic texts. Newmark (1991) has fulminated against the assumption implicit in the ESIT approach that all translation is nothing but communication. However, as was suggested in the previous chapter, Gutt's application of relevance theory to translation may solve this problem by expanding the notion of a communicative translation and thus doing away with the dichotomy between communicative and semantic, dynamic and formal, and so on. Hurtado Albir's definition of *faithfulness* in translation as *fidélité au sens* is another contribution in this direction. The dichotomy loses all relevance if analysis begins with the three basic principles of *la théorie du sens*: (1) *le vouloir dire*, or communicative intention of the author; (2) the specific mechanisms of the TL; and (3) the TL reader.

Bell (1991) has also written about the translation process, drawing from many different disciplines within the cognitive sciences—artificial intelligence, computer science, psychology, logic, and so on—to do so. Bell's findings do not conflict with those of the Paris School; rather, they seem to confirm them.

INSIGHTS FROM CONSECUTIVE AND SIMULTANEOUS INTERPRETING

Interpreting, both consecutive and simultaneous, provides information about the process that transforms one semiotic entity into another and transmits a message in one linguistic code into another. Seleskovitch and Lederer concluded from their experience as interpreters and teachers of interpreting that between the stages of listening (comprehension) and speaking (reformulation), there is a stage of deverbalization. In consecutive interpreting, the speaker breaks his or her SL discourse into fragments (which may be as much as ten minutes in length). At the end of each pause, the interpreter summarizes the contents of the speech in the TL, basing his or her discourse on the notes that he or she has taken. Considerable developments have been made in taking notes for this purpose. Although each interpreter may eventually develop his or her personal system, interpreter training includes lessons in note taking, and very often the symbols used are not part of a linguistic code; the interpreter's notes tend to be ideograms (except for names, dates, and numbers). Seleskovitch (1975) analyzed interpreters' reformulations and concluded that they were produced in function not of the words that had been said but of a deverbalized message.

Note taking in consecutive interpreting gives us some clues to the interaction between cognitive and verbal contexts and clearly suggests that the message is deverbalized: the sheer bulk of notes taken does not depend on the number of words spoken, and the notes are not lineal as in shorthand; the quantity of notes diminishes toward the end of the speech, when the interpreter has formulated a macrostructure that helps him or her to understand the speaker and provides "hooks" on which to "hang" detailed information; the notes are often symbolic and include words that were not used in the speech; and different interpreters take a different set of notes for the same speech and reformulate the same set of notes with different words. The only items that do not change from interpreter to interpreter and are usually written down are words that are essentially referential, such as names and figures.

As Seleskovitch (1976) has pointed out, memory and understanding are inseparable; one is a function of the other. What we store in our long-term memory is semantic information or the mnemonic trace of the verbal message. Experiments in cognitive psychology suggest that our verbal memory is very ephemeral; we tend to store concepts rather than words. In "click" experiments, the subject is asked to remember a list of utterances read aloud and interrupted at intervals by a sound. These experiments show that if the "click" is put at the end of a sense unit rather than in the middle, the subject is much more likely to remember the utterances.

Simultaneous interpreting in its present form has been possible only since the Second World War, because it depends on electronic equipment that allows the interpreter to be in a soundproof booth, hear the SL speaker through a pair of headphones, and without a pause reformulate the message in the TL. The process is much more transparent than that in consecutive interpreting or in other forms of translation. All of the elements of the communicative situation are present synchronically in the same room: the speaker, the audience, the topic, the context. Modern booths are fitted with glass so that the interpreters can see the speaker and be seen themselves. Interpreters can work at a speed that would not be possible if they were interpreting words (about 150 words per minute) rather than units of meaning. If they concentrated on the words, their speech would be awkward, slow, opaque; however, they retain not the words but *le sens*, or the deverbalized meaning, which is defined in the ESIT theory as a cognitive memory.

Seleskovitch (1976: 65) quotes specialists in neuropsychology, in particular J. Barbizet, to support the theory of deverbalization. Research into accidents and strokes affecting the brain in different ways—such as loss of speech but retention of reasoning, or loss of complex reasoning but retention of words—suggests the existence of two types of memory: one lexical and grammatical and the other nonverbal. It seems that linguistic competence and cognitive competence are situated in different parts of the brain and that both are needed to understand a locution. It may also be true that some individuals have more of one than the other, which would explain in part the saying "Interpreters are born, not made." Simultaneous interpreting can be envisaged as unnatural and artificial because the two stages (understanding and reformulation) are syncopated. Not everyone can develop this skill to the same extent, but in a recording of a good professional it is possible to follow the two stages at the same time.

Memory also has an important role to play in understanding, and it is important to distinguish between short-term and long-term memory. Short-term memory retains sensory perceptions just long enough to integrate them into acquired knowledge. Adults can retain seven to eight words for two to three seconds. This grouping of words in the short-term memory also suggests that word-by-word translation is anti-natural. The words in the short-term memory interact with the long-term cognitive memory, which frees the necessary linguistic and extralinguistic knowledge to create a unit of meaning.

> .Les unités de sens sont le produit d'une synthèse des quelques mots qui se trouvent dans la mémoire immédiate et des expériences ou des souvenirs cognitifs préexistants qu'ils éveillent; cette fusion laisse une trace cognitive, tandis que la mémoire immédiate accueille et conserve un instant les mots suivants, jusqu'à une nouvelle synthèse et à la création d'une nouvelle unité qui va s'ajouter à celles que contient déjà la mémoire cognitive. (Lederer, 1986: 252)

From the point of view of translation-teaching methodology, the stage of deverbalization is the most important concept to retain from this research into the process of interpreting. In Bell's (1991: 21) model, the stage of deverbalization is referred to as a stage of language-free semantic representation.

DIFFERENCES BETWEEN TRANSLATING AND INTERPRETING

Translating is based on the written word; interpreting, on the spoken word. Both intervene in an act of communication that has been interrupted due to differences between the codes used by the transmitter and the receiver. However, the interpreter participates in the same communicative context both physically and temporally, whereas the translator is separated from the transmitter and the receiver by both time and space. This distance in time and space makes it more difficult to integrate linguistic and extralinguistic information and transmit the message accurately.

In translating, as in simultaneous interpreting, there are three main stages (understanding, deverbalization, and reformulation), but simultaneous interpreting is an oral activity. It takes place at the speed of normal speech, all the elements of the situation of the SL discourse are present, transmission and reception are synchronized, the words disappear leaving no trace, intonation and gestures are taken into account. Translating is bound to the mechanisms of reading and writing and takes on the characteristics of texts.

Furthermore, the very solidity of the written word tempts the translator to stay with the words rather than the sense. Eugene Nida gave the example of a blind Navajo who was an excellent Bible translator. He was a skilled Braille reader, but he did his best work when someone read out a verse to him and he translated orally. When he was allowed to have his fingers on his Braille Bible, the quality of the translation suffered considerably (Nida, 1992).

Innumerable examples could be given of the failure to transmit the message accurately in translating—"*l'infidélité au sens.*" A recent television guide in *El País* included the blurb for an American sitcom, "The Golden Girls" (*Las chicas de oro*): "*Un terror sagrado* visita a Las chicas de oro en forma de un chico de 13 años" (emphasis added). Viewers, expecting black magic at the very least, must have been disappointed by the appearance of a normally naughty boy, a "holy terror." If the translator had bothered to make sense of his or her translation, had had time to see the episode beforehand, or had deverbalized, he or she would not have written nonsense.

Because the writer and the translator do not share the same communicative situation, the translator can work at his or her own rhythm, unless he or she has a deadline to meet. The written text is permanent and outlives the first communicative situation; each reading takes place in a new communicative situation. Therefore, much that is implicit in an oral discourse, through situation, intonation, or gestures, has to be made explicit in a written text. The coherence of written discourse has to be more obvious, thoughtful, and organized. The writer must know the conventions of the written language (graphic, lexical, grammatical, and textual); he or she has time to think of alternative forms of expression.

The translator has to be an expert reader, capable of activating his or her extralinguistic cognitive memory to interact with and make sense of the text. The interpreter deverbalizes on reception of the message. As the written text is permanent, the reader is not forced to follow the text straight through from beginning to end; he or she may choose to read the conclusion first, to reread certain sections, or to return to the beginning. We do not understand a text when we remember all of the words but when we have made an effort of synthesis, a mental process of understanding that is not verbal. A good translator is not necessarily a good interpreter; he or she may not have a good auditive memory or possess the reflexes necessary to make a rapid synthesis.

THE CYCLE OF INQUIRY

In all aspects of life, we continuously perceive phenomena through sight, sound, smell, and touch. We attempt to understand these phenomena inductively and deductively. In the case of trying to understand the phenomenon of translation, we can start with the end product, a translation, and work backwards (inductively) to understand the process of translating. At the same time, we can work (deductively) from what we know about how our minds work (experience) when translating (the process) to reach an understanding of a translation.

Work in educational psychology suggests that we are most efficient when we combine both the inductive and deductive methods. For example, if we want to know what the minimum unit of translation is, there is good psychological and linguistic evidence to suggest that it is the clause, since the clause (a) tends to be about the right length to be entered on the visuo-spatial scratch-pad in the working memory, and (b) is the focal point of all three macrofunctions of language and the product of three simultaneous semantic processes: a representation of experience, an interactive exchange, and a message (Bell, 1991: 223).

From this hypothesis, we can then work back inductively to see if there is evidence in the process of translation that, in fact, the clause is the unit of translation. This evidence can be found in the experiments quoted by Bell (Jacobvits, 1970, cited in Bell, 1991: 29), which support the notion of concurrence between cognitive "chunk" boundaries and syntactic boundaries within the clause; boundaries within major structural units (subject, predicate, complement, and so on); and the forms that realize them (phrases, for the most part). Therefore, in reading a passage such as "The United Nations Secretary General reported substantial progress in the peace negotiations in Geneva today," the cognitive "chunks," or units of meaning, would probably be:

[the United Nations Secretary General]
[reported]
[substantial progress in the peace negotiations]
[in Geneva]
[today]

At the same time, we can start with this evidence and from it deduce a theory. Understanding is not vertical, nor is it strictly linear. The gradual building-up of composite meaning is known in the field of artificial intelligence as top-down and bottom-up processing. Bell (1991) provides a chart for what he calls the cycle of inquiry, which is followed to reach an understanding of the simplest natural phenomenon. We should bear it in mind when considering how to understand discourse, the translation process, and the learning process. When we perceive a phenomenon, we can attempt to understand it in two ways: by induction, we build a hypothesis, which we then confirm or reject by comparing it with other similar phenomena, or we observe the phenomenon systematically and by deduction propose a theory.

Adding the *Skopos* to the Model of the Translation Process

The three main stages of the translation process are comprehension, deverbalization, and reformulation. Delisle (1980: 82–5) adds a fourth stage to the translation process: *l'analyse justificative*. This is the stage of verification at which the translator returns to the original text to check if he or she has really transmitted the sense of the original—what Newmark calls back-translation. Hurtado Albir (1990b: 71) provides a model of these four stages for interpreting and translating in *La notion de fidélité en traduction*. The model provided by Bell for the translation process derives from work in psycholinguistics and artificial intelligence. Instead of comprehension and reformulation, he refers to analysis and synthesis. He also incorporates elements of discourse analysis, so he includes the concepts of field, mode, and tenor.

These models do not account for the purpose of the translation, or the TLT. Emphasis on the *skopos* has been the principal contribution of recent German writers (see Vermeer, 1983; Reiss and Vermeer, 1984; Nord, 1991). It is an essential element in any professional situation and should also be an essential element in the classroom. If the teacher does not define the purpose of the translation, by default the purpose will be to please the teacher. Language teachers now try to avoid giving colourless, purposeless assignments of the type "My Summer Holidays," or "Autumn." Gombrich (1969) compares the role of medieval art patrons in the production of a work of art with the role of a grain of sand in an oyster that produces a pearl. The constraints of the orders given by bishops and popes helped to produce the masterpieces of Michelangelo and Leonardo. Translation students need to be told why they are translating a text; they need to be given a *skopos*. The context of the translation is an essential element of the translation process.

The model proposed here (see figure 6.1) is intended to remind students of the different dimensions of discourse that have to be accounted for at each stage of the translation process. A flow chart has not been attempted within each stage, as the process is not linear but bottom-up, top-down, and at each stage there is interaction between macro- and microstructures.

The translation process is the same whether it is from English to Spanish or Spanish to English, B language to A language or A language to B language. The difference is only in the time and effort needed at each stage. Depending on the amount of knowledge in the translator's syntactic, semantic, pragmatic, and semiotic memory, more or less time and effort will be required in comprehension or reformulation, analysis or synthesis.

COMPREHENSION

Before embarking upon any translation, the translator should analyze the text or discourse thoroughly, since this appears to be the only way of ensuring that the SL original has been wholly and correctly understood (Nord, 1991: 1). The *Oxford English Dictionary* gives the origin of the word *text* as the Latin, *texere*: to weave; thus, *textus* is the style or tissue of a literary work—literally, that which is woven, a texture, a web. A written text is constructed according to a pattern (obviously, some are better constructed than others). The words and sentences that make up the text are woven into the web of the text. In certain texts, a skilled reader is needed to grasp the whole pattern.

The metaphor of text as web is an ancient one. Another possible metaphor is a text as a skeleton. Following this metaphor, discourse is a skeleton plus blood, flesh, and guts (ideology, emotions, and soul). Linguistics can provide the tools to analyze texts, but other disciplines are required to analyze discourse. Of course, the distinction between text and discourse is not clear cut, because the text producer

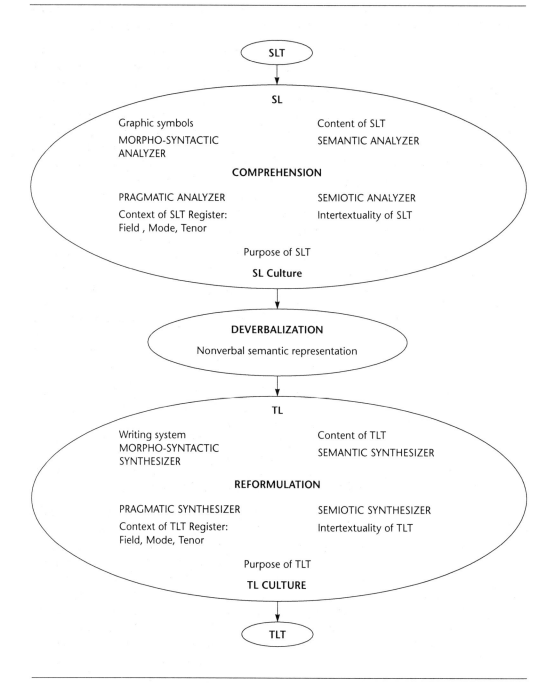

Figure 6.1 Model of Dimensions of Discourse

(writer, reader, or translator) constantly interacts with both. Furthermore, many authors do not maintain this distinction and refer to text as written discourse.

As mentioned above, translation studies have been influenced by developments in related disciplines. One of the most important developments in twentieth-century literary studies has been the re-evaluation of the reader, who is envisaged as taking an active rather than a passive role. For Roland Barthes (1975), the reader is not a *consumer* of texts but a *producer*. Julia Kristeva "sees the reader as realising the expansion of the work's process of semiosis" (Bassnett-McGuire, 1980: 79). Since each reader "translates" or "decodes" the text according to a different set of systems, there is no "correct" reading. It has even been maintained that a text does not have a function until it is defined by the recipient (reader/translator of SLT or reader of TLT) in the act of reading. As a product of the author's intention, the text remains provisional until it is received by its reader; in other words, the text as a communicative act is completed by the recipient (Nord, 1991: 16).

This concept is useful, but only up to a point. There is hardly any reason to teach translators to improve their reading skills if there is no agreement over what constitutes a correct reading. Translation-oriented text/discourse analysis must cover all of the relevant text/discourse features and elements within the framework of the purpose for which the translation has been initiated and the translation context. Even within a variational approach to translation that assumes that there is no one perfect version, the translator should be able to justify each and every decision in terms of the context of the translation.

Intertextuality is one of these relevant text features, the importance of which has been emphasized in the work of poststructuralist literary critics. Laurence Venuti's (1992) *Rethinking Translation*, a collection of essays on literary translations as creations, is concerned with raising the status of the translator, using the arguments of twentieth-century literary criticism (Venuti, 1991). Octavio Paz (1971: 9) has shown how, from an intertextual approach, all SLTs are unique and yet, at the same time, "translations" of other texts, and how all TLTs are "original" creations.

The first Catalan translation (1953) of Milton's *Paradise Lost* is an example of this. The translator, Josep Ma. Boix i Selva, was concerned with reproducing the form and function of Milton's poem as faithfully as possible. However, the translation was published just after the Spanish Civil War, and one of the purposes of the translation was to defend the Spanish republican cause, just as Milton had defended the English republic. The introduction to the translation was carefully designed to convince Franco's censors that the poem was harmless by denying Milton's republican, Protestant views. Fortunately, the censor read only the introduction, and so the poem was published. For skilled readers who progressed beyond the introduction, intertextuality made the translator's political implications clear.[12] Another

---

12. Rosa Flotats i Crispi, doctoral dissertation in progress at Universidad Autónoma de Barcelona.

example of intertextuality in *Paradise Lost* comes from an English-literature teacher at an English secondary school. He claimed that only Muslim students could make sense of *Paradise Lost* because they knew about heaven and hell from reading the Koran. The other students had little or no knowledge of the Bible, and so they found *Paradise Lost* meaningless.

Pre-translating text/discourse analysis provides not only a full comprehension of the SLT/discourse and an explanation of its linguistic, textual, and discourse structures and their relationship with the system and rules of the SL and the SL culture, but also a reliable basis for every decision that the translator has to make in a particular translation process. Therefore, text/discourse analysis for the translator has to be integrated into a general theory of translation that will serve as a frame of reference.

UNDERSTANDING AN A-LANGUAGE TEXT

The fact of translating from the A language does not in any way diminish the importance of the SLT analysis. Trainee translators need to develop their translator-oriented reader expertise in their mother tongue. Problems of meaning in the translation are just as likely to arise from misunderstanding the SLT as from insufficient competence in the TL.

Any reader, or translator, has to possess linguistic competence in the SL. Linguistic competence (syntactic and semantic) is obviously essential, but in isolation it is not sufficient. In order to understand a word, a phrase, or a text, we need to draw on our pragmatic knowledge of the situational, verbal, cognitive, and general socio-historical contexts. This is one of the most important lessons that students learn in the prose-translation class. They assume that because they have native-speaker competence in Spanish, all their problems will arise in the reformulation stage. They sometimes make mistakes in meaning due to insufficient knowledge of their own language and ignorance of the context and intertextuality of the SLT. The mistakes made by Spanish students translating the following text were due to weak reading skills. In some cases, they either did not possess sufficient knowledge of the different contexts or failed to activate their existing knowledge. In other cases, they either had not read enough newspaper articles of this type to grasp the intertextuality or did not draw on their stored knowledge. In either case, pre-translation reading-comprehension exercises could help them to realize the need to develop their knowledge of context through reading and/or to make active use of their own knowledge.

La amenaza del "frente" sur

El avance del integrismo islámico en el norte de Africa
acerca a la frontera española la guerra del Golfo

Mi hijo va a la American School de Rabat. Cada día lo trae y lo lleva al colegio un autobús de aspecto tan inequívocamente americano como la Coca-Cola,

Rambo o el presidente Bush. Dos semanas antes de que se declarara la guerra llegó muy contento a casa.

"Papá, ¿sabes que somos muy populares en el barrio?

Temí lo peor.

"Cuando nuestro bus pasa ante el colegio marroquí del barrio los niños salen a la calle para saludarnos y decirnos cosas, 'Uuuaaa, USA, USA', nos gritan".

Era casi lo peor.

Recordé que el pasado 14 de diciembre, cuando estalló la revuelta de Fez y el lujoso hotel Les Meridines fue asaltado por una horda de desheredados, un grupo de turistas—entre ellos varios españoles—se convirtió en blanco de sus iras y, tras amenazarlos y robarlos, acabaron vejándoles y frotándoles pedazos de cebolla por el rostro. Pocas semanas más tarde, Abdelkader Kaduhi, de 53 años de edad, *se lió la manta a la cabeza* y apuñaló en *Casablanca* a dos ingenieros franceses, Lucien Bonelli y Michel Veyrie, que se encontraban trabajando en el país en virtud de un convenio de cooperación técnica entre las dos naciones hermanas.

Empecé a tranquilizarme una semana después al leer en la prensa oficial un comunicado de las dos viudas—Un gesto de paz lo habían titulado—afirmando que se trataba del acto de un desequilibrado y rechazando cualquier manipulación partidista del luctuoso suceso. Acabó de tranquilizarme el director general de Africa y Oriente Medio del Ministerio de Asuntos Exteriores español, Jorge Dezcallar, cuando en el transcurso de una conferencia de prensa celebrada en la residencia del embajador español en Rabat, aseguró que "los españoles estamos seguros en Marruecos." (Ferran Sales, "La amenaza del 'frente' sur," *El País*, Feb. 1991)

The article is about Islamic fundamentalism in North Africa during the Gulf War. The journalist was reporting on the assassination of two French engineers in Casablanca. Few of the Spanish students knew the expression *se lió la manta a la cabeza*. Most of them recognized it as an idiomatic expression and found suitable solutions: "went the whole hog," "went even further," "went over the edge," "took courage," "took action." One student translated it literally: "Abdelkader Kaduhi *wrapped the blanket round his head* and stabbed the two French engineers in the *White House*." The student's translation of "Casablanca" as "the White House," despite the fact that the text was about North Africa, proved that her real problem was that she was simply translating words; she had not activated her situational, verbal, cognitive, and socio-historical knowledge to interact with the text and make sense of it.

The *situational context* comprises all elements of the situation in which the discourse was transmitted or the speech act took place: location, people, events.

The *verbal context* comprises all the words in the text and how they are grouped. Only the verbal context in *se lió la manta a la cabeza* signals this as an idomatic expression: *se lió* cannot be translated as "he rolled himself a cigarette" as in *se lió un cigarrillo* or "he had an affair with his secretary" as in *se lió con la secretaria*. The verbal context gives us the clues necessary to work through the polysemy of words in order to find the right meaning.

The *cognitive context* comprises all of the information gathered from the text during the reading. The article begins with the journalist recounting his son's experiences going to the American school in Rabat and how the Moroccan children jeered at the American school bus. Abdelkadar went the whole hog a few weeks after a crowd attacked a group of European tourists in a luxury hotel in Fez on December 14. The tourists were threatened, robbed, and even had their faces rubbed with onions! Unpleasant as it must have been, there was obviously a qualitative difference between this and the assassination.

The *general socio-historical context* comprises all the events, codes, and social relationships necessary for understanding the text. Although this article is written in a rather amusing, ironic tone, it expresses serious concern for the safety of Spaniards living in Morocco, which is comprehensible only in the context of the fundamentalists' reaction against the "allies" of the United States during the Gulf War.

When readers process a text successfully, all of their extralinguistic knowledge of context is activated. This activation is still beyond the scope of computers. Therefore, machine translation is effective only with texts that keep within a very limited and controlled context. However, I do regard machine-translation programs with greater respect after a little experiment that took place just before the outbreak of the Gulf War. We were trying out a new translation program, and a colleague typed out a sentence that was very much in our minds at that time: "Mr. Bush is going to start the Third World War." The computer translated: "Sr. arbusto va a empezar la guerra del tercer mundo" (Mr. bush is going to start the war of the Third World).

REFORMULATION

> Language does not give names to pre-existing things and concepts so much as it articulates the world of our experience. The images of art, we suspect, do the same. But this difference of styles or languages need not stand in the way of correct answers and descriptions. The world may be approached from a different angle and the information given may yet be the same. (Gombrich, 1977: 7)

Once the translator, as expert reader, has grasped the sense of his or her text and stored it as semantic representation, he or she is ready to begin the job of writing. In this stage, as in the first, the different levels of context (verbal, cognitive, situational, and general) play an important role. The translator has to take into account a new communicative situation: the purpose for which the text is being translated; the readers of the translation; their social and cultural situation; the extent to which their knowledge sets include the contexts of the original; the linguistic, social, and cultural assumptions they share with the SLT readers.

THE CONTEXT OF SITUATION AND REFORMULATION

The anthropologist B. Malinowski (1923, 1935) first worked out his theory of context to solve a translation problem: how to present the culture of the Melanesian peoples in the Trobriand Islands of the Western Pacific to English-speaking readers. He studied their culture through texts (oral tradition, narration of ceremonies, fishing expeditions, and so on). The distance between their culture and the English-speaking world before the Second World War was immense. (This was before the advent of modern communication techniques and the mass media.)

If he had opted for a free, reader-oriented translation, the texts would have been intelligible but would not have provided information about the SL culture, which was the purpose of his research. A literal, text-oriented translation would have preserved the original at the price of making it totally unintelligible to the English reader. His solution was a translation with commentary to situationalize the text by relating it to its verbal and nonverbal environment. He included every possible aspect of the culture surrounding the production and reception of the text and called it the context of situation.

The distance separating Spanish from English at the end of the twentieth century is not nearly so great: the languages are related, and the two cultures have much in common. A commentated translation is rarely needed, except in the case of some historical documents or "sacred" texts. Nevertheless, the translator can never forget the context of situation. Hatim and Mason believe that translators "have long been aware of the role of situational factors (source, status, client, use to be made of translation)" (1990: 38), but that linguistics has been slow to catch up. Today, under the influence of Malinowski and many others, "description of communicative events is now fairly widely recognized as the proper goal of linguistic analysis." As Gregory points out,

> The difference between situational and other kinds of linguistic description has been greatly exaggerated. Much of the absence . . . of development of contextual and situational statement has been due to what might be termed a remarkable failure of nerve, a fear as to what is a describable relevant situational feature, a situational "fact." (Gregory, 1967: 178)

FUNCTIONAL EFL AND PROSE TRANSLATING

English as a Foreign Language (EFL) teaching has been a booming industry for at least the last twenty years and has been quick to apply situational linguistic description to language teaching. In Spain, for example, the demand for English classes makes the sale of textbooks big business. All of the English-language textbooks in the shops at the moment are based on communicative, functional notions. Nearly all students at the university level have learned English using this type of textbook.

This is an obvious advantage for translation teachers, particularly those teaching translation from Spanish to English: the students have already been "educated" in the notion of appropriateness.

If they have taken Cambridge First Certificate or Proficiency exams, they will have been trained to respond to situations. For example:

> You have gone to the dry-cleaner's to collect your suit and find that it has shrunk. What would you say?

> You have been invited to a party and do not want to go but you don't want to be rude. What would you say?

> You have been stopped by a traffic policeman who is going to give you a ticket for driving down a one-way street. You try to persuade him not to.

REGISTER AND REFORMULATION

In order to respond correctly to these situations, the student has to make choices from the three basic categories of register: field or domain, mode, and tenor.

Field of discourse[13] should not be confused with subject matter or topic. Political discourse is one field, but the subject matter of political discourse may be, for instance, defence, sovereignty, pensions, taxes, or education. Different languages develop different fields of discourse in different ways. For example, the scientific discourse of English is very marked. This may lead to problems of the sort commented on in the previous chapter when translating academic texts from Spanish to English. The English field of law, based on common law and the traditions of the English courts, is very different from the Spanish field based on Roman law and a different legal system. The most difficult translation I ever attempted was of a legal textbook in Spanish on the concept of time in law, based on the work of a German philosopher (yet another field).

Mode of discourse refers to the medium used, basically speech or writing (see figure 6.2). Gregory and Carrol (1978: 47) illustrate the different variations of mode in the following way:

If the President of the United States addresses the United Nations, his field of discourse will be political and the mode will be a text written to be read as speech. His speechwriters will have to take into account the channels through which this speech will reach different audiences: direct to the members of the General Assembly, and via television, radio, and newspapers to the public. The differences that we have established between interpreters and translators are largely questions of mode.

There are many translators in Spain working on dubbing and subtitling for cinema and television, and this is a professional option for translation students. In

---

13. Crystal and Davy (1969) refer to *province,* which emphasizes the occupational, professional, and specialized character of fields (for example, a religious sermon).

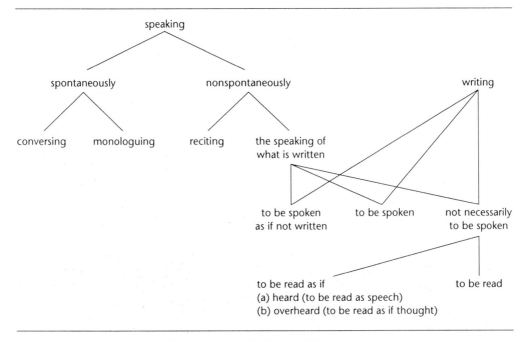

speaking

spontaneously   nonspontaneously   writing

conversing   monologuing   reciting   the speaking of
                                            what is written

                                      to be spoken   to be spoken   not necessarily
                                      as if not written   to be spoken

                                      to be read as if   to be read
                                      (a) heard (to be read as speech)
                                      (b) overheard (to be read as if thought)

Figure 6.2 Variations of Mode

dubbing, the translator is limited by the time of the original speech and has to take into account certain phonological features that are very evident if the spectators can see the mouths of the actors—for example, the labials [b], [m], and [p]. Subtitling is restricted by questions of space on the screen and may have to reproduce aspects of speech such as the slurred speech of a drunkard. Dubbing into the foreign language is not really a viable professional option for prose translators. However, it is certainly a valuable learning activity for the insights it gives to mode switching and deverbalization.

Tenor of discourse reflects the relationship between speaker and audience, writer and reader. Traditionally, this has been described as a continuum from frozen to intimate. Bell (1991: 186) distinguishes four overlapping and interacting levels of tenor: formality, politeness, impersonality, and accessibility.

Formality signals a more distant relationship between writer and reader. The greater care given to the structuring of the message also shows the degree of "importance" of the text. Formality is expressed in different ways. English is particularly rich in lexical alternatives due to the historical development of the language. The lexical alternative of Greek, Latin, or French origin is frequently used when a more formal tenor is required, and that of Germanic origin is used in more informal situations. This means that more formal texts may be easier to translate from the point of view of vocabulary for Spanish students. Of course, they have to be aware of "false friends," but, as Newmark maintains, there are more "close friends" than "false friends," particularly when a formal tenor is used. For example:

Los mismos jefes de <u>Estado</u> y los de los 12 países <u>neutrales</u> <u>europeos</u> <u>ratificarán</u> una <u>Carta Europea,</u> especie de <u>Constitución</u> del Viejo Continente, que <u>incluye</u> las <u>libertades</u> y derechos <u>humanos funda-mentales</u> que deben <u>prevalecer</u> en "la nueva <u>era</u> de <u>democracia, paz</u> y libertad", y a continuación <u>establece</u> un código de <u>conducta</u> para las nuevas <u>relaciones</u> entre vecinos europeos. (*El País,* 18 Sept. 1990)	The same heads of <u>state</u> and the 12 <u>neutral</u> <u>European</u> countries will <u>ratify</u> a European <u>Charter</u>, a kind of European <u>constitution</u>, which <u>includes</u> the <u>fundamental human</u> rights and <u>liberties</u> that should <u>prevail</u> in "the new <u>era</u> of <u>democracy, peace,</u> and freedom" and <u>establishes</u> a <u>code of conduct</u> for the new <u>relations</u> between European neighbours. Translation student X

This version, which relies very heavily on "close friends," is perfectly adequate because it is a formal text. Students have to learn to recognize switches in levels of formality, but when the level is maintained in the SLT they must avoid mismatches. This example comes from Alan Duff's (1981) charming book *The Third Language* about the problems facing English native speakers when they translate into English (most of his examples are taken from French): "However we learn from Sorokin and Hart the lesson that a *plethora* of information is *available* and can be *dug out* from our libraries" (p. 7).

Formality is also marked syntactically. One technique in English is pre-modification, or left-branching. This is a technique that Spanish students recognize as very English; they use it correctly in formal texts but they do not recognize it as a formal marker and tend to overuse it in less formal texts. In the first text below, which is about international relations, it is acceptable, but in the second, which is a more "literary" article about the homeless in New York collecting tins for cash, it is not.

1. Washington se muestra pesimista sobre la mediación que inicia Pérez de Cuéllar

Pérez de Cuéllar, el veterano diplomático peruano de 70 años . . . el acuerdo de alto de fuego entre Irán e Irak . . . (*El País*, 29 Aug. 1990)	The 70-year-old veteran Peruvian diplomat, Pérez de Cuéllar . . . the Iran-Iraq cease-fire agreement . . . Translation student Y

2. Nueva York, el mayor basurero del mundo

Esto es el sonido de los mendigos de fin de siglo . . . Duermen, como Walter, en frente de tiendas abiertas las 24 horas. (*El País,* 3 Sept. 1991)	This is the end of the century beggars sound . . . Like Walter, they sleep in front of 24 hour open shops. Translation student Z

The massively heavy left-branching noun phrases found in some English formal discourse are so difficult to decode that the reader is forced to pay considerable time and attention to the text, which is one of the goals of the writer.

Politeness reflects the social distance between the writer and the reader. There are two main dimensions: power relations between social groups and power relations between individuals, connected with status, seniority, and authority. Spanish has many ways of expressing politeness, but the most obvious is the address system (*usted* versus *tú*). The use of *usted* in Spain is changing. During the democratic transition, it was much less common. Today it is used more frequently in certain formal situations, but other uses seem to have died out. For example, children do not address their parents as *usted*. English has only "you," and politeness has to be expressed by the use of titles and of lexical and syntactic markers. Spanish visitors to England are often surprised by the frequency with which they hear "Excuse me" and "Sorry," and they find the commonly used polite request forms amusing (for example, "Would you mind opening the window?").

Impersonality refers to whether the writer's or reader's presence is made explicit in the text or whether the first- or second-person is used. Typical examples can be found in academic, bureaucratic, and legal texts (for example, "it" as subject, passive constructions, abstract nouns.) Impersonality is highly valued in Spanish formal writing.

Accessibility reflects the assumptions that the writer has made about the extent to which the reader shares his or her knowledge of the universe of the discourse. If a physicist is writing for other physicists, there are certain basic laws implicit in the text, and he or she can use the specific terminology of the field. This text would be inaccessible to the general public. If the physicist is writing for a newspaper, he or she will have to resort to explicature for readers who do not share his or her knowledge of concepts, methodology, and terminology. The translator has to consider how TLT readers differ from the readers of the SLT and whether elements that are implicit in the original have to be made explicit.

Field, mode, and tenor refer to variation in language use. The translator also has to take dialectal—geographical, temporal, social, (non-)standard, idiolect—variations into account.

All of these variables, which may be expressed in macrostructures or microstructures, are interdependent. Together they help us to define[14] and identify registers. A certain level of formality (tenor) influences and is influenced by a particular level of technicality (field) in an appropriate channel of communication (mode).

---

14. This macro/micro interdependence is often described as simultaneous bottom-up and top-down analysis by translation theorists such as Bell (1991) and Hatim and Mason (1990).

CONCLUSION

This description of the translation process is the first step in defining a teaching methodology to help translation students discover the principles that have to be observed for correct development of the translation process. The next chapter looks at a translation (text) and how all of the previously mentioned factors intervene—how the translation process is never lineal but always cascaded—and how they are all interrelated and interdependent.

CHAPTER 7

A Translation (Text)

Microstructural and Macrostructural Interdependence

Micro-structural and macrostructural interdependence is the basis of text consumption and production and of translation. There is ample evidence of this interdependence in human action and language. Delisle's (1980) methodology is based on the interpretive theory of translation proposed by Seleskovitch, who found evidence of this interdependence in an analysis of the work of simultaneous and consecutive interpreters. This interdependence or interaction is also basic to recent work in semantics, narrative theory, rhetoric, psycholinguistics, sociolinguistics, cognitive psychology and pragmatics, action theory, philosophy of language, the theory of speech acts, and the social sciences.

The same trend can be seen in modern physics. Fritjof Capra, author of *The Tao of Physics*, wrote that in subatomic particles "every particle consists of all other particles." Subatomic particles are not separate entities but interrelated energy patterns in an ongoing dynamic process. These particles do not "contain" one another, but "involve" one another. Several theories (Chew's S-matrix theory and Bohm's Holomovement) recognize that consciousness may well be an essential aspect of the universe that will have to be included in future theory of physical phenomena (Capra, 1976: 137, 141).

In the field of human language, it is clear not only that the meaning of the macrostructure depends on the meanings of the microstructures, but that the meanings of the microstructures are determined by the constraints and global meaning of the macrostructure. Any translator worth his or her salt knows this intuitively, and intuitively makes the adjustments required by the global constraints and meaning of the text and context. Nevertheless, it is instructive at least once during an introductory translation course to make a systematic attempt to identify all of these global constraints, from the point of view of both the teacher and the student.

From the teacher's point of view, this effort can be compared to that made when a group of teachers agree on criteria for marking a translation. Of course, these criteria have to be worked out systematically, and even mathematically, so as to give a mark out of 10 for a translation, as is required by the educational system. However, marks are not always given for a translation by adding up half-points or decimals. If a few translations are marked using the criteria systematically and then a more intuitive marking system is used, the results are very similar. This is usually true even when two different teachers correct the same text, one adding up the marks mathematically and the other giving a global grade. For this to be possible, it is necessary to have passed through the analytical stage. For the students, it is also another stage in consciousness raising—consciousness of the problems of translation and of what the teachers are looking for when they correct a translation (which should be very similar to what a translation supervisor or reviser is looking for).

In this chapter, I make a systematic attempt to apply semantic and pragmatic analyses to a Spanish text and to show how the semantic and pragmatic macrostructural constraints influence the morphosyntactic and lexical microstructures.

The influence of the cognitive context on the verbal context—that is, how we understand units of meaning—is confirmed by the interpreting process, in particular by note-taking in consecutive interpreting. As we listen to or read language, we formulate a hypothetical macrostructure, which is confirmed or refuted by the underlying propositions of the text. This macrostructure allows us to understand a text, organize the information in our memory, and retrieve details if they are needed.

T.A. van Dijk began to work out a theory of how semantic and pragmatic constraints work in discourse analysis. This theory is still incomplete. Formal or logical semantics based on artificial languages (such as mathematics and logic) is complicated enough, but any semantic theory based on natural language is far more complex. Semantically speaking, "The meaning of a sequence of propositions is far more than the sum of propositions underlying the sequence. The meaning of sequence as a whole hierarchically orders the respective meaning of its sentences" (van Dijk, 1980: 144). The infinite number of combinations that may make up the context or frame of a sequence of speech acts means that any pragmatic theory has to account not only for the known world but for any possible or imaginary world. Pragmatically speaking, the value of a sequence of speech acts or a global speech act depends on the context. For example, the semantic meaning of the statement "The water's boiling" is "The temperature of the water has reached 100° C." The pragmatic meanings, however, are many: "Make the tea"; "Come for a swim"; "Add some cold water before you put baby in the bath." Although the suggestions made by van Dijk are necessarily incomplete, they do help in discourse analysis, which is the first stage in the translation process, understanding the SLT.

In both producing and understanding language, there is intentional control of lower elements by higher elements, and it is important to distinguish between grammatical laws and cognitive or pragmatic constraints. Cognitive constraints actually govern how we hear and understand phonetic and lexical information. Our understanding of speech depends on the verbal and cognitive contexts. How our brains process phonetic items depends on the understanding of units of meaning.

Children often misunderstand adult language for this reason and interpret unfamiliar words and syntax as familiar ones. Therefore, instead of singing the traditional Christmas carol as it was written, "We three kings of Orient are," they may sing, "We three kings of orange and tar." Alternatively, they may mistakenly choose a familiar pragmatic context to interpret a proposition, as did the little girl who drew a picture of an airplane when her Sunday-school teacher asked her to draw a picture of "The Flight into Egypt."

Adults find it difficult to make sense of texts from cultures that are very different from their own, even if the language itself presents no difficulty. For example, when reading James Joyce's *Ulysses,* my knowledge of Greco-Christian-British-Irish culture made it possible for me to formulate a hypothesis, or cognitive macrostructure, that allowed me to "make sense" of the words, even if my understanding is inferior to that of a Joyce scholar. My reading efficiency was much reduced when I read *The Interpreters* by Wole Soyinka. My ignorance of "the Nigerian context" impeded the formulation of a satisfactory macrostructure that would allow me to understand the book, even though Soyinka writes in English and his syntax and vocabulary are simpler than those of Joyce in *Ulysses.*

This is confirmed by what we know about the process of interpreting. When we read and translate, we accumulate a series of words and anticipate others in our search for sense units. The larger the unit, the better our understanding. A text is lineal only when it is being used for certain functions, such as dictation. Children learn to read letter by letter, then word by word, and then progress to reading with meaning. Translation students, particularly when they are translating into the foreign language, tend to return to infancy and get stuck at the level of the word. This is one reason that pre-translation contextual exercises are so important in training translators. As we read, we formulate a hypothetical macrostructure that is confirmed or refuted by the underlying propositions of the text. This macrostructure allows us to understand a text, organize the information in our memory, and retrieve details when we need them. Cognitive experiments prove how easy it is to remember the details of a story but not a list of unconnected sentences.

TEXT TYPE: ECONOMIC DISCOURSE

The text that has been chosen for analysis is from *Estructura económica internacional* (Tamames, 1980; this is the sixth edition of a work originally published in 1970) and it belongs to the field of textbook economics. The job of the translation teacher can be seen as consciousness raising, making students aware of elements that we do not normally notice when we read and write. These elements may be morphological, syntactic, semantic, pragmatic, or semiotic. Consciousness of text type is a very valuable skill for trainee translators to develop: "Our ability to recognise texts as instances of a type—exposition, argumentation, instruction—depends on our ability to recognise texts as signs. The way we recognise and respond to these signs is a regularity of language use which transcends boundaries of genre" (Hatim and Mason, 1990: 2).

Establishing criteria to distinguish systematically between different types of discourse is not easy. Fowler (1986) argues that the boundary between literature and nonliterature is an artificial one if the distinction is based on "creative use of language." Many of the features that are said to characterize the former will be found in the latter. McCloskey (1986) used the insights provided by modern literary approaches to text and rhetoric to analyze economic discourse. He highlighted the extensive use of abstract language, metaphor, and construction of fictional worlds that provide information about the belief structure of the discipline. In a later publication, he explored the idea of narrative or storytelling in economics. He suggests that a satisfying story for economists is the "Equilibrium Story" found in microeconomics: Equilibrium is the hero, and the story always ends with the triumph or defeat of Equilibrium (McCloskey, 1988).

Some translation teachers argue in favour of teaching literary translation on the grounds that students have to cope with all possible types of translation problems, and the skills they acquire can then be applied to any other kind of course. However, it does seem an unnecessary effort for students to sweat over Angela Carter when their first professional task will be to translate a computer manual.

Nearly all schools of translation in Europe include economics as one of the specialized branches of translation in which students can take extra-content courses. The Tamames text has been chosen for the following reasons:

1. To develop extralinguistic knowledge of the world—in this case, economic concepts and socio-economic information about the United States.

2. To work on the formal aspect of the different treatment of figures in Spanish and English.

3. To develop an understanding of the difference between standardized and nonstandardized vocabulary.

4. To develop vocabulary. This is a neglected area in current EFL teaching; in specialized texts, very often, the semitechnical vocabulary is the most problematic. As Jan Fisher suggests, "There is a clear need for a new approach to teaching vocabulary, but this should be focused on the ways that semitechnical English is used in economics writing rather than on specific technical vocabulary" (1990: 86).

5. To develop awareness of text types by approaching a genre in which the reader's expectations are very often at variance with the intentions and

persuasive devices used by the author. The reader has to make an effort to "see" the author's intentions, because they are often camouflaged under the "outmoded official methodology of economics as science" (McCloskey, 1986: 16). This is an exercise that is best done in *inversa*, when the students are working from their own culture and language.

6. To illustrate how the author's ideology is expressed in the text. This is particularly interesting with Tamames because the 1980 text can be compared with more recent texts by the same author in which the effect of "the new world order" gives rise to ideological ambiguities.

Estructura económica internacional
Ramón Tamames, Alianza, Madrid.
Primera edición: 1970
Sexta edición: 1980

International Economic Structure
Ramón Tamames, Alianza, Madrid.
First edition: 1970
Sixth edition: 1980
Translation: Allison Beeby

19. ESTADOS UNIDOS DE AMERICA

19.1. Datos básicos: El "Melting Pot" y el "American Way of Life".

Con una superficie de 9,4 millones (M en lo sucesivo) de kilómetros cuadrados, EE.UU. tenía a principios de 1980 una población de 222M de habitantes. Al ritmo de crecimiento actual (el 1,7 por 100), se calcula que la población llegará a 300M después del año 2.000.

La proporción de raza negra es de 10,5 por 100, existiendo otras minorías importantes, como los "mexicano-americanos" (unos 7,5 M) los puertorriqueños (unos 3,3M), los indios (0,9M), y otros grupos étnicos y lingüísticos menores todavía en curso de asimilación o que se resisten a ella. El anunciado conjunto de minorías es origen de toda una seria de problemas de racismo y discriminación que afectan—y afectarán—profundamente a la estabilidad de la sociedad norte-americana, todavía muy lejos de la homogeneización que se pretendió con las tesis del "*Melting Pot*" y del "*American Way of Life*".

19. THE UNITED STATES OF AMERICA

19.1. Basic Information: The Melting Pot and the American Way of Life.

The United States covers an area of 9.4 million (M) square kilometres and at the beginning of the 1980s had a population of 222M inhabitants. Calculations based on the present growth rate (1.7%) suggest that the population will reach 300M after the year 2000.

Blacks make up 10.5% of the population, and there are other large minority groups, such as Mexican Americans (some 7.5M), Puerto Ricans (some 3.3M), and American Natives (0.9M), along with other smaller ethnic and language groups. All of these groups are still in the process of assimilating or resisting assimilation. This has led to a series of problems of racism and discrimination, which are seriously undermining the stability of American society and will continue to do so. America is still very far from achieving the homogeneous society that was the aim of the Melting Pot and the American Way of Life.

Las tendencias segregacionistas e integracionistas en pugna se mantienen muy vivas. Y lo que es aún más importante, hay nuevos planteamientos por parte de los propios grupos minoritarios, que de ser espectadores pasivos, han pasado a posturas más radicales y reivindicativas de su propia personalidad frente a lo que "desde siempre" se consideró como el núcleo poblacional del país en términos de *elite*, los WASP (*White Anglo-Saxon Protestants*—Blancos Anglosajones Protestantes).

Si a esos problemas raciales se agregan los fuertes desequilibrios personales y regionales de renta, podemos explicarnos porqué en EE.UU. se ha desencadenado en nuestro tiempo una crisis de confianza frente a la exaltación tradicional de la democracia y las libertades personales. El pretendido sueño de un país socialmente homogéneo y estable se ha visto dramáticamente sacudido por la violencia, el manejo de la información masiva y el complejo industrial militar.

De forma aparentemente anecdótica, pero que da mucho a reflexionar, podría sintetizarse la situación social y psicológica de EE.UU. desde 1963 para acá en personas. J.F. Kennedy, asesinado en 1963 en circunstancias más que oscuras. El ex presidente Johnson que en 1970, por un temor inconfesable, no se atrevió a hacer las revelaciones que había prometido sobre el complot para aquel asesinato. Un candidato a la presidencia como Robert Kennedy, asesinado en 1968, seguramente como una consecuencia más de la intervención norteamericana en el Oriente Medio en apoyo de Israel. Dos líderes del movimiento negro como eran Malcolm X y Martin Luther King, igualmente

The conflict between segregation and integration is still very much a live issue today. Furthermore, and even more important, the minority groups themselves have adopted new tactics. Instead of being mere passive spectators or candidates for integration, they have taken more radical positions and defend their own identity against those who have always been considered the elite nucleus of the population, the WASPS (White Anglo-Saxon Protestants).

These racial problems, combined with a very unequal distribution of wealth, on both a personal and a regional scale, may explain why America is undergoing a crisis of confidence today. The traditional American values of democracy and individual freedom are themselves in question. The longed-for dream of a socially stable and homogeneous country has been dramatically shaken by violence, manipulation of the mass media, and the military-industrial complex.

A synthesis of the social and psychological history of the United States since 1963 could be made by looking at a few individuals. This may seem anecdotal, but it does give much food for thought. J.F. Kennedy was assassinated in 1963 under very shady circumstances. In 1970, Lyndon Johnson, the former president, held back by a dreadful secret fear, did not dare reveal the information he had promised about the plot behind Kennedy's assassination. Robert Kennedy, a presidential candidate, was assassinated in 1968, probably yet another indirect consequence of the American intervention in favour of Israel in the Middle East. Two leaders of the black movement, Malcolm

asesinados en un contexto no aclarado, pero sin duda por su liderazgo de sendos movimientos en pro de los derechos para los negros. Y un presidente como Nixon que violó fronteras, compromisos internacionales y extendió la guerra en el Sudeste Asiático, y que después—en su fase pacifista—cayó a causa del escándalo "Watergate".

X and Martin Luther King, were also assassinated. Again, the reasons were not made public, but the motive was, without doubt, their leadership in the struggle for black rights. President Nixon violated frontiers and international agreements and escalated the war in South East Asia. Later, in his pacifist phase, he was brought down by the Watergate scandal.

19.2. Las raíces del crecimiento económico de EE.UU.

19.2. The Roots of Economic Growth in the United States

Volviendo ahora a los datos económicos de base, registremos que el PNB anual de EE.UU. a nivel de julio 1978 se estimaba en 2.094.900M de dólares, lo que representa casi la mitad del total Producto Social de los paises del OCDE, un tercio del total del mundo. En ese mismo año, el PIB per capita se estimó en 8.670 dólares con salarios promedios en la industria (en 1978) de 250 dólares (semanal) y de 32 dólares (diario) en la agricultura, en la que sólo trabaja el 3 por 100 de la población activa.

To return to basic macro-economic information, in July 1978, the GNP of the United States was calculated at $2,094,900M. This represents nearly half the total social product of the OECD countries, a third of the world total. In the same year, GDP per capita was estimated at $8,670, with average wages of $250 a week in industry and $32 a day in agriculture. Only 3% of the working population is employed in agriculture.

Se trata pues de la fuerza de trabajo mejor retribuida del mundo, cuyos Sindicatos (AFL-CIO) han perdido todas sus aspiraciones de transformar el sistema, para integrarse plenamente en él, con la simple aspiración de obtener no una mejor calidad de vida sino, fundamentalmente, una mejor cantidad de bienes materiales.

Thus, the American work force is the best paid in the world. Their trade unions (AFL-CIO) have abandoned any dreams of transforming the system and have opted for full integration. They aspire simply to accumulate more material goods rather than to achieve a better quality of life.

Estados Unidos es un país de altas concentraciones en todos los aspectos. En términos de urbanización, las grandes áreas metropolitanas de las Costas Este y Oeste y de los Grandes Lagos alcanzan 16M de habitantes (Nueva York), 7M (Chicago y Los Angeles), 5M (Detroit), y las de más de tres millones son cinco.

From every point of view, the United States is a country of extremes, of high concentrations. In terms of urban development, the huge metropolitan areas of the east and west coasts and the Great Lakes are heavily populated: 16M (New York), 7M (Chicago and Los Angeles), 5M (Detroit), and five cities with more than 3M.

Incluso se concibe ya la configuración de verdaderas megalópolis, como San-San (desde San Diego a San Francisco, a lo largo de un amplio segmento de la costa de California), Chipits (desde Chicago a Pittsburg, en la región de los Grandes Lagos) y Boswash (desde Boston a Washington, en la Costa Este). Esas grandes concentraciones urbanas, a la par que permiten un alto nivel de vida y un intenso desarrollo cultural, generan un sinfín de problemas, típicos de la sociedad "postindustrial": la contaminación atmosférica y de las aguas, la deshumanización de la vida en los centros urbanos, el crimen en proporciones alarmantes, el consumo masivo de drogas, etc.

El crecimiento económico de los EE.UU. ha sido el resultado de un avance progresivo hacia el Oeste, desde los 13 Estados iniciales (las antiguas 13 colonias). Esa conquista de la Vieja Frontera se hizo en buena parte a base de una población nutrida por una inmigración masiva procedente de Europa (unos 40 millones de inmigrantes entre 1860 y 1939).

También será preciso recordar los fuertes impulsos que en el sistema productivo tuvieron las inversiones masivas de capital, igualmente procedente de Europa, así como la incidencia expansiva en la economía de los sucesivos conflictos bélicos (primera y segunda guerras mundiales, guerra de Corea y guerra de Indochina).

Alejado del teatro de las operaciones bélicas por dos grandes océanos, EE.UU. fue en la segunda guerra mundial un seguro "arsenal de las Democracias". Así, en tanto que la segunda guerra mundial redujo el potencial industrial de la URSS en casi 2/3, en EE.UU. dobló la capacidad de producción en poco más de cuatro años.

Indeed, the formation is already envisaged of megacities, such as San-San (from San Diego to San Francisco along a wide stretch of the Californian coast), Chipitts (from Chicago to Pittsburgh on the banks of the Great Lakes) and Boswash (from Boston to Washington on the east coast). Although these huge concentrations of urban development permit a high standard of living and intensive cultural development, they generate countless problems typical of post-industrial societies: air and water pollution, degradation of the inner cities, crime on an alarming scale, the massive consumption of drugs, etc.

The economic growth of the United States is the result of a continuous movement toward the West from the 13 founder states (the original 13 colonies). The conquest of the West was undertaken largely by a population fed by massive immigration from Europe (some 40M immigrants between 1860 and 1939).

Moreover, it should not be forgotten that the system of production was boosted by massive capital investment, once again from Europe, and that economic expansion was favoured by a succession of wars (the First and Second World Wars, the Korean War, and the Vietnam War).

During the Second World War, the United States was separated from the fighting zone by two enormous oceans and was a safe arsenal for the Allies. Therefore, whereas the industrial potential of the Soviet Union was reduced by nearly two thirds in the Second World War, the production capacity of the United States was doubled in a little over four years.

Translation-oriented Analysis of a Text

The part of Tamames's book that has been chosen for analysis is the introduction to the section on the United States. It is a text that has been translated (not into English, but into Portuguese and Russian). It introduces information about a country in which the B language is spoken (extends encyclopedic knowledge). It is a good example of a multifunctional text in that both the informative and the operative functions are dominant (Reiss and Vermeer, 1984). It provides interesting examples of specialized and nonspecialized (standardized and nonstandardized) vocabulary and syntax and presents formal typographic difficulties. Furthermore, macrostructural-microstructural interdependence is illustrated in the way the pragmatic context and the semantic topic affect the selection, distribution, and coherence of information and the linguistic medium (vocabulary and syntax).

Pragmatic Context—Cognitive Sets

Dimensions of Language User (Author)

a) The *author* is Ramón Tamames, born in Madrid in 1933.

b) His *idiolect* is unmarked.

c) There is no evidence of any marked *regional dialect*.

d) The *class dialect* is standard, middle-class, educated Spanish.

e) The distance in *time* is not very great. He wrote the first edition of this book in 1970. The sixth, revised edition appeared in 1980.

f) His *knowledge of the topic* is broad. He has spent a great part of his life writing, teaching, and doing research from his chair of economic structure at the Universidad Autónoma in Madrid. He was elected to Congress in 1977–82 and 1986–89. He participated in writing the 1978 Spanish Constitution. He has also served as an economic consultant for the United Nations in Latin America and for the Spanish government in Spain and on missions abroad.

g) His *belief structure* is quite intrusive in most of his work. He started out as a member of the Spanish communist party, but has since changed allegiances several times. Although he is not an "orthodox" Marxist, he does believe in the progress of history and is obstinately optimistic about the future of mankind. He has been the director of *El Anuario del País* for some years, and in his editorial for the 1987 edition he made clear his position on a number of issues: anti-NATO, against American troops in Spain, in favour of a special relationship between Latin America and the European Community, and concerned with improving north-south relationships in general. The *assumptions* upon which his belief structure is based were expressed in the preface to the 1970 edition of the book. The dark clouds of the past are being swept away: "Incluso en los lugares más remotos . . . está germinando la simiente de la rebeldía contra el atraso. . . . Pero la meta está clara, y el enemigo común, por doquier, se halla identificado . . . el imperialismo, el dominio colonial" (Tamames, 1980: 13).

His *wishes* are also made quite clear:

> Estamos en una época en la que se vislumbra como próximo, lo que tal vez ha de ser el definitivo despertar de la humanidad, el final de su larga Prehistoria de luchas y contiendas. (Tamames, 1980: 3) Ojalá que en 1992 nos demos cuenta al final de que todos los hispanohablantes de ambos hemisferios somos por igual ciudadanos de un mismo mundo. (Tamames, 1987: 63)

h) What were Tamames's intentions in writing *Estructura económica internacional*? The title suggests an objective, scientific, academic textbook, but the author states in the introduction that he does not want the book to be a useless exercise in erudition and he intends to follow up on the subjects treated in it. This particular book is very important for him:

> A fin y al cabo, algunos libros se acaban por convertirse en una especie de hijos; no sólo se procrean, sino que además es preciso continuar ocupándose de ellos—si se aspira a que su crecimiento sea un proceso de continuo enriquecimiento cultural que sirva al fin propio de cualquier labor científica: ayudar a mostrar el camino de la verdad. (Tamames, 1980: 7)

Tamames obviously believes in the need for macrostructures in action theory. In *El Anuario del País,* he argues for the importance of a global vision: "Debemos plantearnos una visión perspectiva, esto es, hemos de intentar vislumbrar a donde vamos desde este presente en que vivimos" (Tamames, 1987: 63). *Estructura económica internacional* can be classified as a global speech act in which the purpose is to give people a macrostructure with which to interpret the world and act accordingly.

The World (Context) in which the Text Is Interpreted

The context has changed considerably since the first edition of this book was written. In 1970, most of the students in university today were not born, Spain had not yet begun the transition from dictatorship to democracy, and the PCE (Partido Comunista Español) was still illegal. However, many people in Spain looked to the PCE as a motor of change and felt that it would have an important role to play in Spain after the death of Franco, as indeed it did. In 1992, the PCE is hopelessly shrunk and fragmented, with no support abroad after the collapse of the Warsaw Pact.

Tamames did make changes in the book between 1970 and 1980. There are additional sections on population, food, the energy crisis, and multinationals. There are some changes in the section on the great powers after journeys he made to the Far East, the United States, and the Soviet Union between 1970 and 1978. Nevertheless, the section we are concerned with is almost identical and the illocutionary intention is the same: to identify the enemy—the United States.

The Readers

Probably, Tamames's first objective was to reach university students. In the introduction, he recognizes his debt to his own students at the Universidad Autónoma in Madrid. In the 1970s, *Estructura económica internacional* was used as a textbook in Spain and Latin America. The Portuguese translation was published in 1979 and was used in universities in Portugal and Brazil. The book was also successful and influential among a wider public in Spain in the 1970s, as his latest book, *Un nuevo orden mundial* (Tamames, 1991), is today.

In *Estructura económica internacional*, Tamames writes as a teacher; therefore, the writer-reader relationship is *asymmetrical*. It is a formal teacher-student social relationship in which the writer has information (the power) that the reader needs.

Purpose of the Translation

Although this book has been translated and widely read, it is difficult to think of a reason for translating it in 1992 that is not purely academic. It could, for instance, be translated for a historian who was writing a biography of Tamames. For this analysis, we will imagine a purely fictitious context that would maintain a functional equivalence with the original: a Cuban publishing house sending textbooks to English-speaking parts of Africa.

SEMANTIC CONTENT (TOPIC)

The topics given by the author in the title and headings give an idea of the topic, but, as we shall see, pragmatic constraints govern the actual selection of information. Thus, a book with the same headings by a different author—say, Milton Friedman, or John Kenneth Galbraith—would have a very different content. The structure we are given is the following:

a) Book title: *Estructura económica internacional*. The very fact that he writes *estructura* in singular is a pragmatic choice that illustrates his point of view, which is that we are moving toward a world government because of the total interdependence of the whole of the globe with its parts.

b) Chapter 5: *Las grandes potencias económicas* (the United States, the Soviet Union, Japan, and China)

c) Section 1: *Estados Unidos de América*

d) Subsection 1: *Datos básicos. El "Melting Pot" y el "American Way of Life"*

e) Subsection 2: *Las raíces del crecimiento económico de EE.UU.*

PRAGMATIC AND SEMANTIC SELECTION OF INFORMATION

The selection of information in a text is decided by pragmatic and semantic coherence (van Dijk, 1980: 112). *Pragmatic coherence* is based on what is related to or relevant for the point of view, purpose, or function of the text. Irrelevant, known, or predictable information is deleted. For example, in a detective novel, the description of the town where the story takes place may be minimal or deleted if it is not crucial to the development of the plot, whereas in a travel guide it is essential.

Semantic coherence is based on the interrelatedness of information and its relatedness to the topic or referential identity of the macrostructure. Within the theme of relatedness, coherence is maintained if the information belongs to the same level—that is, if each text or macrostructure has an upper boundary of generalization and a lower boundary of particularization (van Dijk, 1980). In the words of Dr. Johnson (1755: xii), "In all pointed sentences some degree of accuracy must be sacrificed to conciseness." For example, Dick Francis enchants the readers of his detective novels by giving them inside information about the professions of his heroes: steeplechaser, insurance agent, merchant banker, gem merchant. He makes these professions come alive, but his readers would soon lose patience if he overstepped the lower boundary of information by giving too much detailed information of this kind, which would detract from the main purpose of the "whodunnit."

In the Tamames text, pragmatic constraints are of great importance in the *selection of information*. Semantic coherence is sometimes sacrificed for pragmatic coherence.

Subsection 1: Datos básicos

Paragraph 1 begins with two sentences that establish the size of the land and the population. The third sentence breaks the population down into different minority groups. This leads into the last sentence, which is obviously *the topic sentence* and fulfils the pragmatic function of introducing us to the enemy. The United States is an unstable country of racism and discrimination, where minorities have to accept the dominant culture and where the Melting Pot and the American Way of Life are myths with no reflection in reality.

Paragraph 2 develops the idea that the minorities are resisting the tyranny of the dominant culture. The enemy is further identified—the WASPs.

Paragraph 3 develops the theme of instability, which is aggravated by unequal distribution of wealth but still focusses on the problem of racism. The image is of a violent society manipulated by the mass media and the military-industrial complex.

Paragraph 4 breaks the boundaries of particularization set by the text, because here pragmatic coherence dominates semantic coherence. The paragraph is made up of a list of references to individuals who are supposed to represent the violence and corruption of American society. All of the events and individuals would have been familiar to university students in the 1970s but they are not so familiar to the present generation. Furthermore, the list is written in a kind of shorthand with incomplete sentences, which emphasizes the abnormality of the sequence. It provides an excellent opportunity for a brief discussion in class on the history of the United States in the last thirty years and to fill in the gaps and give the students a macrostructure with which to make sense of the paragraph. The topic of the entire section could be that the United States is a social and psychological mess.

Subsection 2: **Las raíces del crecimiento económico de los EE.UU.**

Paragraph 1 begins by admitting that the previous section was not strictly macro-economic information. This paragraph does provide economic information: the United States is the wealthiest country in the world, and its workers are the best paid.

Paragraph 2, however, shows how these workers have been corrupted and their trade unions have sold out to the system. They have no "higher" aspirations, no concern for a better quality of life, but only materialistic greed for more consumer goods.

Paragraph 3 lists the large cities but does not mention the vast areas of unspoiled nature and flourishing agriculture.

Paragraph 4 states that the result of this urbanization is an endless list of problems: pollution, crime, drugs, and so on.

Paragraphs 5 and 6 explain that economic growth in the United States is the result of external factors. The conquest of the West was undertaken by European immigrants, and the economic boom of the twentieth century was due to European investment and a series of wars. The Second World War favoured the United States, while it crippled the Soviet Union.

Tamames's selection of information is pragmatically coherent but not always semantically coherent. No space is given to geographic elements such as latitude, altitude, rain, or raw materials, although in the section on the Soviet Union, the point is made that this country is far less fortunate than the United States with regard to climate. Tamames does not mention the Protestant work ethic or the American workaholic who cannot believe that Europeans have such long holidays. In the section on Japan, he pays credit to the exceptional working qualities of the Japanese people but he does not mention the fact that 50 percent of the university students in California are of Asian descent. Pollution is mentioned as a problem only in relation to the United States.

PRAGMATIC AND SEMANTIC DISTRIBUTION OF INFORMATION

According to van Dijk (1980: 223), the distribution of information in a text depends on four main factors, the first two of which are semantic; the second two, pragmatic. The *fact sequence* has two dimensions: time and space. The normal time sequence is chronological. The normal space sequence is from the whole to the part, from the general to the particular. *Cognitive reasons* may alter the normal order of the fact sequence due to the order of observation, perception, or understanding of the fact sequence. The *communicative context* normally requires a progression from known information—that is, what is known by the writer and the reader—to new information in a sentence: topic → comment, old → new. *Pragmatic constraints,* due to the writer's intentions, the purpose of the global speech act, may alter the topic → comment order.

The study of these four factors in the Tamames text shows that, in general, the normal ordering of information is maintained. There are three exceptions:

1. The time sequence is altered in section 2, paragraph 2, sentence 2. The new attitude of minority groups is described before their old one. The reason for this is pragmatic, to stress the importance of this change of attitude, "Y lo que es aún más importante." The alteration of the topic-comment sequence to produce emphasis is more common in argumentative Spanish texts than in English.[15]

2. Although the sequences are maintained within the sentences, the whole of section 1, paragraph 4 violates the norm of whole to part. Tamames disarms his readers by admitting that his examples might seem anecdotal, but what he does is to give micro-examples in the place of a macrostructure. He presents a list of assassinations and scoundrels upon which to base his macropicture of the United States. The fact that he has descended from the whole to the parts is emphasized by the way he begins the second section: "Volviendo ahora a los datos económicos de base."

3. Section 2, paragraph 4, sentence 1 alters the time sequence (the relation of the present economic growth to the conquest of the West), but only in order to maintain the topic→ comment sequence, because the previous paragraphs are about contemporary American economic growth.

Thus, it could be argued that the writer's intention is to produce the impression of an objective, "scientific" text. The unmarked ordering reinforces this impression and masks the persuasive, emotional, argumentative nature of the text.

SYNTACTIC CONSEQUENCES

In the preceding section, we saw how the normal distribution of information in the sentence was maintained, giving the impression of a scientific, objective economic textbook (field). This impression is maintained in the syntax used. The persuasive, pragmatic force of the text is based almost entirely on the selection of information and, as we shall see in the next section, the selection of vocabulary.

---

15. See appendix, section 9, "Sentences and Punctuation."

Because the distribution of information in the sentences is normal or "logical," textual cohesion is largely semantic, and connectors are used sparingly. They are not essential from the point of view of either meaning or style. Here is a list of the few connectors used in the text and those used in the English translation proposed.

Table 7.1
Connectors in Tamames Text

Spanish	English
Y	Furthermore
Igualmente	Again
Pero	But
Lo que	This
En ese mismo año	In the same year
Pues	Thus
Incluso	Although
A la par que	Also
También	Moreover
Igualmente	Once again
Así	Therefore

The syntactic differences between the SLT and the TLT described below are typical of academic economic discourse (field) in Spanish and English.

The structure of the Spanish sentences is complex and the author uses subordinate clauses that in English would be connected by conjunctions or put into another sentence. The Spanish sentences are longer than the English ones, so there are 26 in Spanish and 34 in English.

Most of the sentences are complete. The verbs are exhaustively analyzable in terms of the transitivity system and the agents realized (Mason, 1990: 16). The only part of the text where this does not apply is section 1, paragraph 4, which begins, "De forma aparentemente anecdótica," followed by the list of individuals. This is also the part of the text that breaks the distribution of information norms by moving part → whole. Agents are systematically omitted and the verbs are not complete. Incomplete sentences of this kind are more acceptable in formal Spanish prose than in English. The translator has to decide whether to maintain the incomplete sentences in English, which would make this section even more shocking, or to complete the verb and perhaps give greater authority to the "anecdote." For example:

J.F. Kennedy, asesinado en 1963 en circunstancias más que oscuras.
J.F. Kennedy, assassinated in 1963 in very shady circumstances.

or

J.F. Kennedy was assassinated in 1963 in very shady circumstances.

There is a *low level of redundancy,* and *parentheses* are used frequently.

There are no examples of imperatives, interrogatives, or exclamations. The preterite and the present are the tenses most commonly used in the Spanish and can be translated into the past simple and the present simple in English. Here is a brief breakdown of some of the features of the verbs:

Table 7.2
Verbs in the Tamames Text

Spanish	English
26 sentences	34 sentences
3 incomplete sentences	24 passive clauses
14 impersonal <u>se</u> clauses	32 active clauses
29 active clauses	

Both tenor and field influence the style used, which, on the whole, is impersonal, typical of objective, scientific, academic writing.

The *presence of the author* is *unobtrusive.* He never uses the first-person singular.

The *reader participation* is *implicit* rather than explicit, except on two occasions, when the first-person plural is used.

Thus, syntactically, the translation problems are not acute in this text. The persuasive, pragmatic force of the text is almost entirely based on the selection and distribution of information and vocabulary.

LEXICAL CONSEQUENCES

Standardized Language

Newmark (1981) makes a distinction between standardized and nonstandardized language. Standardized language is defined as having only one correct equivalent and falls into Newmark's category of the "science" of translation. For example, OCDE can only be translated as OECD. Nonstandardized language has more than one correct equivalent and falls into the category of the "art" of translation. Certain fields of discourse contain no, or very little, standardized language. The field of economics-textbook discourse, for example, contains a high proportion of standardized language.

Names of countries are normally standardized, but there are some debatable cases; for example, the English press is beginning to use "the Netherlands" instead of "Holland." If the Tamames text were more recent, there would, of course, be a problem with "USSR," which is now without a satisfactory name. *The Economist*

Style Guide (Butler, 1991) suggests using "the former Soviet Union" or "the ex-Soviet Union" on first mention and then dropping the "former" or "ex-."

Most Spanish texts use *norteamericano* for citizen of the United States, whereas the unmarked *americano* is associated with people from Latin America. *The Economist Style Guide* states that it is usually all right to talk about the inhabitants of the United States as "Americans," but to bear in mind that the term also applies to everyone from Canada to Cape Horn.

The case of *norteamericanos de raza negra* is more complicated. A few years ago, "black" was perfectly acceptable, and the change from "nigger" to "Negro" to "coloured" to "black" fits in perfectly with Tamames's little history lesson that includes the Kennedys, Martin Luther King, and Malcolm X. Both black leaders provided inspiration for the "black is beautiful" movement.

> It is currently difficult to advise how to refer to Americans whose ancestors came from Africa; preferred usage appears to be no longer blacks but there is no agreed alternative. Avoid giving offence. This should be your first concern. But also avoid mealy-mouthed euphemisms and terms that have not generally caught on despite promotion by pressure groups. If and when it becomes plain that American blacks no longer wish to be called black, as some years ago it became plain that they no longer wished to be called coloured, then call them African-Americans (or whatever). Till then they are blacks. (Butler, 1991: 27)

English Erasmus exchange students from Wolverhampton University (1991–92) were very unhappy about the idea of using "black" in the English context and were therefore unwilling to use it in the American context.

Other cases of standardized language are statistics; names and titles of people, dates, wars; common acronyms: *PNB → GNP, PIB → GDP, OCDE → OECD;* transcription of English expressions: *WASPs, Watergate, AFL/CIO* (American Federation of Labor/Congress of Industrial Organizations); and standardized economic expressions: *nivel de vida → standard of living,* as opposed to nonstandardized *calidad de vida ⇒ quality of life.*

Specific Translation Problems for Spanish Students

Capital letters: The main problem here is to remember to use capital letters for nationalities and countries used adjectivally—for example, *mexicano-americanos → Mexican Americans.*

Articles: The definite article is obligatory in English for *EE.UU. → the USA, URSS → the USSR.* It is not used for titles when the name of the person is given: *el presidente Johnson → President Johnson.*

Numbers: The main difference between Spanish and English is the inverted use of the comma and the period: thousands: period→ comma: *2.094.900 ⇒ 2,094,900;*

decimals: comma → period: *9,4 millones* ⇒ *9.4 million*. When dealing with numbers, students may forget that adjectives in English are never plural: *9.4 millions kilometres*. They may also have problems with prepositions: *9,4M de kilómetros cuadrados* → *9.4M square kilometres; 222M de habitantes* → *222M inhabitants; 2M de dólares* → *2M dollars*. Another common mistake is to retain the article in percentages: *un 10,5 por 100* → *10.5%*.

Nonstandardized Language

If the pragmatic purpose of the text (to identify the enemy) is seen in the selection and distribution of information, it could also be argued that the tenor (formal, impersonal style) of the text reinforces the pragmatic purpose indirectly by presenting the information in an objective, unobtrusive style. However, the choice of vocabulary reflects the pragmatic purpose much more directly. This is particularly true in the first section.

Even the choice of a seemingly neutral word like *asimilación* is significant. *Integración* suggests a two-way process, while *asimilación* is one-way: immigrants have to adapt to the WASP culture. At the 1987 congress in Toledo on the relationship among Jews, Muslims, and Christians previous to 1492, Barkai, from Tel Aviv, pointed out the difference between these two words and concluded, "Sólo se produce simbiosis cultural (*the Melting Pot?*) cuando existe una completa integración" (*El País*, 20 Apr. 1987).

A study of the vocabulary used shows that the enemy is being described. Naturally, given the topic, there is much referential, denotational, standardized language, but there is also a surprising amount of nonstandardized language with a strongly emotional connotational impact. The first section included this set of strongly emotive vocabulary:

> tendencias . . . en pugna . . . viva
> los fuertes desequilibrios
> crisis de confianza
> exaltación tradicional
> el pretendido sueño
> dramáticamente sacudida
> violencia
> asesinado (*three times*)
> complot
> asesinato
> circunstancias oscuras
> un temor inconfesable
> un contexto no aclarado
> violó
> escándalo

Students might be tempted to "neutralize" this vocabulary if they look only at the text and not at the context—that is, if they take into account only the formal, "scientific," impersonal structure of the text and the semantic topic. The pragmatic context is essential to make sense of these words and understand why they are being used here. The macrostructure explains the microstructure and vice versa. One of Tamames's pragmatic intentions in writing this book is to identify the enemy. He does so very successfully.

THE SEMIOTIC DIMENSION OF A TEXT

In the semantic and pragmatic analysis of Tamames's 1980 text introducing the United States, we saw how the main intention was to identify the enemy and how this was achieved by the selection of information and some of the nonstandardized vocabulary. At the same time, this rather atavistic aim was disguised by the complex, sophisticated, specialized language of economics. Specialized language can be used to mask the real intention of a text, hiding it behind jargon, professorial authority, and the structure, syntax, and orientation of a scientific text, which is presumed to be "objective."

As was pointed out in chapter 5, signs, semiotic units, and texts are processed not by empty brains but by individuals who have already formed a world view based on their own experience. The search for meaning is a process of intertextualization as the semiotic units in the text interact with each individual's categories and prototypes. Furthermore, each individual shares the common prototypes or myths of his or her culture, to a greater or lesser extent. This is illustrated by a pre-translation exercise for the Tamames text, using the list of emotive, nonstandardized vocabulary given in the previous section. Students are given the list of words and asked to imagine a context in which they could use these words to write a text (such as an article, a story, or a letter). They are then asked to write their text in English, translating the words according to the context they have chosen. Their texts would enliven the pages of the most sensationalist newspaper: "Murder in the Jet Set," "Shame and Scandal in the Family." It is possible to see differences in the contexts chosen by students of different nationalities. Spanish, Algerian, Italian, and French students sometimes set the scene in the United States, but English and German students rarely do. For French students, the scandal often takes place in the Middle East, whereas Spanish students often situate it in Latin America.

George Orwell, in his essay "Politics and the English Language," provided the example of

> some comfortable English professor defending Russian totalitarianism. He cannot say right out, "I believe in killing off your opponents when you can get good results by doing so." Probably, therefore, he will say something like this. "While freely conceding that the Soviet regime exhibits certain features which the humanitarian may be inclined to deplore, we must, I think, agree that a certain curtailment of the right to political opposition is an unavoidable

concomitant to transitional periods, and the rigours which the Russian people have been called upon to undergo have been amply justified in the sphere
of concrete achievement." (Orwell, 1984: 362)

Hatim and Mason (1990: 101) qualify the subordinate clause "While freely conced-
ing that the Soviet regime exhibits certain features which the humanitarian may be
inclined to deplore" as an example of a thesis cited to be opposed.

The title of Tamames's 1980 introduction to the United States is another example of a thesis cited to be opposed: *Datos básicos. El "Melting Pot" y el "American Way
of Life."* These two clichés (metaphors, signs), "the Melting Pot" and "the American
Way of Life," can be interpreted in many different ways—that is, they have multiple
significants. As signs, they have an endless capacity for commutability. Originally,
certainly, they had positive connotations, and they probably still maintain these in
many cultures. "The Melting Pot" suggested a country in which all races were welcome and integrated, and all contributed to construct a richer, more vigorous society. "The American Way of Life" suggested material comfort, but also a society of
equal opportunity, in which every child had the chance to become president of the
nation or of the Coca-Cola Company. Tamames introduces the United States by
these two signs, but the rest of the text is dedicated to proving that in no way has
the American dream been achieved.

There is considerable confusion over the value of different semiotic entities
within a culture. Spanish students vary widely in their interpretation of the "American Way of Life," although they all associate it to some extent with McDonald's.
However, some are horrified at the unhealthiness of the hamburgers sold at
McDonald's; some would like to throw a stone through the window of that "impe-
rialistic establishment"; some would like to eat at McDonald's, but only if they were
sure they were not going to meet anyone they knew; some adore everything about
the McDonald's experience. This intracultural confusion increases in an intercultural situation.

Even in the 1990s, Spanish students tend to associate the two signs ("the
Melting Pot" and "the American Way of Life") with more negative connotations
than do students from other European countries (class discussions, Universidad
Autónoma de Barcelona, 1992). Anti-American feeling still lives in Spain; therefore,
it is much easier for Spanish students to interact with the original intertextuality of
Tamames's text. Nevertheless, in the last few years it has become increasingly difficult for all students to capture the ideological viewpoint of authors of texts. This is
due to the ideological vacuum produced by recent events in the world, which has
shaken the foundations of our social semiotic systems or cultural myths.

THE NEED FOR SEMIOTIC ANALYSIS IN A NEW WORLD ORDER

It is becoming increasingly difficult to predict the position of a writer. Our expectations are not always fulfilled even with authors who are quite familiar. This is true

with Tamames. His position in 1970 (and 1980) was easy to identify because it was based on well-established European communist or socialist myths. His position now is much more complex, as we shall see when we look at an extract from his book *Un nuevo orden mundial*. Tamames is far from being an isolated example.

For this reason, pre-translation exercises that emphasize the semiotic dimension of the text are particularly useful. In order to understand the whole communicative intention of a discourse, it is necessary to consider not only the pragmatic action but also the semiotic dimension, which regulates the interaction between the different elements of the discourse as signs. This interaction takes place, on the one hand, between signs within the text and, on the other hand, between the sender and the receiver of the signs. The semiotic dimension propels and controls communication.

TRANSLATOR-ORIENTED SEMIOTIC ANALYSIS OF TWO TEXTS: TAMAMES (1980) AND TAMAMES (1991)

This analysis is based on Charles Pierce's semiotic approach described in chapter 5. Pierce breaks down the sign into three parts: whatever initiates identification of the sign; the object of the sign; and the interpretant, or the effect the sign is meant to relay.

In translating, a semiotic entity can be a word, a phrase, a sentence, or an entire text. Two texts have been chosen for analysis according to a simplified version of Pierce's three categories. The first text is the introduction to the United States from Tamames (1980), which has already been studied in considerable detail. The second is in Tamames's book *Un nuevo orden mundial* (1991), the introduction to the United States in the section "Los Poderes del Norte" and titled "Crónica de un declive no irrecuperable."

Tamames (1980): Datos básicos. El "Melting Pot" y el "American Way of Life"

What initiates the sign is an economics textbook written for university students in Spain and Latin America. The style is typically academic, objective, and scientific, both in the distribution of information within the sentence and in its impersonality. Neither the presence of the author nor the participation of the reader is explicit. The level of redundancy is low and there are many examples of parenthesis. There are no imperatives, interrogatives, or exclamations. The vocabulary is, on the whole, denotative, factual, frequently related to size, numbers, amounts, and percentages. However, the pragmatically driven selection of information and the use of emotionally charged, nonstandardized vocabulary provide the intertextual references that make the text interact with the discourse of Marxist propaganda.

The object of the sign is the United States: territory, population, economic, and social situation from the beginning of the nineteenth century to 1970.

The interpretant is to identify the United States as the enemy. There is no need to go into further detail here, as the text was fully discussed in the previous section.

Tamames (1991): **Crónica de un declive no irrecuperable: EE.UU., desde Bretton Woods a la Guerra del Golfo**

What initiates the sign is a text from a book written for a wider public than was the earlier university textbook, although it shares many of the same characteristics. The differences are as follows: the presence of the author is often explicit; he expresses his own opinions and does not rest on the authority of Marxist discourse; sentences and paragraphs are shorter and the print is larger; it is easier to read—there are fewer details, numbers, and statistics—but much of the language is still denotative, technical, typical of the specialized language of economics. The nonstandardized vocabulary of the text reflects uncertainty:

> un declive no irrecuperable
> toda una serie de incertidumbres
> toda una serie de problemas
> ya no es el dueño y señor de otro tiempo
> esa tendencia de declive global
> se debaten mil problemas
> la inquietud
> no tuvo más remedio
> tienen pánico
> ve con impotencia
> un acicate y una inquietud permanentes
> motivo de preocupación

Once again, the object of the sign is the United States: its social and economic position from the end of the Second World War to the Gulf War.

The interpretant could be expressed as uncertainty about the future of the United States. The title, *Un declive no irrecuperable,* is significant; the syntactic double negative has semiotic meaning. Tamames is by nature optimistic; he has not totally abandoned his belief in "the progress of history," although he can no longer believe that "the dawn is red." Therefore, the United States is not in *un declive irrecuperable,* but neither is it in *un declive recuperable.* If the translator is not aware of the semiotic dimension, it would be very easy to iron out that double negative to avoid *not without hope of recovery.* English students translating this text usually simplify it to *with hope of recovery.* The intertextuality of this text can be recognized only in interaction with articles and books written after the fall of the Berlin Wall.

In 1970 and 1980, Tamames was certain who the enemy was and whose side he was on, but in 1991 he is not so sure. The title of this book, *Un nuevo orden mundial,* also expresses this uncertainty, which he stresses in the prologue:

> ¿De qué nuevo mundo se trata? El anterior, bipolar, eso parece claro, está feneciendo ante nuestros ojos. El nuevo, ¿será unipolar, o compartido? ¿Habrá la hegemonía autoritaria de unos pocos con un criterio autogratifi- cante, o vamos a un mundo solidario? Esos son algunos de los interrogantes

> a los cuales pretendo responder al referirme a *un* nuevo orden. Así, con
> artículo indefinido, como indefinida está su configuración.

It is very difficult to define Tamames's position today. On occasion, he appears to be
an ecologist who has caught some of Margaret Thatcher's obsessions. In this book
he offers an ecological-economic alternative *(Eco-Eco)*. In 1992, he wrote an article
about the Treaty of Maastricht for the *Anuario El País*, in which he attacked the
Spanish government for its inward-looking, falsely social system of protectionism:

> por medio de toda clase de dispositivos de *asistencia al paro* (en vez de esti-
> mular el empleo), de creación de *ocupación ficticia, prebendaria y electorera* en
> las administraciones públicas, *de cubrir* sine die *los números rojos de las empre-
> sas públicas* que no tienen ninguna posibilidad racional de supervivencia, etc.,
> etc. (emphasis added)

In the 1991 text, the selection of information about the United States is still critical,
but the novelty is that the criticism is all from American sources, such as *Time* magazine and *The International Herald Tribune*. Tamames concludes the section by saying,

> Todo lo dicho no supone, porque sería necio, anunciar otra vez más, una
> catástrofe económica en EE.UU.; porque el país tiene portentosas capacida-
> des de recuperación. . . . Tampoco hay en las palabras anteriores ningún anti-
> americanismo. El diagnóstico más duro sobre la realidad lo hacen los propios
> estadounidenses: Grunwald, Chomsky, Cronkite, etc.

He even suggests that the Americans may reinvent capitalism: "sencillamente
porque no es eficiente."

SEMIOTIC ANALYSIS IN TRANSLATING IRONY

Recognizing irony in one's own language is not always easy. When Jonathan Swift
wrote *A Modest Proposal* to shock England into awareness of the suffering caused by
the potato famine in Ireland, he used irony, writing as though the Irish were not
really human, and even suggested recipes for cooking Irish babies as a solution to
the problem. Some English readers, taking him seriously, were horrified.

As I mentioned in the introduction, in a pre-translation exercise on *Un hombre
providencial* by Haro Tecglen, only about half the Spanish students recognized the
irony, and none of the foreign-exchange students (English, German, and French)
recognized it at all. The recognition of irony (and humour) in a foreign language
involves awareness of the many different referential, ideological networks (intertextuality) that make up the world view of the speakers of that language at a particular
time in history. The translator needs to be aware of the semiotic dimension of the
SLT, the signification of all the signs that make up the full interpretant of the text.
Without knowledge of the ideological networks in the SL and TL cultures, the translator cannot identify intertextuality and carry out the cultural transfer necessary to
translate irony. This is very clearly illustrated by *Un hombre providencial*.

EL PAIS, domingo 24 de noviembre de 1991

INTERNACIONAL
ANALISIS

Un hombre providencial   Eduardo Haro Tecglen

De 13 candidatos para sustituir a Javier Pérez de Cuéllar en la Secretaría General de las Naciones Unidas, cuatro eran europeos, y nueve de lo que aún llamamos Tercer Mundo: puede que por mucho tiempo, porque es una denominación con tal suavidad semántica, tal calidad de eufemismo, que será difícil encontrar otra mejor.

Desde el principio, en la Conferencia de Bandung, donde se redactó una carta del nuevo enciclopedismo que correspondía a la época (1955), se descubrió que entre sus políticos, pensadores y poetas aparecían unos característicos hombres de buena voluntad, templados, con amplias ilusiones, reducidas a la modestia de la práctica posible de cabalgar entre las distintas civilizaciones internas y externas. Eran hombres dúctiles, razonables y útiles, de donde podían salir excelentes Secretarios Generales para las Naciones Unidas. Pérez de Cuéllar ha llevado su servicio al cargo con tal abnegación que ha sido capaz de gastar sus últimos tiempos permitiendo que las Naciones Unidas realizaran una terrible guerra, sin dejar de utilizar para ella la terminología pacifista; un poco pudoroso ante el ultimátum del Consejo de Seguridad, capaz de viajar a los centros más comprometidos para explicar que no tenían más salida que la aceptación de las condiciones y, por tanto, investido del manto del negociador, del intermediario. Convenía creerle, y se creyó. Gracias a él, las Naciones Unidas han aparecido justicieras al fin.

El puesto justo

El egipcio Butros Ghali tiene las condiciones que le califican como providencial para la sustitución, teniendo en cuenta que no siempre la voluntad humana encuentra por sí sola el hombre ideal para el puesto justo. Arabe pero cristiano, oportunamente casado con una judía; egipcio pero de civilización francesa; político de un país y de una época que produjo la primera reconciliación árabe con Israel, y que ha trabajado siempre en ese sentido. Con 70 años que quizá no le estimulen para apurar su mandato (cinco años) si, antes, llega a coronar una obra sustancial, pero que le dan el vigor, la experiencia y el sentido común que se necesitan para ayudar al establecimiento del nuevo orden del presidente Bush; que ya comenzó desde el momento en que su país, del que es vice-primer ministro, envió soldados a esa guerra frente a un caudillo árabe que pretendía alzar el islam en contra del buen sentido; incluso en contra de Israel, con el cual es eterno negociador favorito. Su puesto de vice-primer ministro, y los que ha desempeñado en su carrera, no le han obligado a tomar posiciones demasiado visibles y personales. Su condición de hombre de Occidente no sólo no le compromete ante los gobiernos árabes, sino que le hacen especialmente útil como creador de puentes; no tener ni un solo voto en contra en la primera votación del Consejo de Seguridad, y sólo cuatro abstenciones de paises tímidos, le califica especialmente. Va a tener en contra a los integristas musulmanes, a las organizaciones extremistas y quizá a partes populares que se consideran irredentas. Pero son grupos con poco porvenir en un tiempo próximo. A extinguir.

Sobre este hombre de confianza podrán ahora transferirse algunas de las formas de presión y negociación que está realizando directamente Estados Unidos a través de Baker para que se extienda la Conferencia de Madrid y, bajo su manto funcionen las conversaciones bilaterales o multilaterales que lleguen a apurar todas las consecuencias de las nuevas relaciones de fuerzas en la amplia zona en disputa, hasta llegar a un posible equilibrio de grupos, naciones y fronteras.

En ello se incluye una reducción de las posibilidades palestinas: hay que considerar que los palestinos perdieron la guerra con Irak. Arafat sabía que razones de seguridad para Israel había tras esa guerra, más allá del *casus belli* de Kuwait, del asunto del petróleo y de la inverosimilitud de la bomba atómica iraquí.

El reconocimiento de los derechos nacionales de los palestinos decidido el jueves por el Partido Laborista va en esta misma corriente: en la de la sonrisa de la paz y la posibilidad de la negociación. Sobre todo, la ocasión de abrir un frente en la acalorada política interna, donde Shamir no va a poder resistir mucho tiempo entre la presión de los norteamericanos y de las comunidades israelís en Estados Unidos y la intemperancia de sus *ultras* y sus partidos religiosos. Parece que todo está percutiendo en la opinión pública de Israel: van creciendo los partidarios de una negociación con resultado ventajoso, puesto que ahora las fuerzas reales y políticas son favorables a la continuidad extenuante de un estado permanente de vigilia y ansiedad. No quiero decir que los laboristas fueran a ganar hoy unas elecciones, pero sí que representan esa nueva voluntad que parece corresponder a la tranquilidad que puede darles tener teóricamente enfrente a un hombre como el egipcio Ghali, tan dúctil y tan eficaz para la política de Estados Unidos en la zona.

A semiotic analysis of this article using Pierce's (1931–58) categories shows that the author's purpose is to present Butros Ghali as a providential tool for American interests. What initiates the sign is an elegantly written newspaper article that occupied a full page of the international section of *El País* on 24 November 1991 and was classified as *Análisis*. The sentences are very long, between 50 and 100 words. There are many examples of subordination. The text shows aspects of abstract language (for example, a great number of adverbial and adjectival phrases, connotational vocabulary with multiple meanings, metaphor, personification, verbal agents not realized).

The object of the sign, the man sent by providence, is Butros Ghali, newly elected Secretary General of the United Nations.

The interpretant is the opposite of what is indicated in the title. *Un hombre providencial* is another example of a thesis presented to be refuted: Butros Ghali is a man for all seasons, whose varied past allows him to see every side of an argument, a perfect Secretary General of the United Nations. Do not be fooled. Butros Ghali, like Perez de Cuéllar, his predecessor, is providential only for the United States.

Unlike the two Tamames texts, this one is deliberately ironic. Taken in isolation, each word used to describe Butros Ghali is positive. The irony becomes evident through the cumulative effect of the exaggerated praise. The United States is still the bully, but it is clever enough to hide its fists of iron in velvet gloves, and Butros Ghali is a velvet glove. He is therefore a traitor to the Third World.

There are many linguistic clues to the irony. We will consider a few of these linguistic clues, and why the non-native Spanish speakers did not recognize the irony at all.

Clues to Irony

The *use of* "tal" in the text:

> . . . lo que aún llamamos Tercer Mundo: puede por mucho tiempo, porque es una denominación con *tal suavidad semántica, tal calidad de eufemismo*, que será difícil encontrar otra mejor.

The *juxtaposition of conflicting qualities*. The successors of Bandung, men such as Perez de Cuéllar and Butros Ghali, are depicted as both quixotic heros and pragmatic politicians:

> . . . unos característicos *hombres de buena voluntad, templados, con amplias ilusiones, reducidas a la modestia de la práctica posible, cabalgar* entre las distintas civilizaciones. . . . Eran hombres *dúctiles, razonables y útiles* de donde podían salir excelentes Secretarios Generales para las Naciones Unidas.

The *connotational force* of much of the vocabulary conflicts with the superficial message of the text. For example, the use of *justicieras* instead of *justas* evokes all kinds of connotations related to *pistoleros* who take the law into their own hands:

> . . . ha llevado su servicio al cargo con *tal abnegación*. . . . Gracias a él, las Naciones Unidas han aparecido *justicieras* al fin.

The word *providencial* also has conflicting connotational meanings. German students translating this text avoid using the word "providential," perhaps for the reason that Katerina Reiss (in a lecture at the First International Congress of Translation, Barcelona, 1992) gave for a German translator's avoidance of the word "providence" in Camilo Jose Cela's *Pascual Duarte*. The translator substituted "luck" for "providence" in the phrase, "No obstante, y si la Providencia dispone que . . ."

Reiss assumed that in this case the translator had avoided the use of "providence" because of its associations with or (intertextual reference to) Hitler's discourse.

Many of the Spanish students also avoided the word "providential" in the title of *Un hombre providencial* and looked for a paraphrase. Their suggestions included "the right man for the job," "the ideal candidate," "the perfect candidate." In fact, Haro Tecglen is a proclaimed atheist and the title is the first clue to the irony in the text. The English students did not avoid "providential," perhaps because the religious, messianic connotations are not so strong in English. "A gift from God" would reinforce the irony more effectively.

> . . .tiene las condiciones que le califican como *providencial* para la sustitución, teniendo en cuenta que *no siempre la voluntad humana encuentra por sí sola el hombre ideal para el puesto justo.* Arabe pero cristiano, *oportunamente* casado con una judía; egipcio pero de civilización francesa.

Why the Irony Was Difficult to Recognize

The article was difficult because it was unexpected, unpredictable. All of the other articles published in the Spanish press on the occasion of the election of Butros Ghali took the same position as Angeles Espinosa:

> El nuevo secretario general de la ONU cuenta con su prestigio en el Tercer Mundo y la simpatía occidental para emprender la renovación que todos esperan de la organización. ("Perfil: Butros Ghali," *El País,* 5 Jan. 1992)

Like Tamames, Haro Tecglen wanted to change the world. He was the assistant editor of *Triunfo*, the magazine that played such an important role in Spain in the last years of Franco and during the transition. According to Juan Cruz, Haro Tecglen wrote much of the magazine:

> En España era difícil hablar de España. En cierto modo, *Triunfo*, exiliada, obligada, como dice Escurra, a referirse al exterior para hallar allí la metáfora de lo que ocurría dentro. Para hacerlo, en seguida contó con la presencia polivalente de Eduardo Haro Tecglen, que unas veces era Pablo Berben—cuando escribía temas científicos—, otras era Haro propiamente dicho—cada vez que no se prodigaba demasiado—y en otras ocasiones resolvía convertirse en el comentarista de política internacional Juan Aldebarán. Después, pasado el tiempo, fue Pozuelo, donde inauguró *la ironía* que ahora le hace uno de los columnistas más prestigiosos de España.[16]

Triunfo ceased publication in 1982, and its disappearance coincided with what Haro Tecglen defined as "la llegada de la vida práctica a lo que antes estaba ocupado por

---

16. "*Triunfo*, el eslabon perdido: La revista con la que formaron generaciones de españoles cumple 30 años de vida y 10 de desaparición," *El País*, 6 June 1992.

la utopía."[17] He now writes a daily column, "Visto/Oído," on the penultimate page of *El País*. A few extracts from this column illustrate the ideological crisis that is a part of the new world order.

Miedo al miedo, 2 February 1992.

Me costará trabajo admitir que el mal es decisivo en la especie humana. Seguiré creyendo que la sociedad está mal hecha. ¿Está más pasado de moda Rousseau que Nietzsche? Ser escéptico, o desalentado, es grave: pero ¡como son los que tienen creencias firmes, los seguros de sí mismos, de su patria, de su sangre, su fe, su dinero!

Los jesuitas, 8 December 1991.

Me asombro de mí mismo cuando me veo creyendo que los jesuitas son una de las últimas reservas del pobre, del desvalido, del explotado. ¡Quién me iba a decir que sólo habría este clavo ardiente al que pudiera agarrarse un ateo al terminar el siglo XX!

Medios Seres, 19 January 1992.

Lamento haber creído con Lévi-Strauss o con Toynbee que lo suyo era tan bueno como lo nuestro y podían vivir sólo con ello: no es verdad, la punta de lanza de la calidad de vida está entre nosotros, y la base ha quedado inmóvil en Africa, en Asia, en América.

Querida democracia, 12 December 1992.

Es la nueva democracia. Todo viene del nuevo orden. Veo pasar, en el prodigioso televisor, la reconversión de la democracia universal. Yo no soy reconvertible. Ni quiero. Me daría vergüenza, si no, protestar cuando Castro mate a sus nuevos condenados.

There are at least three reasons why non-Spanish exchange students found the irony more difficult to recognize than did Spanish students. The first is obviously linguistic. There was much unfamiliar vocabulary for them (even some of the Spanish students did not know *irredentas*). They did not pick up syntactic clues of irony, such as the repeated use of *tal:* "tal suavidad semántica," "tal calidad de eufemismo," "tal abnegación." The second reason is that freedom of the press was a much more recent phenomenon in Spain than it was in the other European countries represented in the class. Although Franco was already dead when most of the students learned to read, it is still perhaps more necessary to read between the lines in the Spanish press. The third reason is definitely semiotic. This article was written after the Gulf War, when feelings were still running high. In certain quarters in Spain, there was a considerable amount of anti-American feeling. Although Spain was one of the "Allies," there were no signs of the jingoism that appeared in some sectors of the British and American media.

---

17. Quoted in ibid.

One of the questions in the pre-translation exercise referred to networks of extralinguistic references. The most evident network here is related to the crisis in the Middle East. A close study of each of these references as semiotic entities would probably reveal very different associations for Spanish readers from those for English, German, or Danish readers. After the Gulf War, a group of exchange students produced the associations in the second column. Those in the third column are the ones used by Haro Tecglen in this article. Even if Spanish readers did not share these associations, many would recognize them.

Table 7.3
Extralinguistic Associations

References	English Associations	Haro Tecglen's Associations
United Nations	useful	suspect
Security Council	reliable	manipulated
Gulf War	justifiable	wicked
Kuwait/Iraq	victims/bullies	bullies/victims
Arabs/French	unreliable/reliable	victims/bullies
Extremists	dangerous	heroes
PLO/Israel	dangerous/victims	victims/bullies
East/West	unreliable/reliable	victims/bullies
North/South	reliable/unreliable	bullies/victims

Despite, or perhaps because of, the difficulties presented by this text, it proved an extremely fruitful subject for study. Once again, the presence of exchange students provoked a very educational debate in the classroom. Some of the Spanish students, stimulated by the challenge of the task, produced excellent translations that transmitted the interpretant of *Un hombre providencial* much more successfully than those of the English speakers. The English students tried to "fix" the hyperbole and smooth out the contrasts to suit their interpretation of the original, and in some cases their translations made no sense. Some of the students were hard to convince; one German student resisted to the end. All of the students profited from the experience.

The full analysis of a text for translation purposes involves many theoretical principles that are essential for correct development of the translation process. Professional translators do not sit down and undertake this kind of analysis before attempting to translate; an understanding of the underlying principles behind the analysis is a part of their translator competence. Trainee translators cannot be expected to understand these principles and put them into practice after a few lectures on translation theory. The aim of the translation teacher is to delimit these principles and present them systematically and actively so that the students can fully apprehend them and practise using them in the translation process. A fuller definition of the teaching objectives and a method for achieving them is the subject of the next chapter.

PART 3

METHODOLOGICAL FRAMEWORK

The methodology described here is based on the definition of learner-centred objectives. It has been developed to help students become translators and, in particular, to translate into the foreign language. The methodology has to be student-centred—in this case, centred on students whose mother tongue is Spanish and for whom English is a foreign language, albeit at an advanced level.

The first step is to define general objectives, knowledge, and skills needed by translators: ideal translator communicative competence. This is achieved by looking at what the translator does at each stage of the translation process, as described in the theoretical framework. The second step is to determine how the "artificial" and "unnatural" process of translating into the foreign language differs from translating into the native language and to adapt the objectives to the starting point, which is student-translator communicative competence. The third step is to define the teaching context (employment opportunities, students' motivation, ability, expectations, and so on) and give a specific profile to the objectives of the prose-translation program. Finally, translation strategies are defined as putting into practice the theoretical principles that allow for correct development of the translation process. These principles are used to delimit translation difficulties and establish an ordered and rational learning progression. The students learn to use these strategies through a variety of activities, in a variety of discourse fields. Frequently, the activities and fields chosen are directly related to the employment opportunities available to prose translators.

CHAPTER 8

IDEAL TRANSLATOR COMMUNICATIVE COMPETENCE

According to Chomsky, competence is an ideal, abstract concept, whereas performance refers to what people actually do in the real world. This distinction is similar to de Saussure's *langue-parole* dichotomy. Therefore, if we define translation as "a communicative transaction taking place within a social framework" involving the transfer of "equivalent" meaning from the SLT to the TLT (Hatim and Mason, 1990: 3), we are obviously concerned with performance.[18] However, Chomsky's dichotomy need not be developed here, as our purpose is to define a teaching methodology. Thus, competence here is used to mean knowledge and skills, which is how Bell uses it:

> To deny the competence-performance dichotomy which we have been implicitly accepting and redefine our objective as the specification of a multicomponent "communicative competence" which would consist minimally of four areas of knowledge and skills: grammatical competence, sociolinguistic competence, discourse competence and strategic competence. (Bell, 1991: 41)

Many linguists, literary theorists, and translation theorists assume that all communicators are, in a sense, translators. They receive written or spoken signals that they decode, and if they wish to maintain the communication they must encode their responses in such a way that they will be received by the other participants in the communicative process. This idea is confirmed by George Steiner's hermeneutic approach:

> Any model of communication is at the same time a model of translation, of a vertical or horizontal transfer of significance. No two historical epochs, no

---

18. The term "equivalence" in translation theory opens up a series of pitfalls because it implies the possibility of total equivalence. Two valuable recent publications have contributed to clarifying the notion of equivalence in translation: Amparo Hurtado Albir's *La notion de fidélité en traduction* (1990b) and Rosa Rabadan's *Traducción y equivalencia* (1991). Hatim and Mason (1990) suggest that "adequacy" may be a more useful concept: "Adequacy of a given translation procedure can . . . be judged in terms of the specifications of the particular translation task to be performed and in terms of users' needs."

two social classes, no two localities use words and syntax to signify exactly the same things, to send identical signs of valuation and inference. Neither do two human beings. (G. Steiner, 1975: 45)

However, professional translator communicative competence is different from that of the average communicator. Ideally, it consists of the specific grammatical, sociolinguistic, discourse, and transfer competences defined as follows:

Ideal translator grammatical competence. Knowledge of the rules of both languages, including vocabulary and word formation, pronunciation, spelling, and sentence structure—that is, the knowledge and skills required to understand and express the literal meaning of utterances.

Ideal translator sociolinguistic competence. Knowledge of and ability to produce and understand utterances appropriately in the situational context of both cultures—that is, as constrained by the cognitive context, the general sociohistorical context, the mode, the field, the tenor, the status of the participants, the purposes of the interaction, the *skopos* of the translation, and so on.

Ideal translator discourse competence. The ability to combine form and meaning to achieve unified spoken or written texts in different genres in both languages. This unity depends on cohesion in form (the way in which utterances are linked structurally to facilitate interpretation of the text) and coherence in meaning (the relationships among the different meanings in a text: literal meanings, communicative functions or social meaning, intertextuality).

Ideal translator transfer competence. The mastery of communication strategies that allow transfer of meaning from the SL to the TL and may be used to improve communication or to compensate for breakdowns (caused by limiting factors in actual communication or insufficient competence in one or more of the other components of communicative competence).

GENERAL OBJECTIVES IN TEACHING TRANSLATION

Some breakdowns in the communicative situation are due to differences between spoken and written communication and were mentioned in the comparison of interpreting and translating in chapter 6: absence of a shared communicative situation (temporal and spatial); loss of oral aids to understanding, such as intonation; gestures; conventions of writing; and permanence of the written text. The absence of these clues (context) can obstruct the resolution of lexical and syntactic difficulties of polysemy; the translator has to be able to recognize the difference between deliberate polysemy (ambiguity) and accidental polysemy in the SLT.

As García Yebra points out, solving ambiguity is one of the most interesting aspects of the translation process:

La polisemia es una propiedad de las lenguas. Pero la traducción no opera sobre las lenguas en cuanto tales, sino sobre sus manifestaciones en el habla, sobre textos concretos. Ahora bien, la polisemia puede producir en los textos ambigüedad e incluso polisignificación. En sentido estricto llamaríamos ambigüedad a la posibilidad de que un texto o parte de un texto pueda interpretarse de dos maneras distintas; si las posibilidades de interpretación son más de dos, hablaríamos de plurisignificación. . . . A la teoría de la traducción le interesa la ambigüedad más directamente que la polisemia. (García Yebra, 1983: 73)

The principles of polysemy and ambiguity comprise one aspect of translation theory that must be understood by the translator in order to develop strategies with which to overcome translation difficulties. Therefore, an understanding of these principles should be an objective of any translation program. However, a distinction should be made between pure theory , on the one hand, and processes and principles, on the other. This is a methodology not for teaching translation theory but for teaching translating.

A general list of translation teaching objectives would include the following:

1. The metalanguage for talking about translation (theory).

2. Understanding of the cognitive process of translating (theory).

3. Expert reading skills in the SL (grammatical, sociolinguistic, and discourse competence).

4. Expert writing and composition skills in the TL (grammatical, sociolinguistic, and discourse competence).

5. Documentation techniques essential for translating (sociolinguistic competence).

6. Work habits (essential for developing competence!).

7. Knowledge of typographical differences between the SL and the TL and transfer competence (grammatical and transfer competence).

8. Knowledge of lexical differences between the SL and the TL (grammatical, sociolinguistic, discourse, and transfer competence).

9. Knowledge of syntactic differences between the SL and the TL (grammatical, sociolinguistic, discourse, and transfer competence).

10. Familiarity with text types in the SL and the TL (sociolinguistic, discourse, and transfer competence).

11. Knowledge of discourse differences between the SL and the TL: textual coherence and textual cohesion (sociolinguistic, discourse, and transfer competence).

12. Knowledge of pragmatic and semiotic differences between the SL culture and the TL culture (sociolinguistic and transfer competence).

TEXT TYPES—CRITERIA FOR SELECTING A TEXT

Obviously, texts provide the content of the translation class. The above list of translation teaching objectives includes knowledge of different aspects of how texts are put together. Therefore, it is hardly surprising that text types have often been taken as the basis for the organization of translation training programs. Reiss (1971, 1976) developed a complicated model for pricing a translation based on subject matter, level of language, textual function, transmitter, receiver, and distance in time and space from the translator. Arntz proposed a text type model based on the extralinguistic context of the text. His model can be reduced to three main text categories:

Table 8.1
Arntz's (1982) Text Categories

TRANSMITTER	→	RECEIVER
1. Nonspecialized	→	General public
2. Specialized	→	General public
3. Specialized	→	Specialist(s)

This distinction between general and specialized texts is used by some translation agencies to establish the price of a translation—the more specialized, the more expensive.

Neunzig et al. (1985) worked out an elaborate set of criteria for translation teaching purposes based on Arntz's model for judging the difficulty of a text. The model is divided into fifteen components, each of which is judged according to four degrees of difficulty. The purpose was to establish a "scientific" basis for the choice of texts for translation class on a continuum from easy to difficult.

Newmark (1969) distinguishes four main text types: literary, institutional, scientific, and technological. He does not believe that one type can be said to be "easier" than another. Literary translation presents the problem of the author's idiolect; institutional translation always includes terms that cannot be translated because of cultural and institutional differences between the two language communities; technological translation in recent years has been plagued by neologisms. The scientific community may be said to be the most international, but the translator almost has to become a member of that community to be able to understand the SLT and translate it adequately. Scientific texts are expected to be coolly objective, but scientists are often obliged to persuade and convince, even though they may use resources other than those used in advertising.

All texts are multifunctional; therefore, any attempt to classify texts must be very complex. Even the most unemotional, informative text will have connotative undertones.

Aucun texte ne relève uniquement du notionnel ou de l'affectif; tout texte littéraire possède des contenus informatifs, tout texte technique une orientation sinon des émotions. Ce qui permet de classifier les uns en affectifs et les autres en notionnels est beaucoup plus une dominante qu'une caractéristique exclusive. (Lederer, 1981: 339)

The general tendency in translation schools has been to consider specialized texts the most difficult and to begin the program with general texts and then progress to specialized texts. It is not true that specialized texts are necessarily more difficult than general texts. Vázquez Ayora (1977) holds that good general translators can always develop their own specialties by doing documentary research and consulting experts. Furthermore, the area covered by specialized texts is too enormous to be learned in four years, or even in a whole lifetime. However, some specialized texts should be worked on during the translation program, both to expand students' knowledge of text types and to train them in the process of documentation. Students at the University of Ottawa in 1992 asked for more general translation classes instead of specialized ones because they considered general texts more difficult to translate. They also tend to be more interesting.

In fact, assigning texts to a particular type does not provide any magical solutions for the translation teacher. Nevertheless, the various attempts to define text-type categories can contribute to a comprehensive and useful model of text analysis, as Nord suggests:

By means of a comprehensive model of text analysis which takes into account intratextual as well as extratextual factors the translator can establish the "function-in-culture" of a source text. He then compares this with the (prospective) function-in-culture of the target text required by the initiator, identifying and isolating those ST elements which have to be preserved or adapted in translation. (Nord, 1991: 21)

RECENT METHODOLOGICAL APPROACHES

The different competences are interdependent, and, as was seen in the chapter on the translation process, there is a continuous bottom-up/top-down interaction. In practice, it is impossible totally to isolate work on each area of competence. It is possible only to emphasize one or more aspects of competence in each teaching unit. For example, reference within a text provides cohesion: it is situationally bound and comes into the area of discourse competence. However, reference depends on the use of pronouns, tenses, and so on, which are part of the grammar of a language (grammatical competence) and vary according to the system of that language. For example, English has a two-term set of demonstratives—*this, that*—whereas in Spanish the set comprises three terms—*este, ese, aquel*—corresponding, respectively, to proximity to speaker, proximity to addressee, and distance from both. During the translation process, the four aspects of translator communicative competence are brought into play simultaneously to cope with the different macro- and microstructures of the text and context.

Authors concerned with teaching *directa* have taken different approaches to the problem of delimiting difficulties and establishing progression. In a recent book, Mona Baker takes a bottom-up approach, although she admits that a top-down approach is more valid theoretically. She starts with single words and phrases, not the text as situated in its context of culture. She justifies her decision pedagogically: "It is much easier to follow for those who have had no previous training in linguistics" (Baker, 1992: 6).

It is indeed justifiable if the aim is to teach about linguistics rather than the skill of translating. If the aim is to teach the latter, the "textual analysis which is an essential preliminary to translation, should proceed from the 'top down', from the macro to the micro level, from text to sign"(Snell-Hornby, 1988: 69). Discourse analysis is the approach favoured by Delisle (1980) and Hatim and Mason (1990). The methodology proposed in this book is basically top-down, from macro to micro, but always bearing in mind the interdependence of macro- and microstructures. Thus, the main focus in some of the exercises is on microstructures. However, Baker is right to draw our attention to the dangers of an excessive emphasis on "text" and "context" if it obscures the fact that although "a text is a semantic unit, not a grammatical one . . . meanings are realized through wordings; and without a theory of wordings . . . there is no way of making explicit one's Interpretation of the meaning of a text" (Halliday, 1985: xvii).

As project manager of Cobuild, the Collins/University of Birmingham International Language Database, Baker made some interesting suggestions about how to introduce the concept of meaning at and above word level. However, her work *In Other Words* focusses mainly on teaching *about* translation, not teaching translating. Baker draws her examples from a wide variety of languages, including Arabic, Chinese, and Japanese. The SLT is always English, and there is no reference to whether the author is writing for foreign students translating into their own language or for English students translating into the foreign language. These points are not considered important because the author is writing *about* translation.

Thinking Translation: A Course in Translation Method: French-English, by Sándor Hervey and Ian Higgins (1992), is a real course (tried and tested at the University of St. Andrews), designed to improve *quality* in translating. They propose a scheme of textual filters as a guide to translation problems.

1. CULTURAL FILTER

Items involving choice between exoticism, cultural borrowing, calque, grammatical transposition, communicative translation, cultural transplantation.

2. FORMAL FILTER

Intertextual level, discourse level, sentential level, grammatical level: structure and lexis, prosodic level, phonic/graphic level.

3. SEMANTIC FILTER

Literal meaning, attitudinal meaning, associative meaning, reflected meaning, collocative meaning, allusive meaning, affective meaning.

4. VARIETAL FILTER

Dialect, sociolect, social register, tonal register.

5. GENRE FILTER

Oral genre types, written genre types: fiction, text book, etc. (Hervey and Higgins, 1992: 246)

The authors admit that theoretical notions have been "freely borrowed and adapted from translation theory and linguistics merely with the aim of facilitating and producing a rationale for problems of methodology." They assume "that higher quality is achieved by translating into the mother-tongue than into a foreign language; hence the predominance of unidirectional translation from French into English, in this course" (Hervey and Higgins, 1992: 1). However, they provide an appendix of four chapters devoted to topics selected from contrastive linguistics, in the hope that the exercises from these chapters will be used as specific problems arise in the translation class and not in sequence. In these chapters, they frequently reverse the direction of translation to translating from English to French; "this is to bring into the open certain possibilities in English which it is easy to overlook when translating from French" (ibid.: 202).

For various reasons, the St. Andrew's approach cannot be adapted to teaching translation into the foreign language. First, the borrowing from translation theory has been so free that it would be difficult for students to grasp an over-all vision of the translation process. However, the authors' ordering of filters is useful and makes their program much more than a taxonomic list of results, even though they use the same vocabulary as do comparative linguists (calque, transposition, transplantation, and so on). Second, when translating into the foreign language, more attention has to be paid to basic grammatical and sociolinguistic micro-elements, but problems such as prosody and alliteration are beyond the scope of most prose translating. Third, the focus on exotic language varieties in texts and varieties of genre makes this an interesting textbook for students translating into their mother tongue, but introduces text types that are quite outside the range of the *inversa* class. For example, they suggest an outline for a Spanish course that includes texts from Teresa de Jesús and García Lorca.

Christiane Nord's theoretical framework in *Text Analysis in Translation* (1991) is impeccable. The didactic implications of her text analysis and *skopos* model are that she chooses texts for teaching according to the relations between intention and effect, subject matter and effect, function and recipient. She analyzes three texts to illustrate different aspects of text and context in translation: for the relationship between intention and function, Alejo Carpentier, "Acerca de la historicidad de

Victor Hugues"; for the relationship between subject matter, text structure, and effect, Miguel de Unamuno, "Niebla"; and for the relationship between text function and recipient, Tourist Information Text, "Spezialitäten." However, the "general" texts (Carpentier and Unamuno) are much more difficult than is the "specialized" text, and Nord does not suggest pre-translation exercises to potentiate the students' ability to recognize these functions and understand the translation principles involved.

Jean Delisle's *L'Analyse du discours comme méthode de traduction* (1980) and *La Traduction raisonnée* (1993) really opened up the field for a new approach to teaching translation based on a solid theoretical model. He proposed translation objectives and developed introductory exercises that helped students to grasp the principles of the translation process. Some of the objectives he proposed for an introductory translation course were to establish the difference between equivalences of signifier and of signified (exercises on words out of context and in context); to develop the ability to grasp the main points of a text and the organization of a text; and to establish syntactic differences between French and English (the French superlative and the English comparative, the preference in French for nominalization, and so on).

Delisle's ideas have influenced many teachers, but nothing new was published using the same approach until Alan Duff's *Translation* (1989) and Françoise Grellet's *Apprendre à traduire* (1991), which are ostensibly for teaching language.

CHAPTER 9

STUDENT TRANSLATOR COMMUNICATIVE COMPETENCE

The constraints of translating into the foreign language are obviously important when considering student-translator communicative competence. The current trend in translation theory is to regard translating into the foreign language as unsatisfactory and artificial. This is made explicit in UNESCO's 1976 "Recommendations on the Legal Protection of Translators and Translations": "A translator should, as far as possible, translate into his, or her, mother tongue or into a language of which he or she has a mastery equal to that of his or her mother tongue" (quoted in Picken, 1989: 245).

The assumption that direct translation is the only viable professional option is particularly dominant in English-speaking countries. The Institute of Linguists' diploma in translation tests only translation into the candidate's mother tongue or language of habitual use; "above all, never ask a translator to translate from his/her own language" (Keith, 1989: 163).

However, translation from and into both classical and modern languages played a central role in European education right up to the first part of this century. Learning Latin and Greek was the basis of the sixteenth-century educational reform. The future Queen Elizabeth I was made to translate from English into Latin verses in the style of Virgil. Very little distinction was made between translating into or out of the foreign language—so much so that, even today, modern-language graduates have problems finding an English equivalent for the Spanish *traducción directa* or *traducción inversa*; they are not accustomed to talking about prose translation but just translation.

Furthermore, most translation training programs today include *inversa*. It is a popular subject with students because they learn so much and know that most translators have to translate at some point in their careers into their B language, particularly if their B language is English.

As was explained in the introduction, I have not adopted the term "service translation" (Newmark, 1988: 52) because it suggests an extremely limited scope for translating into the foreign language. Nevertheless, it is indeed true that many professionals only do service translations when working into the foreign language. On the other hand, we could compare *inversa* to Cinderella, the stepdaughter who was obliged to do the dirty work and yet outshone her stepsisters at the ball.[19]

The constraints of teaching translation from Spanish to English in undergraduate degree programs in Spain are provided by the limitations in the students' "ideal bilingual competence" and by their youth. Lanna Castellano suggests that a translator does not mature until the age of fifty (!):

> Our profession is based on knowledge and experience. It has the longest apprenticeship of any profession. Not until thirty do you start to be useful as a translator, not until fifty do you start to be in your prime. The first stage of the career pyramid—the apprentice stage—is the time we devote to *investing in ourselves* by acquiring knowledge and experience of life. Let me propose a life path: grandparents of different nationalities, a good school education in which you learn to read, write, spell, construe and love your own language. Then roam the world, make friends, see life. Go back to education, but to take a technical or commercial degree. Spend the rest of your twenties and your early thirties in the countries whose languages you speak, working in industry or commerce but not directly in languages. Never marry into your own nationality. Have your children. Then back to a postgraduate translation course. A staff job as a translator, and then go freelance. By which time you are forty and ready to begin. (Castellano, 1988: 133)

"Get Rich—But Slow" was the title of Castellano's paper at the Second ITI Conference. Not everybody has the patience—or the opportunity—to follow the life path she suggests, and a good undergraduate translation course can provide some shortcuts and speed up the maturing process somewhat.

STUDENT TRANSLATOR GRAMMATICAL COMPETENCE

A profile of the average Spanish second-year student at the Universidad Autónoma de Barcelona starting to translate into the foreign language is as follows. A few students may be nearly bilingual in Spanish and English (parents of different nationalities, residents in English-speaking countries), but, of course, the majority are not. The majority are intelligent and hard-working.[20] They tend to have a passion for languages and are, by nature, full of curiosity. Few of them imagine that they are

---

19. Frequently, the Spanish students' *inversa* translations are functionally more effective than the English students' *directa* translations of the same text. See questionnaire on *Un hombre providencial* in the introduction.
20. The entrance requirements for English as a B language in the School of Translators were the highest of all centres in the four universities in the Barcelona University District in 1991.

going to get rich—quickly or slowly—but they do hope to find a career that they will enjoy.

KNOWLEDGE OF THE SL RULES

These students have some vocabulary, collocation, and idiomatic limitations due to their youth and lack of experience.[21] However, they know more about the graphic, morphological, and syntactic rules of Spanish than do British students about English. This is due to the analytical nature of Spanish classes in secondary schools. They can give you the *tercera persona singular del preterito pluscuamperfecto del subjuntivo* of any verb and label correctly any type of *complemento circunstancial*. English classes for British secondary students tend to concentrate on language in use rather than language analysis.[22]

KNOWLEDGE OF THE TL RULES

Spanish students' knowledge of the rules of the TL has changed over the last decade. Fifteen years ago, the grammar approach to English-language teaching still dominated in Spanish secondary schools. In the last decade, communicative, functional teaching methods have taken over entirely, and students enter translator training with hardly any metalinguistic vocabulary in English. This means that first-year language-teaching programs should adapt to the times.

Previously, the first-year language teacher could enjoy the pleasant task of activating passive language skills with students who had little experience of participating in communicative situations in English. Today, students have been taught to "communicate" at school and to talk to English speakers in Spain and abroad. Therefore, the first-year language teacher is obliged to concentrate on the more formal aspects of the language. To a certain extent, the prose-translation class can contribute to this "perfecting" of the foreign language by developing accuracy and clarity (Duff, 1989: 7).

STUDENT TRANSLATOR SOCIOLINGUISTIC COMPETENCE

SL UTTERANCES IN SITUATIONAL CONTEXT

Given the analytical nature of their Spanish-language classes at secondary school, the students need practice in SL in use when the situational context transcends

---

21. In Catalonia, the bilingual (Catalan and Spanish) background of the students causes interference between the two A languages.
22. There has been much concern in the United Kingdom about English-language standards in British schools. The Prince of Wales has made it the object of one of his campaigns. The problem in the United States seems to be even more serious.

everyday social situations, journalism, textbooks, and certain areas of literature, and training to recognize register, pragmatic purpose, and intertextuality in different text types. Perhaps their greatest limitation, due to youth and lack of experience and reading, is their knowledge of the world—of general sociohistorical contexts—that would allow them to interpret the SLT. Building up their encyclopedic knowledge within the fields that are most likely to be useful for them professionally is certainly part of the translation class.

TL Utterances in Situational Context

In the TL, their competence is much more limited, particularly their ability to produce utterances appropriately and their knowledge of text types.

Student Translator Discourse Competence

Discourse Coherence in SLTs

On the whole, Spanish secondary education does not give much practice in combining form and content to produce coherent spoken or written SLTs in different genres. Some individual teachers may ask for summaries and essays, but in general the course content, in all subjects, is so packed that there is little time to learn to write. Some students begin translator training with little idea of structuring a text, from the point of view of either coherence or cohesion.

Discourse Coherence in TLTs

The students' limitations in the SL are all the more evident in the TL. However, it is a satisfying area to work on because much progress can be made in a relatively short time. Cohesive norms in English are well defined and can be learned. The choice of which text types to work on is essential to the prose translation class; obviously, not all types are appropriate.

Student Translator Transfer Competence

This involves the mastery of strategies that may be used to improve communication or to compensate for communication breakdowns. These breakdowns may be caused by limiting factors in actual communication or by insufficient competence in one or more of the other components of communication. The students have already had a year of translation into their A language, so they have developed certain strategies, procedures, or techniques. In the beginning, they beg for *técnicas de traducción,* as if there were a few simple techniques that can make translating easy. However, they must first discover and internalize the principles that lead to correct development of the translation process. In theory, these principles are not complicated, and once assimilated they seem just common sense, but, in fact, much experience is required if they are to be fully apprehended and put into practice. One of the goals of the translation class is to delimit these principles so that the students can fully apprehend them through personal experience and practice.

WHAT TRANSFER COMPETENCE IS NOT

When the first comparative studies of languages were formulated (see Vinay and Darbelnet, 1958; Malblanc, 1961), it was assumed by some that translator transfer competence had been defined. As Vinay and Darbelnet's famous book was subtitled *Méthode de traduction*, it was assumed that the comparative description provided a method for teaching translation.

However, as Hurtado Albir (1990b) has pointed out, this method was insufficient theoretically and pedagogically. The theoretical basis was weak for three main reasons. First, the comparisons were based on products, rather than on process. Second, the comparisons were made using isolated examples out of context. Third, the comparison fixed equivalences in a one-to-one relationship that did not take into account fuzzy sets of language, polysemy, and ambiguity. Pedagogically, comparative lists, even supposing they were pragmatically based using notional-functional principles, could lead, in the classroom, only to learning lists by heart. It would be impossible to list all possible equivalences for all possible contexts in the real and fictional worlds. Comparative studies provide the teacher with material for organizing the content of a class, but not for teaching it.

One outcome of the comparative method has been the development of *strategies, techniques,* or *procedures* to explain the structural differences between comparative equivalences. The problem is that they are not really strategies, but descriptions of results or products. If students have learned discourse analysis as a way of translating and have to translate *¡Jesús!* in a context in which someone has just sneezed, they do not need to know that they are applying the technique of modulation when they write, "Bless you!" However, these strategies have been adopted by certain Spanish authors (García Yebra, 1983; Vázquez Ayora, 1977), and some translation teachers use these taxonomies of descriptive strategies as a basis for teaching translation.

Brinton et al. (1981) do not use such taxonomies as a basis for their course, but they include an appendix, "Hints on Handling, Some Useful Techniques," which comprises eight topics: proper names, rephrasing, omissions, insertions, transposition, modulation, adaptation, and stock phrases. Newmark (1988: 81–91) gives a list of eighteen "translation procedures: transference; naturalization; culture equivalent; functional equivalent; descriptive equivalent; synonymy; through translation; shifts or transpositions; modulation; recognized translation; translation label; compensation; componential analysis; reduction and expansion; paraphrase; other procedures; couplets; and notes, additions, and glosses.

Of course, comparative studies can help. One of the basic translation principles is the difference between standardized and nonstandardized language. There are areas of language use that are completely standardized. For example, *nivel de vida* is a standardized expression in economics and must always be translated as *standard of living*. *Calidad de vida* is not a standardized expression and may be translated as "quality of life," "the way people live," "the cultural aspect of life," "leisure time," and so on, depending on the context. Comparative lists can help us with standardized language. In the *Collins Bilingual Dictionary*, the entry for *nivel* includes *nivel de vida*, while the entry for *calidad* does not include *calidad de vida*. Unfortunately, dictionaries cannot solve even all the problems of standardized language. Furthermore, even standardized language is not fixed for all eternity, but changes and evolves over time.

CHAPTER 10

THE TEACHING CONTEXT

EMPLOYMENT OPPORTUNITIES

Employment opportunities for prose translation were discussed in the introduction. It was suggested that there are opportunities for oral translating, in which TL errors may be acceptable if they do not interfere with the informative communicative intent of the discourse or break politeness rules in the TL culture. It was also suggested that formalized prose translations in restricted registers will be asked of translators as a part of their job. It is important for translators to know their own limits and recognize which texts they can cope with and how much documenting they will need to do. They should also know if their translation is a rough draft that will be edited.

STUDENTS' MOTIVATION

Motivation is obviously the clue to any successful learning situation. Trainee translators are usually motivated when they start, and it is the teacher's job to organize the course in such a way that this precious motivation is not lost.[23]

The person who has chosen to work with languages will usually find the puzzles provided by translation infinitely beguiling, at least in the relaxed atmosphere of the classroom, if not when hurrying to meet a deadline or in an exam. Surprisingly, Spanish students usually enjoy translation into English. At the beginning of the year, the task before them appears enormous, so it is important to start with exercises that they can do without too much difficulty to build up their confidence in the achievability of the task. If they have been learning English for a long time, they have probably reached a plateau at which it is difficult to realize that progress is being made. In the translation class, the approach allows progress to be observed.

---

23. This has been the case in Spain, where there has been a very limited number of places for translation training.

They are at a stage in their language development at which it is constructive to reflect on the differences between the two languages and the reasons for these differences.

STUDENTS' EXPECTATIONS

The maintenance of motivation is closely linked with students' expectations and whether or not they are fulfilled. Of course, when students begin a new discipline, they may have expectations that are unfounded, and these should not be encouraged. For example, students should not be led to think that the teacher has a list of secret techniques and that, if they receive this list, they will become skilled translators. However, most students are more sophisticated than this, and some teachers would be surprised at how aware they are of incoherence and lack of cohesion in a teaching program. Certainly, students' expectations should be taken into account when planning teaching.

At an impromptu seminar with a small group of teachers during the International Congress on Translation held at the Universidad Autónoma de Barcelona in April, 1992, Delisle described the results of a questionnaire that he had administered to Canadian translation students about what they expected of teaching and evaluation. These were the students' main ideas with regard to course organization:

1. They are aware of the organization or lack of organization of the classes.

2. They appreciate attempts by the teacher to give variety to their teaching.

3. They like problems to be delimited.

4. They find "sight translation" boring and uninstructive. (By sight translation, they mean a class in which the teacher brings a text to the classroom and they translate on the spot.) They make the distinction between a translation class and a *stage* (training course). In a translation course one learns to translate, while a *stage* is an opportunity to develop one's translation skills through practice.

5. They would like to cover a wide variety of fields in one course.

6. From the second year on, they would like to see more "theory" in the practical translation classes. By theory, they seem to mean "rational, systematic presentation of translation problems."

7. They would like to take as many courses of "general translation" as possible, as opposed to specialized translation. General translation is considered more difficult.

Discussion with students from the Universidad Autónoma de Barcelona showed that their hopes and expectations were very similar to those of the Canadian students. They, too, appreciate an effort on the part of the teacher to provide an organized, systematic, and yet varied approach to overcoming translation difficulties. This is no easy task, because, as I have shown, translation is a complex process that involves a variety of skills and different types of knowledge. Although we can draw diagrams separating hierarchically the different levels of the process in a theoretical model, in practice, all elements, both macro- and micro-, are continuously interacting and essentially interdependent.

SPECIFIC OBJECTIVES OF TEACHING PROSE TRANSLATION

Having compared student translator competence with ideal translator competence within the teaching context, it is now possible to adapt the list of general translation teaching objectives to the specific demands of the prose translation class.

The following objectives are suggested:

1. Gaining the metalanguage necessary for talking about the translation process at an elementary level.

2. Understanding the process of translation, according to Delisle's four stages—comprehension, deverbalization, reformulation, and verification.

3. Achieving advanced reading skills in the SL and recognition of limitations in this area.

4. Learning grammatically correct, pragmatically adequate "plain language"[24] writing and composition skills in the TL.

5. Getting an introduction to documentation techniques: first from parallel texts, encyclopedic articles, and "experts" brought to the class by the teacher; later, using documentary searches as a pre-translation task.

6. Maintaining work habits by executing regular assignments, which will be corrected individually and returned promptly.

7. Gaining knowledge of typographical differences between the SL and the TL.

8. Gaining knowledge of lexical differences between the SL and the TL within certain fields and registers (defined by the students' competence and the demands of the work market).

9. Gaining knowledge of syntactic differences between the SL and the TL.

10. Achieving familiarity with text types, with an emphasis on pragmatic texts (predominant informative function) and restricted fields and registers now in demand in the work market.

---

24. Principles of intelligibility defined by the Plain English Movement started by lawyers and administrators in the United States in the 1960s.

11. Gaining knowledge of discourse differences between the SL and the TL: textual coherence and cohesion.

12. Expanding knowledge of pragmatic and semiotic differences between the SL culture and the TL culture: (a) by choice of texts, (b) by taking advantage of exchange programs (students visiting countries where the TL is spoken/ TL speakers in the translation class), and (c) by reading newspapers, magazines, and books, and seeing films and television programs in the TL that reflect that culture.

13. Improving communicative oral skills for professional use (conversation interpreting, contact with clients, public relations, etc.).

CHAPTER 11

ACHIEVING OBJECTIVES

THE CYCLE OF INQUIRY—INDUCTIVE AND DEDUCTIVE LEARNING

The aim of this methodology is to teach a skill—translating. As has already been stressed, the translation class is above all a practical class, and yet the students have to understand the principles behind the process that they are taught to follow. They have to understand the "why" in order to be able to answer the "how." Whenever possible, the cycle of inquiry should be simplified. The students should be given teaching units (texts and tasks) that help them to formulate a hypothesis about the principles of translation. At the end of each unit, they should be able to confirm their hypothesis. Just as beginners learning a language find it easier to remember conclusions that they have reached from their own observations, trainee translators find it easier to remember what they find interesting, and a real-life example is often more interesting than a theory. Skills, whether playing the violin, show jumping, or translating, can be developed only by practising, and by practising in the right way.

GROUP DYNAMICS

The teacher's responsibility in the translation class is to maximize opportunities for students to develop their learning potential. Although it is hoped that the teacher is in the enviable position of knowing more than anybody else in the class, there will be areas in which the students' knowledge surpasses the teacher's. If the teacher's A language is English, Spanish students will know more colloquial Spanish than he or she does , even if he or she is a more skilled reader. If the teacher has spent a long time out of the UK, British students will know more about the UK today: what it is like to live in Wolverhampton in a recession, the latest slang and "buzz" words, and so on. Exchange students from other countries can contribute insights from their own languages and cultures. It is essential to pool all of the resources in the class and not to be restricted to a single channel of communication (teacher ↔ students), but to open up communication channels among the students.

Like the language teacher, the translation teacher has to devote some thought to achieving a communicative situation in the classroom. It is particularly important to integrate the foreign students from the beginning. A couple of class hours spent on getting to know each other will pay dividends throughout the year. It is also important to obtain a classroom that lends itself to group work: large enough for the students to move around in, and with chairs that are not secured to the floor. The more comfortable the students are with each other, the teacher, and the classroom, the easier it is to achieve active participation of all members of the class.

Some group work, both in the classroom and as homework, yields good results. As in the language class, it has been found that the whole is greater than the sum of the parts. There are advantages in asking the students to do some of their translation homework in groups of two to four people. The text is worked on very thoroughly because it goes through four stages:

1. In-class discussion of the general sociohistorical context of the SLT or a discourse-analysis questionnaire.

2. Individual first-draft translation of the text at home.

3. Group discussion of the different versions and selection of group version, identification of problems, and search for solutions.

4. Corrected translations returned in class and discussion of the problems and different solutions.

The students gain confidence working in this way. In groups, they often find solutions to problems themselves, which is a much more efficient learning process than obtaining a solution from the teacher. The final in-class discussion is often very lively because they have already invested so much time and effort in the translation that they are really interested in the outcome, and also because as a group they do not feel as threatened (Weymouth, 1984: 167). The success of this system depends largely on good organization on the part of the teacher. Texts must be given well in advance, deadlines must be respected, and all groups must hand in all translations.

We saw from the Ottawa questionnaire that students appreciate variety in the classroom. A variety of activities and tasks is invaluable for maintaining motivation and high levels of participation and for potentiating learning.

Delimiting Difficulties

To a great extent, students' expectations coincide with my opinion about how to program a translation course. The course should have a structure with clearly established objectives. Translation difficulties should be delimited and presented in a rational order (within a theoretical, methodological, and contextual framework). Motivation should be maintained by providing a variety of activities and fields of discourse. However, for prose translation a greater emphasis should be placed on specialized translations, which, with the aid of parallel texts, are easier than general translations. This preference is confirmed by the demands of the market and the students' own abilities. Nevertheless, general texts can also be used to provide variety, interest, and encyclopedic knowledge, illustrate specific translation principles, and provide experience in SLT analysis.

Most of the units in part 4 are intended for the first year of prose translation. Each task sheet is designed to concentrate on a specific, delimited difficulty so that the students can induce the "why" behind the "how"—the principle behind the practice. The following basic translation principles (drawn from theoretical and methodological considerations) are used to establish progression and delimit difficulties in the teaching of prose translation from Spanish to English.

SOME BASIC TRANSLATION PRINCIPLES

1. The translation process is made up of three stages: comprehension, deverbalization, and reformulation.

2. Different languages organize meaning and lexis in different ways. Semantic fields are rarely exactly equivalent—for example, *correr* and *run*.

3. Lexical polysemy is solved by context—for example, *double the money, double the blanket, he has a double, the families doubled up, he was doubled up in pain, daily double, he hit a double, he rented a double room, they have a double bed.*

4. Syntactic polysemy is solved by context—for example, *his car, his house, his arm, his father, his partner, his country, his work, his boss, his punishment, his God, his heir, his wife, his memory, his growth, his death, his attacker, his folly, his party, his hearing.*

5. Collocation is not rule-based.

6. Standardized language must be distinguished from nonstandardized language.

7. Context affects register (field, mode, and tenor).

8. Multiple contexts are involved in translation: the contexts of the SLT author, the SLT reader, the translation initiator, the *skopos*, the translator, the TLT reader.

9. Negotiating meaning requires awareness of pragmatic purpose and intertextuality.

10. Discourse cohesion and coherence are expressed differently by different languages.

ESTABLISHING PROGRESSION

The teaching units in part 4 are aimed at a first level of prose translation, and each one has one or more of the above principles as learning objectives. The units are grouped into five chapters: "Words in Context" (chapter 12); "Sentences in Context" (chapter 13); "Deverbalization" (chapter 14); "Restricted Codes and Transcoding" (chapter 15); and "Cohesion and Coherence" (chapter 16). The chapters have been ordered in this way to attempt a rational presentation of translation difficulties. Chapters 14 and 15 fulfil a double function of illustrating translation principles and preparing students for professional translating. They include the kind of translating that is most commonly asked of prose translators which is the kind they are most able to do.

Hurtado Albir (1994a) is generous in allowing *inversa* a pedagogical role as a good contrastive exercise and in improving the foreign language, but she advises teachers (a) only to introduce it after the students have got used to *directa*, (b) to adjust the tasks to the students' level, and (c) to prepare the reformulation stage with great care.

The aim here is more ambitious, as students may have to translate into English at some point in their working lives. Whether they go any farther than the simplest service translations will depend on their own circumstances, abilities, and inclinations. The work they do in *inversa* should be reflected in their *directa* and should make them better translators into their own language. Nevertheless, Hurtado Albir's advice is sound. The principal difference between the *inversa* class and the *directa* class will be the greater attention paid to reformulation at all levels: lexical (the dire problem of collocation), syntactic, and textual.

One way of preparing the reformulation stage with care is to begin with texts written in restricted codes, in which there is a high degree of standardized language with accepted equivalents in the TL. Working with parallel SL/TL texts in restricted codes provides the students with reliable, useful guidelines for their translation. Examples of standardized language include commonly used metaphors, idioms, proverbs, public notices, expletives, usual ways of stating the date and the time of day, dimensions, performatives expressed in accepted formulae, the language of weather reports, recipes, games, company reports and accounts, the formats of agendas and minutes, business letters, and medical reports (Halliday, 1973).

Some of the texts using standardized language could also be considered specialized language or language for special purposes and, in most *directa* courses, would be introduced only later on as practice in specialized translation. However, simple examples of this type of SLT, accompanied by a parallel text or texts in the TL, are introduced quite early on in the *inversa* program.

Another advantage of using standardized texts is that it is precisely these text types (service translations) that make up the bulk of the prose translator's work. Therefore, motivation is reinforced on two scores: the task is within their scope and they can see a practical professional application in the future. On the other hand, the *inversa* class should not be limited to this kind of text, because the content is not, on the whole, very interesting. Motivation can be stimulated toward the end of the year, when students are more confident about their ability to translate into English, by choosing texts that are intrinsically interesting and for which an investigation of their pragmatic purpose and semiotic value can lead to valuable discussions in class.

PART 4

UNDERSTANDING PRINCIPLES AND LEARNING SKILLS

CHAPTER 12

WORDS IN CONTEXT

TEACHING UNIT 1. WORDS OUT OF CONTEXT

Objectives

1. To make students aware of the principle that lexical polysemy is solved by textual context.

2. To help students see the difference between dictionary meaning and contextual meaning, understand the limitations of bilingual dictionaries, and learn not to depend blindly on the dictionary (see Delisle, 1980).

Tasks

1. The students are given Task Sheet 1, a sheet of paper divided into three columns. The left-hand column contains a list of words taken from a Spanish text unknown to the students. Individually, as homework, they are asked to fill in the second column with the English entries given in their bilingual dictionaries.

2. In class, the definitions from the different dictionaries are compared.

3. Task Sheet 2, the original text, is distributed. In groups of three or four, the students decide which, if any, of the dictionary definitions are adequate in this context. They will put their final choice in the third column of Task Sheet 1, and defend their decision to the rest of the class.

4. Individually, for homework, the students are asked to translate the words in their verbal context, at the bottom of Task Sheet 2.

Commentary

The meaning of a word for a translator is decided by its general situational and verbal context, by its distribution and collocation. The context makes it possible to neutralize the polysemy of a word in a sentence and discover the meaning of the message. For example, *Collins* gives seven alternatives for *saldo: settlement, payment, balance, clearance sale, remnant, remainder, leftover.* However, in the context of the text below, an appropriate translation is *outcome*, which was not given as a definition in any of the bilingual dictionaries.

El *saldo* provisional de los combates en las últimas 24 horas es de 40 muertos y un centenar de heridos.	The provisional *outcome* of the fighting in the last 24 hours is 40 dead and approximately 100 wounded.

TASK SHEET 1. LEXICAL POLYSEMY AND CONTEXT

1. Write in the second column all the definitions you know or can find in dictionaries for the words in the first column.

Words	Out of Context	In Context
luchas		
confesional		
justo		
ocupación		
saldo		
apostadas		
degenerado		
cabo		
pueblos		

TASK SHEET 2. *LUCHAS EN EL LÍBANO*

1. Read the following text carefully. When was it written? Where was it published? Why was it published?

2. Tell your neighbour what the text is about in English.

3. In groups of three or four, decide (a) which of your definitions are appropriate for the words that are underlined in the text and (b) which is the best definition for the context.

4. Translate the phrases at the end of the text into English.

El País, el 13 de noviembre de 1985.

40 muertos en <u>luchas</u> entre musulmanes y cristianos en el sur de Líbano

La batalla <u>confesional</u> entre milicias cristianas y musulmanas anunciada para inmediatamente después de la evacuación israelí de Sidón ha empezado con más de un mes de retraso, <u>justo</u> antes de una segunda retirada del Ejército de <u>ocupación</u>. El <u>saldo</u> provisional de los combates en las últimas 24 horas es de 40 muertos y un centenar de heridos, según el alcalde de la ciudad, Admed Kalash.

Primero circunscritos a choques entre las Fuerzas Libanesas (milicias cristianas y unificadas), <u>apostadas</u> en los barrios cristianos del este de Sidón, y el Ejército regular, los combates han <u>degenerado</u> rápidamente con la participación al lado de las fuerzas armadas, de milicias musulmanas y de *fedayin* de la resistencia palestina.

Por otra parte, el Ejército israelí llevó a <u>cabo</u> ayer en una zona colindante su tercera incursión desde su evacuación de Sidón contra <u>pueblos</u> shiíes.

luchas entre musulmanes y cristianos: _____

la batalla confesional: _____

justo antes de: _____

el Ejército de ocupación: _____

el saldo provisional: _____

las fuerzas apostadas en los barrios: _____

los combates han degenerado rápidamente: _____

llevó a cabo: _____

contra pueblos shiíes: _____

TEACHING UNIT 2. THE SAME WORD IN DIFFERENT CONTEXTS

Objective

To make students aware that different languages organize meaning and lexis in different ways (that words may belong to several different semantic fields or lexical sets).

Tasks

1. The students are given Task Sheet 3, containing nine sentences from a novel by Eduardo Mendoza, *El año del diluvio* (1992). The word *correr* appears in all of the sentences, in different verbal contexts, with different meanings. In groups, the students are asked to paraphrase the sentences in Spanish, avoiding, if possible, use of the word *correr*. They are asked to suggest possible translations for each sentence.

2. For homework, they are asked to read the five pages that the *Collins Cobuild Dictionary* devotes to the word *run* and try to find it used in the same ways as is *correr* on Task Sheet 3. They are asked to find two examples of *run* used in an English text and suggest ways of translating them into Spanish.

Commentary

The distribution and use of *correr* may overlap with that of *to run* but their distributions are not equivalent (see Grellet, 1991). *Correr* cannot always be translated as *run*. In some cases, the distribution is the same—for example: *una mujer corría* and *a woman ran*, or *una galería que corría a lo largo de la fachada trasera de la casa* and *a veranda that ran all along the back of the house*. In other cases, they do not coincide— for example, *los visillos corridos* and *the drawn curtains*, or *su vida corre peligro* and *his life is in danger*.

TASK SHEET 3. *EL AÑO DEL DILUVIO*

Instructions

1. Paraphrase the following sentences in Spanish, avoiding the use of *correr*.

2. Suggest possible translations for each sentence.

3. Look up the word *run* in the *Collins Cobuild Dictionary* and try to find the word *run* used in the same contexts as *correr* in these sentences.

4. Find two examples of *run* used in an English text. Suggest ways of translating them into Spanish.

Context

All examples are taken from *El año del diluvio* by Eduardo Mendoza (1992). This novel is situated in Catalonia in the years just after the Spanish Civil War. It tells the story of the relationship between Don Agosto, a powerful local landowner, and the mother superior of a nearby convent. Don Agosto lives in a beautiful old house guarded by two huge dogs, León and Negrita. The nun visits him to ask for his help in building a new hospital. He is a Don Juan and she falls in love with him. The plot is not at all predictable, and the ending is quite a surprise!

1. Era el último descendiente de una antigua estirpe de terratenientes . . . y aunque su edad <u>corría</u> pareja con el siglo, permanecía soltero. (p. 5)

   _____

   _____

2. Abrió los ojos y vio una mujer que <u>corría</u> por el sendero repitiendo a voces: ¡León! ¡Negrita! ¡Aquí! (p. 7)

   _____

   _____

3. . . . pues apenas iniciada la guerra civil . . . había <u>corrido</u> a poner su persona y sus bienes al servicio de nuestro invicto caudillo, el generalísimo Franco. (p. 12)

   _____

   _____

4. Las persianas estaban echadas y los visillos <u>corridos</u>. (p. 14)

   _____

   _____

5. Seguido de la monja, separó la cortina y salió a una galería que <u>corría</u> a lo largo de la fachada trasera de la casa. (p. 25)

   _____

   _____

6. En otro lugar, dos mujeres más, una madre y una hija, habían estado a punto de <u>correr</u> la misma suerte, pero habían podido ser salvadas en el último momento. (p. 46)

   _____

   _____

7.   Asistía a la <u>corrida</u> de toros que echaban de cuando en cuando en Bassora. (p. 55)

_____

_____

8.   ¿De verdad cree usted que la vida de don Agosto <u>corre</u> peligro?, preguntó la Superiora. (p. 58)

_____

_____

9.   Un buen día dejamos de verla, se había ido y no volvió más, pasado el tiempo <u>corrió</u> el rumor de que había muerto de un modo horrible, más no sé. (p. 68)

_____

_____

TEACHING UNIT 3. SEMANTIC FIELDS AND LEXICAL SETS

Objectives

1. To use the concept of semantic fields and lexical sets to help students (a) to appreciate the value that a word has in a given system, and (b) to develop strategies to deal with nonequivalence.

2. To make the students aware of some reformulation problems related to English verbs of speech (*me dijo que era verdad* → *he told me it was true* (S+V+O+O) but *he said to me it was true* (S+V+to+O+O). One of the lexical sets that is presented is that of verbs of speech. To reinforce this concept, a text is used that includes a large number of verbs of speech. This text is also useful for clearing up problems with reported speech in English.

3. To work on a very common Spanish → English reformulation problem: differences in sentence length and organization.

4. To have students start to think about the importance of typography in transmitting information—in this case, the use of italics.

Tasks

1. The students are given Task Sheet 4, consisting of three lexical sets in English: *speaker, traitor,* and *father.* They are asked to comment on differences in meaning between the items in the sets and to think of suitable contexts for each item.

2. They are asked to make up the same lexical sets in Spanish, and comment on the differences between the individual items and the differences between the Spanish and English sets.

3. They are given Task Sheet 5 and asked to make a list of English verbs of speech and order them from general to specific.

4. They are asked to do the same in Spanish and to comment on the differences between the two sets.

5. They are asked to research the rules governing the verbs of speech in English, in particular, the pattern (V+O+O) and (V+to+O+O).

6. Task Sheet 6 is based on a pragmatic text about Kim Philby, the famous double agent. The text is read aloud in class and the students are asked to make notes of the facts that are reported. Together, the class constructs an outline of the facts on the blackboard.

7. The students are asked to comment on the use of italics in the text and to translate it into English, paying particular attention to the register of the vocabulary they choose according to context, sentence length, and grammatical structures related to the verbs of speech.

Commentary

The idea of semantic fields is an oversimplification of how language actually works because a great number of words cannot be classified under any heading. As a concept, however, it can be useful for the translator. Fields are abstract concepts. An example of a semantic field would be *speech*, or *plants*, or *vehicles*. The actual words or expressions that belong to each field are called lexical sets. Lexical sets include general and more specialized words. General words in the lexical set of *verbs of speech* would be *say* and *tell*; more specialized words would be *murmur, whisper, mumble, mutter*. It is easier to find equivalences between general words than between specialized words.

A good introduction to Task Sheet 6 (the text on Philby) is to show on video the episode from the BBC series *Yes Minister* entitled "One of Us." This will lead to a discussion about famous "moles" in the British Secret Service. Below is a possible outline of the facts that will emerge from the students listening to the text being read. This is a good introductory text because it is pragmatic, the informative function is dominant, and the expressive function is weak. At the same time, the length and complexity of the Spanish sentences make it difficult to translate literally into English. The students are obliged to deverbalize and reformulate. The deverbalization is helped by presenting the text orally.

Here is an outline of facts from the Philby text:

1. Philby died in Moscow yesterday, aged 76.

2. The Soviet Embassy told the FO.

3. The FO told the BBC.

4. The BBC broadcast the news.

5. Philby's nickname was Kim.

6. He worked for the KGB and MI6.

7. For thirty years he gave British secrets to Moscow.

8. He was made a general of the Soviet Army.

9. He fled to Moscow in 1963.

10. He was a student at Cambridge.

11. He was recruited by the KGB at Cambridge.

12. The other recruits were his friends Burgess, MacLean, and Blunt.

13. They are all dead.

14. Burgess and MacLean fled to Moscow in 1951.

15. Philby was suspected in the 1950s.

16. He was responsible for MI6 anti-Soviet operations in the 1940s.

17. He was accused of betraying many British agents.

18. He organized the landing in Albania of a group of anti-communist rebels.

19. They were killed in an ambush.

20. He wrote an autobiography called *My Secret War.*

21. He supported the USSR because the West was weak and corrupt.

22. He opposed the Nazis.

23. He never gave interviews.

24. In March, 1987, he gave an interview to the *Sunday Times.*

25. He was not homesick.

26. The British let him escape to avoid a scandalous trial.

27. He was ill.

28. The Soviet medical care for high-ranking officers was first class.

TASK SHEET 4. SPEAKER, TRAITOR, FATHER

1. Comment on any differences in meaning between items in the following sets. In which context would you expect to find them? If you are not familiar with any of the words, look them up in the *Collins Cobuild Dictionary.*

2. List all of the words and expressions you can think of in Spanish for *speaker, traitor,* and *father.* Comment on the differences in meaning between the individual items in each set and differences between the English set and the Spanish set.

	Meaning	Context
a) speaker		
lecturer		
orator		
public speaker		
spieler		
spokesman		
spokesperson		
b) traitor		
apostate		
back-stabber		

defector   _____   _____
deserter   _____   _____
double-crosser _____   _____
fifth columnist _____   _____
informer   _____   _____
Judas   _____   _____
rebel   _____   _____
renegade   _____   _____
snake in the grass _____   _____
double agent   _____   _____
turncoat   _____   _____

c) father   _____   _____
   dad   _____   _____
   daddy   _____   _____
   pa   _____   _____
   papa   _____   _____
   pop   _____   _____
   pater   _____   _____
   sire   _____   _____
   old man   _____   _____
   padre   _____   _____

TASK SHEET 5. VERBS OF SPEECH

1. Make a list of all the English verbs you can find that have to do with speech, such as *say, suggest, complain, mumble, mutter, murmur, whisper, speak, tell,* and so on.

2. Try to group them in sets, starting with the more general ones.

Verbs of speech

_____

_____

_____

_____

3. List all the verbs of speech you can think of in Spanish, starting with the more general ones.

   Verbos de habla

   _____

   _____

   _____

   _____

4. Comment on the presence or absence of any semantic gaps in Spanish when compared with English, or vice versa.

   _____

   _____

   _____

   _____

TASK SHEET 6. KIM PHILBY

Instructions

1. The story of Kim Philby will be read out loud twice. Take notes of the main points.

2. Now read the text. Five words or expressions in the text are written in italics. Explain the reasons for its use in each case:

   (1) *Kim* (2) *Foreign Office* (3) *guerra fría* (4) *tercer hombre* (5) *Mi guerra secreta* (6) *Sunday Times*

3. As homework, translate the text. Pay particular attention to the context, register, and emotive value of the vocabulary you choose. Be careful with the verbs of speech.

   El País, el 7 de noviembre de 1989.

   Fallece Kim Philby, el famoso doble espía británico que huyó a Moscú en 1963

   Harold Philby, apodado (1) *Kim*, el mundialmente famoso doble espía británico que trabajó en los servicios secretos de su país suministrando información al Kremlin durante tres décadas antes de huir a Moscú en 1963, murió ayer en la capital soviética a la edad de 76 años, reveló anoche la cadena de televisión BBC citando fuentes del ministerio de Asuntos Exteriores británico.

"La Embajada soviética nos ha informado que Philby murió ayer en Moscú," explicó anoche un portavoz oficial del (2) *Foreign Office*.

Philby, que fue funcionario del Comité de Seguridad del Estado (KGB) desde su puesto en los servicios de información británicos (MI6) y posteriormente general del Ejército soviético, era el único superviviente de la red de estudiantes de la universidad de Cambridge que reclutó el KGB, integrado por sus amigos Guy Burgess y Donald MacLean y Anthony Blunt, el asesor de la pinacoteca de la reina Isabel II. Suministró a Moscú abundante información de secretos militares británicos y norteamericanos durante la época de la (3) *guerra fría*.

Burgess y MacLean huyeron a la Unión Soviética doce años antes de que Philby lo hiciera, en 1963, y hasta ese año las autoridades británicas desconocían la identidad del famoso (4) *tercer hombre*, si bien algunas sospechas habían empezado a alimentarse en los años cincuenta. Philby, responsable del departamento de operaciones antisoviéticas del MI6 durante los años cuarenta, fue acusado de traicionar a numerosos agentes británicos durante sus años de servicio. Organizó el desembarco de un grupo de emigrantes rebeldes anticomunistas en Albania, que serían luego asesinados en una emboscada.

En su autobiografía, titulada (5) *Mi guerra secreta*, escrita en Moscú, justificó su colaboración con la URSS argumentando que las democracias occidentales eran muy débiles y corruptas para combatir el nazismo en los años treinta.

En marzo pasado, el famoso tercer hombre rompió años de silencio sobre su deserción en una entrevista con el (6) *Sunday Times* en la que confesaba no añorar su patria. En la entrevista afirmaba también que sus superiores le dejaron escapar para evitar así un juicio escandaloso. Philby declaró al dominical londinense que se encontraba enfermo y que estaba recibiendo un tratamiento médico de primera clase como correspondía a su rango de general.

TEACHING UNIT 4. STRATEGIES FOR NONEQUIVALENCE

Objective

To provide examples of nonequivalence at word level and strategies used by translators to overcome the problem (from categories in Baker, 1992: 26–38).

Tasks

The students are asked to study the examples in groups of four and then to find examples in the context of other Spanish words that are difficult to translate into English, explain why, and suggest translation alternatives.

Commentary

The two previous exercises are designed to show the students how languages such as Spanish and English organize their experience of the world differently. This will inevitably lead to nonequivalence at all levels.

1. It is often easier to find an equivalent word at a more general level than at a more specific level (*wash → lavar*).

2. *Simpático* has a false friend, *sympathetic,* and no direct equivalent. Several words are needed in English in order to express all the meanings of *simpático.*

3. Institutional terms can be translated by cultural substitutes if the text is not an institutional one. An American cultural substitute for *el juez del Juzgado de Guardia* would probably be *Police Court* rather than *Magistrate's Court.*

4. *Cantaor*, like *simpático*, does not have a direct equivalent in English, but in this case it was considered necessary (the text was from the album cover) to paraphrase and break down the different elements that make up the word: flamenco composer and singer (which does not include the element of extemporizing).

TASK SHEET 7. Strategies at Word Level

Instructions

The following are some examples of strategies used by professional translators.

1. **Translation by a more general word** (*superordinate*).
    SLT: <u>Shampoo</u> the hair with mild WELLA SHAMPOO and lightly towel dry.
    TLT: <u>Lavar</u> el cabello con un champú suave de WELLA y frotar ligeramente con una toalla.

2. **Translation by a more neutral, less expressive word.**
    SLT: Uno de los asistentes, hombre <u>simpático</u>, de verbo ágil, buen conversador, se hallaba en el uso de la palabra.
    TLT: One of the guests, a <u>nice</u> man, a gifted speaker, and a good conversationalist, was speaking.

3. **Translation by cultural substitution.**
   SLT: En el pequeño despacho del <u>Juzgado de Guardia</u>, el <u>juez</u>, con traje negro un poco desgastado, firme y firme.
   TLT: In the small office of the <u>Magistrate's Court</u>, the <u>J.P.</u>, wearing a worn black suit, was signing papers.

4. **Translation using a loan word (plus explanation).**
   SLT: Las estelas de "<u>Los Danzantes</u>" en Monte Albán, Oaxaca, fechadas entre 600 y 300 a.C. constituyen en el Nuevo Mundo el más antiguo registro de aconteceres.
   TLT: The stelae known as *danzantes* (dancers) at Mount Alban in the Oaxaca Valley constitute the oldest known chronicle (600–300 B.C.) of the New World.

5. **Translation by paraphrase.**
   SLT: Su padre es el legendario <u>cantaor</u> José Reyes.
   TLT: His father is the legendary <u>flamenco composer and singer</u> José Reyes.

Make a list of five Spanish words that you feel are particularly difficult to translate into English. Comment on the source of difficulty in each case and suggest possible translations.

CHAPTER 13

SENTENCES IN CONTEXT

TEACHING UNIT 5. SENTENCES OUT OF CONTEXT I
(See Delisle, 1980)

Objectives

1. To stress the importance of reading the whole text in order to contextualize words and sentences.
2. To reinforce notions of textual coherence and cohesion in English.

Tasks

1. The sentences of a text are copied out onto separate cards. Each student is given one to translate without having seen any of the others.
2. They are then asked to read out their translated sentences in the order of the SLT and the sentences are written on the blackboard.
3. The sentences are edited to form a text, adjusting meaning, coherence, and cohesion. This text is then compared with the SLT and any additional changes are made.
4. Task Sheet 9 provides semantically correct alternatives in different registers. The students are asked to choose the most appropriate for their translation or provide a better alternative.

Commentary

The sentence will not always provide enough information to contextualize words; syntactic polysemy is solved by context. Sentences translated out of context and put together will not form a coherent and cohesive text and may even produce non-sense. Solving semantic ambiguity is the first stage in translation, but selection of lexis also depends on the register of the SLT.

The sentences translated out of context and written on the blackboard will not form a text. There will be breakdowns in cohesion, for example, between sentences

2 and 3. The student has no way of knowing the subject of *Llegó* and may translate it as *He arrived*. Babies are always masculine in Spanish, so in sentence 6 the little girl is referred to as *este*, which, out of context, will be translated as *he*, or even *it*.

The last sentence on its own is not sufficient to resolve the polysemy of *caballo* and the student will naturally think of the primary meaning, the animal *horse*, not the drug *heroin*.

Here is a possible translation:

Carmen is an attractive young woman of 24, but drugs have aged her. She has two daughters, now four and two. She first came to Barcelona's Hospital del Mar four years ago when she was going to have her first baby. The little girl was born with withdrawal symptoms and was under medical treatment for 15 days, suffering from eye and ear defects. However, Carmen was able to stay in hospital with her baby, thanks to the support of her parents and the close control of the doctors. Finally, the right treatment was found for her daughter.

After this experience Carmen tried to kick the heroin habit, but she was able to keep away from the drug only for a few months. A year and a half later, she was pregnant again, and she was admitted to hospital when she was almost five months pregnant. She was given methadone as a substitute for heroin and told to follow a balanced diet. The second child's withdrawal symptoms were less pronounced.

Carmen is now separated from her husband, whom she met when she was already a drug addict. He is also a heroin addict. Drugs were not only a source of excitement for the couple but also a source of income. Economically, the separation has been a serious blow for her. She is so short of money that a few months ago she had to wait for the first bus at seven in the morning to take one of her little girls to Emergency at the Hospital del Mar because she could not afford a taxi. She had given up drugs and was determined to stay off them but, given the failure of her first attempt, she knew she needed to change her whole environment.

Only 15 days ago she was admitted to hospital suffering from a heroin overdose, which had brought on a heart attack. She has recovered this time but it was the drug's last warning.

TASK SHEET 8. *ENTRE EL PICO Y LA MATERNIDAD*

Translate the sentence you have been given.

1. Carmen es una joven de 24 años, de aspecto agraciado, a la que la droga hace aparentar mayor.
2. Carmen es madre de dos niñas, de 4 y 2 años de edad.

3. Llegó por primera vez al Hospital del Mar hace cuatro años.

4. Fue cuando iba a dar luz por primera vez.

5. El bebé nació con síndrome de abstinencia y tuvo que ser tratado con fármacos durante 15 días.

6. Este presentó trastornos visuales y auditivos, pero Carmen, con el apoyo de sus padres y la estrecha vigilancia de los médicos del hospital, pudo quedarse.

7. Finalmente se logró conseguir una correcta estimulación.

8. Tras esta experiencia, intentó desengancharse del caballo.

9. Sólo lo consiguió durante unos meses.

10. Al cabo de un año y medio volvió a quedarse embarazada.

11. Cuando ingresó estaba casi de cinco meses.

12. Se le administró metadona como sustitutivo del caballo y se le recomendó una alimentación equilibrada.

13. La segunda niña presentó un síndrome más discreto.

14. En la actualidad, Carmen se ha separado de su marido, que es también heroinómano y al que conoció siendo ya adicta.

15. La droga para la pareja no era sólo una fuente de sensaciones sino también una fuente de ingresos.

16. Esta ruptura ha supuesto un duro golpe a la economía de la joven.

17. Hasta el extremo de que hace unos meses tuvo que esperar al primer autobús, a las siete de la mañana—ya que no pudo tomar un taxi—para ingresar a una de sus pequeñas en urgencias del Hospital del Mar.

18. Ahora, ya lo ha dejado.

19. Su decisión de abandonar la droga es firme, pero sabe que necesita un contexto distinto, a la vista del fracaso de su primer intento.

20. Hace apenas 15 días ingresó en el hospital con un sobredosis de heroína, que le provocó un paro cardiaco del que ha podido recuperarse.

21. Fue la última advertencia del caballo.

TASK SHEET 9. ALTERNATIVES

Now that we have the whole text, analyze the context and the register and consider which of the following alternatives would be most appropriate for your translation. Have you any better suggestions?

1. Fue cuando <u>iba a dar luz por primera vez</u>.
   a) She was going to have her first baby.
   b) She was about to experience childbirth for the first time.
   c) She was going to give birth to her first child.
   d) She was about to become a mother.

2. El bebé nació con <u>síndrome de abstinencia</u>
   a) went cold turkey
   b) withdrawal symptoms
   c) had the sweats

3. Este presentó <u>trastornos visuales y auditivos</u>
   a) ear and eye defects
   b) seeing and hearing difficulties
   c) visual and auditive problems

4. intentó <u>desengancharse del caballo</u>
   a) give up heroin
   b) quit taking the hard stuff
   c) forswear the deadly drug
   d) kick the habit

5. estaba <u>casi de cinco meses</u>
   a) in the fifth month of her pregnancy
   b) nearly five months pregnant
   c) in the fifth month of gestation

6. <u>La segunda niña presentó un síndrome más discreto</u>
   a) The second child's withdrawal symptoms were less pronounced
   b) The second baby had less serious symptoms
   c) The second little girl manifested less acute symptoms

7. <u>La droga para la pareja no era sólo una fuente de sensaciones sino también una fuente de ingresos</u>
   a) Heroin wasn't just how they got their thrills but how they paid the rent
   b) Not only was the drug a source of excitement but also a source of income
   c) Drugs gave them their kicks and paid the bills

8. Esta ruptura ha supuesto <u>un duro golpe a la economía</u> de la joven
   a) a grave economic set-back
   b) Economically, the separation has been a serious blow
   c) has left her without a penny

9. le provocó <u>un paro cardiaco</u>
   a) a heart attack
   b) a cardiac arrest
   c) a heart seizure

TEACHING UNIT 6. SENTENCES OUT OF CONTEXT II

Objectives

1. To show that ambiguity at the sentence level cannot be solved without context.

2. To demonstrate that metaphorical use of language cannot be recognized out of context.

Tasks

1. The students are given six sentences out of context (Task Sheet 10) and asked to imagine a communicative situation and a translation for each one.

2. They are given the whole text (Task Sheet 11) and asked to reconsider their translations of the six sentences now that they are in context.

3. They are asked to translate the whole text.

Commentary

Sentences with a literal and metaphorical meaning have been taken out of the context of the first scene of Valle-Inclán's *Luces de Bohemia*.

Le toca ir delante: A possible situation might be a family setting out on a car trip and the children arguing about whose turn it is to sit in front. The father might settle the argument by saying, *It's John's turn to sit in front.* Madama Collet means that Buey Apis is older than Max and should die first: *He'll be carried out first.*

¡Oh! No te pongas a gatas, Max: A possible situation might be a romantic declaration of love in which the object of the declaration says impatiently to her lover, *Get up off your knees!* Alternatively, a mother to a small child who has just been washed and dressed, *Stop crawling around!* Madama Collet means, *Stop feeling sorry for yourself! Don't grovel!*

TASK SHEET 10. AMBIGUITY

Instructions

1. Read the following sentences and imagine a context for each one. Who is speaking to whom? What is the situation?

2. Suggest one or more translations for each sentence.

	Communicative Situation	Possible Translation(s)
1. Ten paciencia, Max.		
2. Le toca ir delante.		
3. Otra puerta se abrirá.		
4. También se matan los jóvenes.		
5. ¿En qué redacción me admiten ciego?		
6. ¡Oh! No te pongas a gatas, Max.		

TASK SHEET 11. *Luces de Bohemia*

Instructions

Now read the first page of Ramón del Valle-Inclán's *Luces de Bohemia* and you will find the sentences from Task Sheet 10 in context. Do you have to rethink your translations? If you do, try to explain why.

Ramón del Valle-Inclán, *Luces de Bohemia:* Escena primera.

Hora crepuscular. Un guardillón con ventano angosto, lleno de sol. Retratos, grabados, autógrafos repartidos por las paredes, sujetos con chinches de dibujante. Conversación lánguida de un hombre ciego y una mujer pelirrubia, triste y fatigada. El hombre ciego es un hiperbólico andaluz, poeta de odas y madrigales, Máximo Estrella. A la pelirrubia, por ser francesa, le dicen en la vecindad Madama Collet.

Max. — Vuelve a leerme la carta del Buey Apis.

Madama Collet. — Ten paciencia, Max.

Max. — Pudo esperar a que me enterrasen.

Madama Collet. — Le toca ir delante.

Max. — ¡Collet, mal vamos a vernos sin estas cuatro crónicas! ¿Donde gano yo veinte duros, Collet?

Madama Collet. — Otra puerta se abrirá.

Max. — La de la muerte. Podemos suicidarnos colectivamente.

Madama Collet. — A mí la muerte no me asusta. ¡Pero tenemos una hija, Max!

Max. — ¿Y si Claudinita estuviese conforme con mi proyecto de suicidio colectivo?

Madama Collet. — ¡Es muy joven!

Max. — También se matan los jóvenes, Collet.

Madama Collet. — No por cansancio de la vida. Los jóvenes se matan por romanticismo.

Max. — Entonces, se matan por amar demasiado la vida. Es una lástima la obcecación de Claudinita. Con cuatro perras de carbón, podíamos hacer el viaje eterno.

Madama Collet. — No desesperes. Otra puerta se abrirá.

Max. — ¿En qué redacción me admiten ciego?

Madama Collet. — Escribes una novela.

Max. — Y no hallo editor.

Madama Collet. — ¡Oh! No te pongas a gatas, Max. Todos reconocen tu talento.

Max. — ¡Estoy olvidado! Léeme la carta del Buey Apis.

Madama Collet. — No tomes ese caso por ejemplo.

Max. — Lee.

Madama Collet. — Es un infierno de letra.

Max. — Lee despacio.

TEACHING UNIT 7. IMAGINING CONTEXTS—REGISTERS

Objective

To make the students aware of the relationship between context and register: field, mode and tenor (see Duff, 1989: 37).

Tasks

1. The teacher writes a stimulus word or expression on the blackboard. This should be a short, relatively neutral statement that lends itself to transformation into different registers. For example:
   - Gracias
   - Estoy de acuerdo/No estoy de acuerdo
   - Prohibido fumar
   - Lo siento
   - Siéntate

2. Ask the students to call out various ways of conveying the same message in different words (*Gracias, muchas gracias, muchísimas gracias, muy amable, ¡qué amable!, te estoy muy agradecido, le estaré eternamente agradecido, ¡qué sorpresa!, has acertado, es justo lo que quería, no tenías por qué*).

   For each suggestion, the students should say as precisely as possible in what context they would expect to see or hear the words (Who is speaking to whom? Where are they? Where would the words be seen?).

3. In groups of three or four, they now work in the same way on two of the other stimulus phrases. If they have difficulty imagining contexts, some suggestions could be written on the blackboard, such as lists of people and places.

GENTE	LUGARES
banquero	tren/autobús/avión
vagabundo	tribunal
guardia civil	ascensor
diplomático	teatro
director de cine	aula magna
niño	mercado
dependienta	laboratorio
vecina	sala de espera del dentista
juez	recepción de un hotel
azafata	fábrica

Ask them to write down their suggestions and compare notes with other groups.

4. Finally, keeping the imaginary contexts clearly in mind, they should look for similar expressions in English.

Commentary

Here are some possible English expressions:

THANK YOU

(mainly spoken)	**(mainly written)**
(I'm) most obliged.	Please convey our thanks to . . .
Thanks a lot.	We should like to acknowledge our thanks to/for . . .
Many thanks.	And in conclusion, a word of thanks to . . .
I can never repay you!	Finally, I should like to express my gratitude to . . .
Ta.	I should like you to know how grateful I am for . . .
I'm extremely grateful.	It was most kind of you to . . .
How (very) kind.	We thank you for your consideration/understanding.
You shouldn't have!	
What a lovely surprise!	
Oh, thank you!	

I DO NOT AGREE

(mainly spoken)	**(mainly written)**
You're wrong.	There are, however, certain points with which I take issue . . .
Have it your way.	Far be it from me to criticize, but . . .
Surely not?	The mistaken assumption here is that . . .
With all due respect . . .	This is simply not so.
No. No. No!	The argument is fallacious in several respects.
Nonsense!/Rubbish!	To such a proposal, in all conscience, I could never agree.
I don't agree./I do not agree.	
You may have a point, but . . .	
I beg to differ. . .	
I think it would be unwise.	
Yes, but . . .	
Hmmm . . .	

TEACHING UNIT 8. IMAGINING CONTEXTS AND READERS

Objectives

1. To establish the register of the SLT.

2. To show how multiple contexts are involved in translation: the contexts of the SLT author, the SLT reader, the *skopos*, the translator, the TLT reader.

Tasks

1. A procedure similar to the one described in the previous exercise can be used as a preliminary exercise to establish the context and register of a text that is to be translated. Choose an expression from the text that illustrates the register clearly. Give the students a list of expressions that serve the same function and ask them to imagine a context for each one. The following example is based on an interview with Santiago Carrillo in *Cambio 16* (3 December 1990). The register of Santiago Carrillo's discourse is typical of the old-style Spanish politician and the expression that has been chosen is *¡Mire usted!* (which is also one of Felipe Gonzalez's catchwords).

2. The students are asked to define the field, mode, and tenor of the interview with Carrillo.

3. They are asked to identify the words and expressions that are culturally bound and suggest strategies for translation.

Commentary

The field of the discourse is Spanish political discourse. The mode is an oral interview with Santiago Carrillo. The tenor is the relationship between a well-known politician and a journalist.

In particular, this exercise is concerned with establishing what *implied* information needs to be made *explicit* for the TLT readers. The students are asked to translate the interview for *The Economist* (*skopos*). There are several references to Spanish institutions and personalities that would not be familiar to English readers of *The Economist* (TLT readers). The translator never knows exactly what readers of the translation know. He or she has to make an educated guess and, in informative, pragmatic texts of this kind, decide which explicatures have to be made.

TASK SHEET 12. *¡MIRE USTED!*

Instructions

Imagine a context (Who says it? To whom? Where? When? Why?) for each of the following expressions:

WHO SAYS IT?	TO WHOM?	WHERE?	WHEN?	WHY?
¡Escucha!				
¡Eh! tío				
Hijo mío				
¡Mire usted!				
¡Cuidado!				
¡Atención!				
¡Ten cuidado!				
En mi opinión				

TASK SHEET 13. *ENTREVISTA CON SANTIAGO CARRILLO*

Instructions

1. Read the following text and compare the context you imagined for *¡Mire usted!* with this one. Do the two contexts have anything in common? Can you find an English expression that would create a similar impression to *¡Mire usted!*?

2. a) What is the **mode** of the text (spoken, spoken as if not written, not necessarily to be spoken, read in silence, etc.)?
   b) What is the **tenor** of the text (superior to inferior, equal to equal, frozen, formal, consultative, casual, intimate)?
   c) What is the **field** of the text?

3. You have been asked to translate this interview for *The Economist*. There are several references in the text that are culturally bound and that may not be familiar to English readers. Underline these references and decide which translation strategies would be appropriate in each case.

4. Translate the whole text.

   Cambio 16, el 3 de diciembre 1990.

   Entrevista con Santiago Carrillo

   ¿Quiénes son los auténticos comunistas hoy en España?

   Mire usted, no voy a hacer una declaración diciendo que el comunista en España soy yo. Hoy precisamente he leído en la prensa una declaración de Julio Anguita en la que dice que yo me voy al PSOE porque es natural que cada uno se vaya a su sitio. Si Julio Anguita se refiere al decir eso que en mi primera juventud estuve en la Juventud Socialista, le puedo responder que su sitio sería Falange, que es donde él estaba. Estoy seguro que en España hay muchos comunistas que no están en mi partido ni en el PCE, sino en su casa.

¿Es la *perestroika* el eurocomunismo a la rusa?
Creo que sí. La desgracia es que si eso hubiera nacido en la época de Kruschev que se acercó bastante, pero no vio todo el fondo de los problemas, a estas horas otro gallo nos cantaría.

Si Lenin levantara la cabeza . . .
Mire usted, a mí esas fórmulas de si fulano levantara la cabeza nunca me han gustado, porque es intentar poner en boca de esa persona lo que uno piensa para darle más autoridad. No sé lo que diría Lenin si levantara la cabeza, lo que sé es que no puede levantarla.

¿Ve posible la sustitución de Anguita por Antonio Gutiérrez?
No creo que Antonio Gutiérrez se proponga dejar una realidad, que es Comisiones Obreras, para encabezar un fantasma como es IU y el PCE.

Un fantasma con algunos vivos notables. Por ejemplo, Cristina Almeida.
Cristina Almeida tiene una cierta personalidad, pero no hay que exagerarla. Tiene sus límites, a lo mejor en el futuro se transforma en la Margaret Thatcher española, pero hoy no lo veo posible.

TEACHING UNIT 9. COMIC STRIPS

Objectives

1. To make the students aware that, depending on the translation, the importance of the multiple contexts will vary. Some theorists speak of author-centred translating, text-centred translating, and reader-centred translating. The choice of approach will depend on the status of the SLT and the purpose of the translation.

2. To consider the priorities (SLT readers) and constraints (mode) of translating comic strips. The priority is to create a humorous response, and in some cases to drive home a form of social criticism. They have to be immediately accessible to a wide readership. If the SLT contains too many culturally bound implicatures, it cannot successfully be translated.

Tasks

1. The students are given five *Mafalda* comics (Task Sheet 14) and asked to identify cultural references and decide which, if any, have to be adapted to make them accessible to British readers.

2. They are asked to identify the field and tenor of each comic.

3. They are asked to consider strategies for transferring the cultural references, field, and tenor within the constraints of mode (picture and bubble).

Commentary

Translators of modern literature, often working closely with the author of the SLT, may be author-centred (for example, William Weaver, the excellent English translator of Umberto Eco's *The Name of the Rose*). For translators of European Union directives or legal contracts, authorship is far less important than the nature of the text itself and its range of possible meanings. Certainly, they are not concerned with making the texts accessible to readers other than those skilled at working their way through this type of document (a select band, if we are to judge by those who have actually read the Maastricht Treaty). Where translation is reader-centred the demands of author and text are still present but priority is given to creating a particular kind of reader response.

The format of the comic does not allow space for paraphrases, amplification, translator's notes, or other explicatures. The mode of the comic is a text written to be read as spoken. The translator is bound by the space in the bubble, the message of the picture, the SLT, and the coherence of the sequence. The English translations of Claire Bréchter's comics make her characters British. References to French political institutions are exchanged for equivalent British ones. There is nothing in the pictures that makes this unbelievable.

There are excellent Spanish political cartoonists who have not been translated; this may be because they are too culturally bound to be effective. Some of Romeu's comic strips could be translated into English if it were not for the pictures; non-Spanish readers would wonder who the character in the striped overalls and a black beret is. Two famous French comic-strip characters that have been translated into many different languages are *Tintin* and *Astérix*. Both are typically French, and they remain French in the English version. However, they represent archetypes that are familiar to readers of English, and the situations in which they find themselves are also archetypal.

Some of the *Mafalda* comic strips by the Argentinian writer Quino can be successfully translated into English. Through the American comic strip *Peanuts*, readers of English are familiar with the genre: the child's view of the adult world in comic form. The references to Argentinian politics are vague, seen through the eyes of a child (there are no concrete references to political personalities and institutions), and the basic humour and social criticism can be transmitted. This does not mean that there are no problems in a reader-centred translation of *Mafalda*, but they are manageable ones. The purpose of this exercise is for the students to consider what adaptations are needed. Once again, the presence of exchange students makes the task easier.

Here are some translation problems in the *Mafalda* comics

1. The Columbus reference is all right because everybody knows about him:

    In fourteen hundred and ninety-two,
    Columbus crossed the ocean blue.

    The register is that of a child's composition with spelling mistakes, colloquial vocabulary, repetition, and syntactic co-ordination rather than subordination. All of these elements can be used in the translation.

2. *Hacendado* and *oligarca* could cause problems because the oligarchy of large landowners is not a central issue in the English-speaking world. An adaptation could be a *Texas rancher* or a *millionaire* and a *capitalist*.

    The register is that of the classroom, and, in particular, the "contextualized" math problem. It is important to maintain the contrast between the educated *oligarca* and the colloquial *roñica*. A possible solution might be *capitalist pig/cruel oppressor of the people* and *old meanie*.

3. The main translation problem here is based on a play on words. Susanita interprets *cualquiera* as *un cualquiera, a nobody*, instead of the idea that Mafalda is trying to transmit, which is that we are as human as anyone else (perhaps an idea might be found in Shylock's "If you prick us do we not bleed" speech in *The Merchant of Venice*). *Common* might be a solution, as it can be interpreted as either *normal* or *vulgar*.

The register is that of a political speech and the comments are those that might be heard from the government benches in the House of Commons during question period: *Hear! hear! Well said! Bravo!*

4. *Mercado* should probably be adapted to *shops* or *supermarket*.

    ¡Sunescán!! ¡¡dalúna búso!! is not easy to transmit. Breaking up words in different places is a common technique in Spanish and Catalan to signify difficulties in communication. It is often used in children's comics to convey the language of foreigners, particularly Africans and Native Americans. One possibility is to mix capitals and lower-case letters, reduce the size of the letters and run the words together as if muttering:

    DAYlight ROBbery!!!!! thaswhatitis.

5. The students should recognize the Old Testament register of *Desdichado de aquel—Woe is he/Woe unto him*—and take to heart as translators Susanita's advice: It's not <u>what</u> you say but <u>who</u> said what, <u>how</u>, <u>when</u>, about <u>whom</u>, <u>why</u>.

TASK SHEET 14. *MAFALDA*

Instructions

1. Identify the cultural references in the following comic strips and decide if any adaptations are necessary to make them accessible to English-speaking readers.

2. Identify the registers used. What are the characteristics of each register in the SL and the TL?

3. Suggest possible strategies within the constraints imposed by the picture and the size of the bubble.

A.

1. Se acerca el 12 de octubre y cada año la misma historia. Composición Tema: Cristobal Colón.

2. Hace muchísimos años Colón inbentó que la tierra era toda redonda.

3. Entonces agarró y empezó a machacar con que la Tierra es redonda y con que la Tierra es redonda, pero nadie le creía.

4. Lo triste es que al final resultó que era redonda no más y el pobre nunca vió un centavo de "ROYALTY".

B.

1. Un hacendado posee una estancia de 5.000 metros de frente por 6.000 de fondo.

2. Para alambrarla en todo su perímetro encargó al corralón los postes que irá colocando, uno cada 20 metros. ¿Cuántos postes compró?

3. Revisa. ¿Te parece que compró tantos?

4. Ah ¿Por qué? ¿Además de oligarca, roñica?

C.

1. ¡Es absurdo! ¿Por qué los chicos no podemos votar? ¡Bien dicho! ¡Ahí está! ¡Eso! ¿Por qué?

2. ¿Acaso nosotros no formamos también parte del país? ¡Sí señor! ¡Muy bien! ¡Bravo!

3. ¿Acaso no somos tan ciudadanos como el que más?

4. ¡Sí que somos! ¡Claro que sí!

5. ¿Y tan del pueblo como cualquiera?

6. ¡Ah, no! ¡A mí, insultos no!

D.

1. ¡Sunescán! ¡¡dalúna búso!!
2. ¿Y eso?
3. "Es un escándalo, un abuso" en dialecto de madre volviendo del mercado.

E.

1. Encontré algo especial para vos, Susanita, escuchá.
2. "Desdichado de aquél a quien sólo le importa el qué dirán."
3. ¡Por supuesto, si en realidad lo que importa es el *qué* dijeron, *quiénes* lo dijeron, *cómo* lo dijeron, *cuándo* lo dijeron, *de quién* lo dijeron, *por qué* lo dijeron.

TEACHING UNIT 10. TEXTUAL INTERACTION

Objectives

1. To show that, as Susanita says in the last *Mafalda* cartoon, "It's not what you say but how you say it" and that all the micro- and macrostructures that make up a text are interdependent.
2. To stress the differences between denotational and connotational meaning and standardized and nonstandardized language.
3. To work on the formal treatment of measures and numbers in Spanish and English.

Tasks

1. As a pre-translation activity to make the students aware of Tamames's pragmatic intentions, they are given a list of emotive vocabulary taken from the text. They are asked to work in groups of three or four and imagine a context for this vocabulary, and then to write a story, newspaper article, or report using this vocabulary in the context they have imagined. They are asked to write directly in English, translating the Spanish vocabulary according to the context they have chosen.
2. The stories are read aloud in class, discussed, and compared from the point of view of the translation of the emotive vocabulary. The students are then told about the original context and given the Spanish text.
3. The students are asked to analyze the text using a discourse-analysis questionnaire.
4. The students are asked to underline the standardized language in the text and to consider the specific problems related to translating measurements, statistics, and numbers from Spanish to English.
5. Translation of the text is given as homework.
6. When the translations have been corrected and discussed in class, the final exercise in this unit is to translate individually, in class, the first three hundred words of Tamames's introduction to the Soviet Union in the same book. The purpose is to ensure that the students have really assimilated the techniques involved in translating statistics related to size of land, population, and income and the common acronyms that are repeated in both texts. Translation in class, within a time limit (two hours) is also good practice for exams and meeting professional deadlines.

Commentary

This exercise is based on the Tamames article analyzed in chapter 7, which is used to show that all the micro- and macrostructures that make up a text are interdependent.

In previous years the students imagined fantastic contexts: "Murder in the Jet Set," "A Coup d'État in a Banana Republic," "Al Capone." In 1992, this kind of story cropped up, but there were many more about current events, particularly related to the breakdown of the Warsaw Pact, the former Soviet Union, and the war in the former Yugoslavia. One group wrote about Kennedy's assassination, probably because the film *JFK* had just been released.

The lexical polysemy of the emotive vocabulary is resolved differently, depending on the context chosen. For example, *asesinato* may be *killed, murdered* or *assassinated; violó* may be *violated* or *raped.*

TASK SHEET 15. EMOTIVE VOCABULARY

Instructions

Read the following group of words and try to imagine a context in which you might find them all together. When you have imagined a context, write a story, article, or report in English, including all the words and translating them according to the context you have chosen.

> tendencias . . . en pugna viva
> los fuertes desequilibrios
> crisis de confianza
> exaltación tradicional
> el pretendido sueño
> dramáticamente sacudida
> violencia
> asesinado (3 veces)
> complot
> asesinato
> circunstancias oscuras
> un temor inconfesable
> un contexto no aclarado
> violó
> escándalo

TASK SHEET 16. *Los EE.UU.*

Instructions

1. Analyze the text by answering the following questions:

   a) **AUTHOR**
      Who is the author?
      Idiolect: marked/unmarked?
      Regional dialect: marked/unmarked?

Class dialect: marked/unmarked?
When did he write? **Time**: distant/recent?
Why did he write? **Motive**: complex/simple?

b) **MODE**
Is the text meant to be (i) spoken, (ii) spoken as if not written, (iii) not necessarily to be spoken, (iv) read in silence ?
Structure: simple/complex?
Style: personal/impersonal:passives/imperatives/interrogative/exclamations/parenthesis?

c) **TENOR**
Is the relationship between author and reader:
symmetrical/asymmetrical,
permanent/temporary?
Style: frozen/formal/consultative/casual/intimate?

d) **FIELD**
What is the field of the text?
What background knowledge is needed to understand the text: knowledge/beliefs /wants/wishes/intentions?

2. Underline all the **standardized** language in the text:
   a) Names of countries, races, cities, regions
   b) Names and titles of people, dates, wars
   c) Economic expressions
   d) Statistics and numbers
   e) Acronyms

Estructura económica internacional

Ramón Tamames, Madrid: Alianza
Primera edición: 1970. Sexta edición: 1980.

Estados Unidos de América

Datos básicos. El *"Melting Pot"* y *"El American Way of Life"*

Con una superficie de 9,4 millones (M en lo sucesivo) de kilómetros cuadrados, EE.UU. tenía a principios de 1980 una población de 222M de habitantes. Al ritmo de crecimiento actual (el 1,7 por 100), se calcula que la población llegará a 300M después del año 2.000. La proporción de raza negra es de un 10,5 por 100, existiendo otras minorías importantes, como los "mejicano-americanos" (unos 7,5 M), los puertorriqueños (unos 3,3M), los indios (0,9M) y otros grupos étnicos y lingüísticos menores todavía en curso de asimilación o que se resisten a ella. El enunciado conjunto de minorías es origen de toda una serie de problemas que afectan—y afectarán—profundamente a la estabilidad de la sociedad norteamericana, todavía muy lejos de la homogeneización que se pretendió con las tesis del *"Melting Pot"* y del *"American Way of Life"*.

Las tendencias segregacionista e integracionista en pugna se mantienen muy vivas. Y lo que es aún más importante, hay nuevos planteamientos por parte de los grupos minoritarios, que de ser espectadores pasivos o candidatos a la integración, han pasado a posturas más radicales y reivindicativas de su propia personalidad frente a lo que "desde siempre" se consideró como el núcleo poblacional del país en términos de la *élite*: los WASP (*"White Anglo-Saxon Protestants"*, o "Blancos Anglosajones Protestantes").

Si a esos problemas raciales se agregan los fuertes desequilibrios personales y regionales de renta, podemos explicarnos por qué en EE.UU. se ha desencadenado en nuestro tiempo una crisis de confianza frente a la exaltación tradicional de la democracia y las libertades personales. El pretendido sueño de un país socialmente homogéneo y estable se ha visto dramáticamente sacudido por la violencia, el manejo de la información masiva y el complejo industrial-militar.

De forma aparentemente anecdótica, pero que da mucho a reflexionar, podría sintetizarse la situación social y psicológica de EE.UU., desde 1963 para acá en personas. J.F. Kennedy, asesinado en 1963 en circunstancias más que oscuras. El ex presidente Johnson, que en 1970, por un temor inconfesable, no se atrevió a hacer las revelaciones que había prometido sobre el complot para aquel asesinato. Un candidato a la Presidencia como Robert Kennedy, asesinado en 1968, seguramente como una consecuencia más de la intervención norteamericana en Oriente Medio en apoyo de Israel. Dos líderes del movimiento negro como eran Malcolm X y Martin Luther King, igualmente asesinados en un contexto no aclarado, pero, sin duda, por su liderazgo de sendos movimientos en pro de los derechos para los negros. Y un presidente como Nixon, que violó fronteras, compromisos internacionales y extendió la guerra en el Sudeste Asiático, y que después—en su fase pacifista—cayó a causa del escándalo "Watergate".

TASK SHEET 17. *LA URSS*

Instructions

You have two hours to translate the text. Dictionaries are not allowed.

Estructura económica internacional

Ramón Tamames, Madrid: Alianza
Primera edición: 1970. Sexta edición: 1980.

La URSS: ¿un socialismo anquilosado?

El nacimiento del primer estado socialista.

La URSS, con 22,4 millones (en lo sucesivo, M) de kilómetros cuadrados, es el país mayor del mundo, más del doble del que le sigue en extensión

(Canadá, 9,9M). Por su población—266M de habitantes en 1980—ocupa el tercer puesto mundial, inmediatamente después de China y de la India.

Desde el punto de vista económico, la URSS es la segunda potencia mundial, detrás de EE.UU., con un PNB difícil de cifrar en los términos de Contabilidad Nacional convencionales en el mundo capitalista, pero que se estima actualmente en unos 1.000.000M de dólares, en torno, pues al 48 por 100 del PNB de los EE.UU. Ello sitúa a la URSS en términos de PNB per capita en 3.760 dólares por año.

A falta de datos macroeconómicos homogéneos, en el cuadro 25 figura una comparación entre producciones de EE.UU. y la URSS al nivel de 1976, para un conjunto de 12 productos seleccionados.

Aunque dotada de un clima mucho menos favorable que el de EE.UU., en cúmulo de riquezas naturales, la URSS es probablemente la primera potencia mundial en orden a reservas. La progresiva explotación de los recursos propios de su inmenso territorio ha forzado un cierto avance de la población hacia el Este, a lo largo de toda Siberia y hacia el Asia Central.

Lo que hoy llamamos URSS, territorialmente casi idéntica al imperio de los Zares, era en 1914 la quinta potencia económica mundial (detrás de EE.UU., Reino Unido, Alemania y Francia). Pero en comparación con esos cuatro paises. la economía rusa era claramente subdesarrollada.

CHAPTER 14

DEVERBALIZATION

TEACHING UNIT 11. INTERSEMIOTIC TRANSLATION

Objective

To give the students practice in deverbalization.

Tasks

The students are given a number of common signs and asked to verbalize them in Spanish and English—that is, to imagine the context and what would be said.

Commentary

Roman Jakobson (1971) defined three types of translation: intersemiotic translation, interlingual translation, and intralingual translation. This exercise is based on the first type. Every day we practise intersemiotic translation by verbalizing signs and notices: speed limits, maps, washing instructions, computer programs, our personal and banking identification numbers, and so on. It is a useful introduction to interlingual translation because there are no words to stand in the way.

   Another, more relaxing variation of this exercise is to divide the class and the blackboard in two. Give one student from each group a word and ask each to make a drawing to represent the word. Half the class guesses in English and the other half in Spanish.

TASK SHEET 18. TRANSLATING SIGNS

	English	Spanish
⧖⃠ △ ⬓ On clothing		
(40) By the road		
ⓅO̷ By a gate		
★★★★★ Outside a hotel		
$\dfrac{100}{18}$ = 5.555		
✝ On a map		
• • • On a map		

TEACHING UNIT 12. ORAL SUMMARY OF ORAL TEXT

Objectives

1. To give the students practice in deverbalization through a simplified form of consecutive interpreting.

2. To develop concentration and memory.

Tasks

1. The teacher divides the class in half, sends one group (Group A) out of the class for five minutes, and reads the rest (Group B) a short informative text or recounts a news item (possibly an item from that morning's news heard on the car radio) in Spanish.

2. The Group A students are invited back and asked to choose a partner from Group B. The Group B students tell their partners what the text was about in English.

3. One Group A student tells the whole class what he or she has understood, with corrections and enlargements from the rest of his or her group if their stories do not coincide.

4. Finally, if the Group B students are not satisfied with the version, they are given the opportunity to intervene.

5. The teacher reads the original text again.

Commentary

Short, pragmatic texts with a simple message should be chosen for this exercise; if possible, however, they should be texts that are difficult to translate literally into English.

TASK SHEET 19. Sample Texts for Oral Summaries

1. UN CANDIDATO PARA SANT CUGAT

En Sant Cugat también tenemos candidato, se trata de Luis Lemkov. Luis se presenta en la sexta posición de la lista de Iniciativa per Catalunya por Barcelona, en calidad de miembro destacado de la lista del movimiento pacifista y ecologista, temas sobre los cuales ha escrito varios libros. Es profesor de la Universidad Autónoma de Barcelona y asesor de la Organización Mundial de la Salud. Ha sabido combinar su trabajo teórico y práctico en el movimiento ecologista con la defensa del medio ambiente de su entorno, como lo demuestra su actividad en la campaña desarrollada hace dos años contra la aprobación del proyecto del túnel y autopista de Vallvidrera, la devastación ecológica del cual estamos viviendo los santcugatenses desde hace unos meses.

¡Vota Luis! ¡Vota Iniciativa!

(Propaganda electoral, octubre 1989)

2. PISANDO LOS TALONES A URRUSOLO

La detención de Fernando Díez desbarata la infraestructura etarra en la franja mediterránea.

El terrorista etarra Fernando Díez estaba contento aquel sábado 21 de marzo cuando regresaba a su casa tras cortarse el pelo en un complejo comercial de Tarragona. Los dos atentados cometidos el jueves día 19, en poco más de ocho horas, en la provincia de Barcelona, habían sido *perfectos* : dos personas asesinadas y se hablaba de que ETA recuperaba su poderío terrorista en Cataluña a cuatro meses de los Juegos Olímpicos.

Poco imaginaba este joven de Barakaldo, cuando estaba en la barbería, que cuatro *geos* le esperaban dentro de su casa y que el edificio estaba atestado de agentes. A las ocho de la tarde era detenido, pero consiguió dar una contraseña telefónica para que sus compañeros lograran huir.

El País, el 29 de marzo de 1992

3. MALLORCA, EL SUEÑO DEL ARCHIDUQUE

Era el año 1876 cuando un joven extranjero de unos veinte años, descrito como "flacucho, rubio y de ojos azules," llegaba a Mallorca amparado por el nombre de Luis Salvador de Hapsburgo. Aquel muchacho de mirada huidiza que acababa de llegar acompañado de su preceptor, el caballero Sforza, huía del primer acontecimiento trágico de su vida. Matilde, hija del Archiduque Alberto y prometida de Luis Salvador, había muerto de forma horrible. En el curso de una fiesta de disfraces, su atuendo de mariposa se prendió fuego, abrasándola viva. Como remedio para escapar a ese recuerdo, Luis Salvador emprendió un viaje. Gracias a él, tomaría contacto con las Baleares, sobre todo con la costa norte de Mallorca, un lugar que cambiaría su vida.

RONDAIBERIA, septiembre de 1991

TEACHING UNIT 13. ORAL TRANSLATION OF ORAL TEXT

Objective

To avoid the written word and, by deverbalizing, to escape the temptations of a literal translation.

Tasks

1. The teacher finds a text that lends itself to discussion and reads the text to the whole class. The text chosen here is an article by Antonio Gala about a skinhead. The teacher starts a discussion about the text by asking questions about the author: Who is he? Where does he live? What do you know about his achievements, life-style, beliefs? Then, questions are asked about the text: Where do the events take place? Is fascism a problem today? Are we all racists?

2. The students are divided into groups of three and the teacher reads the text, stopping after each sentence or unit of meaning and asking different groups to suggest a translation. The other groups are asked to approve of or improve the translation.

3. They are given the written text and asked to write their own translation for homework.

Commentary

Antonio Gala's style is suitable for this exercise because he usually writes short sentences and yet the word order he uses makes it impossible to translate them literally. Very often, his articles include dialogue or monologue. Because of his experience as a playwright, producing written texts to be read out loud, his texts are suitable for oral work in class. Furthermore, he always has something interesting to say. The most difficult texts to translate are those in which the author says nothing.

TASK SHEET 20. *Cabeza rapada*

Instructions

1. Now that you have translated this text in class, reformulate your own written version.

> Vino a ofrecérseme como guardaespaldas. Vestía el uniforme convencional: debajo de la cabeza afeitada, la cazadora, el pantalón estrecho y botas de caña alta. Me sorprendieron sus aceptables modales, salvo algún desgarro verbal y la manía de crujirse los dedos. Tendría veinticinco años. Era alto, fornido, con un rostro redondeado, aún infantil, y nada feo. Charlamos casi dos

horas. Él parecía decidido a quedarse, hasta tal punto se instaló con naturalidad, cerveza en mano, en el estudio.

"Tú y yo nos parecemos. Yo he estudiado con curas; sacaba buenas notas. Los otros, no. Ya sabes, gente fracasada, de familias obreras . . . Yo es que tengo ideales: limpiar la sociedad, y todo eso". Le pregunté si eran violentos sólo porque eran jóvenes. "Hombre, la violencia demuestra que tú eres superior, que eres persona. Cuando te temen, te das cuenta del poder que tienes. Los otros—él pretendía, en todo caso, diferenciarse de los otros—son así por resentimiento o por venganza. Les gusta asustar, salir en los periódicos, que los retraten y eso. Pero cuando están solos, son cobardes. Por eso les gusta que en el grupo seamos iguales, y a la vez diferentes de los de fuera. Una tribu, ¿comprendes?"

Lo que yo comprendía es que se han enterrado las ideas utópicas que podían iluminar a la juventud, sin suministrarle ninguna de respuesta, y que el fascismo, con su deslumbramiento por la acción y su irracional exaltación de la violencia como síntoma vital, conquista a los más indefensos. Tenían que inventarse un enemigo, y lo habían descubierto muy cerquita: los drogadictos, los pequeños narcotraficantes, los gitanos, los homosexuales, los travestidos, los inmigrantes y hasta los mendigos. No razonan; son nihilistas inconscientes; no tienen preparación, ni fundamentos, ni esperanza. Tienen sólo fuerza y juventud, y actúan.

Antonio Gala, *El País*, enero de 1992

TEACHING UNIT 14. SUBTITLING

Objectives

1. To provide practice in changing mode.

2. To provide practice in maintaining the tone of discourse (the level of formality or social relationship between the speakers) when there is a change of mode.

3. To provide experience in coping with the limitations imposed by the physical constraints of the subtitle.

4. To provide experience in a field in which prose translators may find work. Dubbing is beyond the scope of the prose translator but subtitling is a possibility.

Tasks

The following exercise is based on an extract from one of the episodes of Ian Gibson's series on Spain, *Fire in the Blood*, which was shown on BBC 2 in the first part of 1992. The episode is called "Breaking Free" and is about the changing place of women in Spain. Subtitles were used extensively in this program. Gibson introduced the subject and made some comments throughout the program in English, but the rest of the program was made up of interviews and conversations in Spanish, with English subtitles.

1. First, the students are shown the whole program, which, being quite controversial, may give rise to much discussion. The program is based on Andalusia, and Gibson's presentation is dramatic. The video, recorded from the BBC, comes with the original subtitles, but for the first viewing they can be covered with paper and adhesive tape.

2. The students are then given the script of the first part of the program in which a young couple, Pepe La Reina and Inma Sánchez, explain how they met, fell in love, and decided to get married. Pepe is a food inspector and Inma a civil servant. In this first scene the couple are in a rowboat on the river. The second scene is at Inma's "hen party," where she talks about what she expects from married life. The students are asked to work in groups on subtitles for this part of the program. The versions are compared and the class chooses the "best."

3. Finally, the students are shown the original subtitles and these are compared with their version.

Commentary

Film and television subtitling comprise a shortened form of translating in which the shift of mode from speech to writing obliges the translator to deverbalize to compensate for the prosodic elements of speech: intonation, accent, tone of voice, and so on. Colloquial expressions are more difficult to reproduce in writing and there are even some taboo expressions that are more or less accepted in speech but not in writing. As well, physical constraints are imposed by the speed with which the average reader can take in a subtitle, the speed of the speakers in the film or video, and the space on the screen. The subtitles cannot take up half the screen: in England, the limit is two lines, each with a maximum of forty typographical spaces. (In Spain, it is thirty-two.) To avoid confusion, each speech turn is represented (exceptions may be greetings, affirmatives, negatives, exclamations).

1. Spanish film and television viewers are very familiar with subtitles. Many foreign films are shown in the original version with subtitles. In cities, the most successful films may be shown in two or more cinemas at the same time, some in the original with subtitles and the others dubbed. Television also uses subtitling, both for films and for interviews. Many graduates in Catalonia find work in dubbing and subtitling—above all, in dubbing for the Catalan independent television station TV3. Some of the BBC television comedies have been tremendously successful here in their Catalan version. The cultural difficulties of translating programs like "Yes Minister," ("Si, Ministre") and "Black Adder" ("L'Escorçó Negre") are daunting and complex.[25]

2. My students found the original subtitles for *Fire in the Blood* very bald. Their own were rather longer and attempted to preserve a little of the hesitancy and tenderness of the lovers. They managed to preserve the rhythm and rhyme of the skipping song, which they thought was important and was not maintained in the original subtitles:

    Spanish original:

    > *Con ésta, sí, con ésta, no,*
    > *Con esta señorita me caso yo.*

    BBC translation:

    > *This one yes, this one no.*
    > *This is the girl I'll marry.*

    Prose students' translation:

    > *This one no, this one yes,*
    > *This is the girl I like the best.*

---

25. Their success here is due in great part to the skill of translators such as Juan Fontcuberta. See Zabalbeascoa (1993).

TASK SHEET 21. *FIRE IN THE BLOOD*

Instructions

Write subtitles for the following three scenes. Remember you are not allowed to write more than two lines with forty typographical spaces per line.

"Breaking Free" from *Fire in the Blood* by Ian Gibson (BBC, 1992)
(Original script)

Scene One

Pepe La Reina and Inma Sánchez are in a rowing boat on the Guadalquivir River.

Inma. — Pues nos conocimos en el trabajo. El estaba trabajando cuando yo llegué. Entonces todo el mundo me decía, "Ahí está tu hermano, ahí está tu hermano".

Pepe. — Entonces, un compañero me dijo, "He visto a tu hermana por ahí dando un paseo, ha pasado por ahí.". Yo dije, "¡Qué raro! Que yo no tengo hermanas.".

Inma. — Un día, pues, nos vimos en el pasillo, y coincidimos, luego nos miramos.

Pepe. — La vi, al principio me gustó mucho y me dije, "¡Oh, qué chica más guapa!".

Inma. — Entonces, pues, así empezamos a conocernos, empezamos a ir al cine, y ya está.

Pepe. — Entonces, sí, me di cuenta de que yo estaba con muchas ganas de casarme ¿ no? y se lo propuse. Nada romántico, le dije, "¿Qué, nos casamos?".

Inma. — ¡Qué va! Que no eres nada romántico.

Scene Two

A group of girls in a playground are singing a skipping song:

Con ésta, sí, con ésta, no,

Con esta señorita me caso yo.

Scene Three

Inma's "hen party" in a Seville restaurant.

Inma. — Si yo fuera una mujer antigua, como mi madre o su madre, todo el día dentro de casa.

Inma. — Mi madre se casó para estar en casa. Yo me caso para estar en la calle.

Inma. — Pues, pues, yo creo también que estar ahí trabajando en la calle hace mucho, conoces gente.

TASK SHEET 22. Original Subtitles

"Breaking Free" from *Fire in the Blood* by Ian Gibson (BBC, 1992)
(Original subtitles)

Scene One

1. We met at work.
2. He was already there when I joined.
3. Everyone thought he was my brother.
4. A colleague said he'd seen my sister.
5. How strange! I have no sisters.
6. One day our eyes met.
7. I thought, "What a pretty girl!"
8. We started going out.
9. And here we are.
10. I really wanted to get married.
11. I proposed, nothing romantic.
12. Too bad, you're not romantic.

Scene Two

13. This one yes, this one no.
14. This is the girl I'll marry.

Scene Three

15. I'd hate being like my mother.
16. Staying at home is not for me.
17. My mother wanted to be a housewife.
18. I want to be out in the world.
19. Working is very important to me.
20. I want to mix with people.

TEACHING UNIT 15. CONVERSATION INTERPRETING—ROLE PLAY

Objectives

1. To provide practice in deverbalization.

2. To provide experience in adapting register to context.

3. To offer professional training in a field that is open to prose translators.

Tasks

1. The presence of exchange students in the prose-translation class makes it easy to simulate conversations for interpreting. In recent years, exchange students have made up about 30 per cent of the prose-translation class. The class is divided into three groups: exchange students as English speakers, a group of Spanish speakers, and a group of interpreters.

2. Role-play cards are prepared for the Spanish and English speakers and distributed. When they have found their opposite numbers, the pairs choose an interpreter.

3. These groups of three work together, the speakers playing out their roles in Spanish or English and the interpreter interpreting both ways.

Commentary

Conversation interpreting is a useful translation training technique, but it is also an area in which translation graduates and undergraduates can learn to work effectively in both directions: into Spanish and into English.[26] Anthony Pym (1992) suggests that this is one of the areas where students can work into the foreign language. He calls these areas non-100% situations, in which active competence in the B language may be less than complete, and in which a foreign accent and a few grammatical slips are far less disconcerting than would be their correlatives on the written page.

TASK SHEET 23. ROLE PLAY

Mr. Wilson is interested in buying a house in the Pyrenees. He is a writer and is looking for peace and quiet. He doesn't drive and will have to depend on public transport.	**Jordi Arnau** is working for a real-estate agent in Ribes de Fresser. Mr. Wilson is his first client, and he is very anxious to make a sale because he is getting married next month.

---

26. During the 1992 Olympic Games, many did this work either as volunteers or with companies such as Coca-Cola or NBC.

Lady Di is visiting the Prado on a private visit to Madrid.	**La Reina Sofía** is showing her round the gallery.
Sting will be giving a concert in Barcelona and he is being interviewed by a journalist.	**Carles Juvé** is a journalist working for *El Periódico*.
Rosalynd Russell is a buyer for Selfridges. She is 50, sophisticated, and drives a hard bargain.	**Agata Redó** is a talented young clothing designer who has been selling her apparel on a small scale from her boutique in Gerona.
Frank Healey is the general manager of Lucas. He is having lunch with the manager of the factory in San Cugat.	**Fernando Savater** is the manager of Lucas in San Cugat. He wants to make sure Mr. Healey enjoys his stay in Barcelona.
Magic Johnson is being interviewed on TVE after competing in the Barcelona Olympics.	**Jesús Hermida** is interviewing Magic Johnson for TVE.

TEACHING UNIT 16. POLICE AND COURT INTERPRETING

Objectives

1. To provide practice in deverbalization.

2. To make the students aware of the translator's power to influence people and events.

3. To provide professional training in a field that is open to prose translators.

Tasks

1. As in the previous exercise, the students are divided into groups of three. Since in this case we are using scripts from American trials, the students take the roles of the prosecuting attorney, the witness, or the interpreter.

2. The prosecuting attorney (PA) and the witness are given copies of the script (Task Sheet 24), which the PA reads in English and the witness reads in Spanish. After each intervention, the interpreter translates into Spanish or English.

3. The interpreter is instructed to be as polite as possible, first, to make the witness feel comfortable in the alien atmosphere of the courtroom, and, second, to help the witness make a good impression on the jury.

4. After the groups have practised for half an hour on their own, they are asked to stage the trial for the rest of the class.

5. Finally, they are given the script of the original interpreting (Task Sheet 25) and asked to comment on the tenor used by the interpreter. They are also asked to decide whether the interpreter was a native speaker of English or Spanish.

Commentary

The tenor used by the court interpreter can influence the police and the courts. Berk-Seligson's (1988) interesting article "The Impact of Politeness in Witness Testimony: The Influence of the Court Interpreter" shows how the use of the polite form of address affected jury trials in the United States. The texts she worked with provide useful classroom material.

As was pointed out in the introduction, whereas the translation of legal documents, laws, and legal texts from Spanish to English presents considerable difficulties and should not be attempted in the prose-translation class, interpreting for the police and the courts does not present the same difficulties. The language has to be accessible for a woman reporting the theft of her handbag or a witness in the court. Police and court interpreters are expected to be able to work into their A and B languages.

TASK SHEET 24. *MIRTA CHAMORRO*

Instructions

Imagine you are in court. The witness, Mirta Chamorro (MC), is in the stand, under oath, and the prosecuting attorney (PA) is questioning her. The PA and MC should read their parts with feeling, allowing the interpreter time to do his or her work. The interpreter should be as polite as possible so that the witness feels comfortable and makes a good impression on the court.

FIRST WITNESS: Mirta Chamorro

PA: Would you state your name, please?

Interpreting _____

MC: Mirta Chamorro.

Interpreting _____

PA: And, uh, what is your occupation?

Interpreting _____

MC: En Colombia vendía loteria.

Interpreting _____

PA: And, uh, where were you born? In Colombia?

Interpreting _____

MC: En Bogotá.

Interpreting _____

PA: And are you a citizen of Colombia?

Interpreting _____

MC: Sí, señora.

Interpreting _____

PA: Are you a citizen of the United States?

Interpreting _____

MC: No, señor.

Interpreting _____

PA: Uh, did you enter the United States, uh, on May the 15th, 1983?

Interpreting _____

MC: Sí, señora.

Interpreting _____

PA: Uh, when you entered did you have any papers or documents that allowed you to enter or gave you permission to enter?

Interpreting _____

MC: No, señorita.

Interpreting _____

PA: Did you know you were entering the country illegally?

Interpreting _____

MC: Sí, señorita.

Interpreting _____

PA: And did you pay anybody money in Colombia to make arrangements for you?

Interpreting _____

MC: Um, nos cobraron noventa y cinco mil.

Interpreting _____

PA: Uh, that would be Colombian pesos?

Interpreting _____

MC: Colombianos.

Interpreting _____

PA: When you entered the United States, when you actually entered the United States, were you in an aircraft?

Interpreting _____

MC: Sí, una avioneta era.

Interpreting _____

PA: Was the girl that just testified before you also in that aircraft?

Interpreting _____

MC: Sí, señora.

Interpreting _____

TASK SHEET 25. POLITENESS

Instructions

1. Here is the same script with the transcript of the original interpreter. Compare the original version with yours.
2. Is the interpreter polite? Give reasons for your answer.
3. Do you think the interpreter is a native speaker of Spanish or English?

FIRST WITNESS: Mirta Chamorro

PA: Would you state your name, please?

     Int.: *Señora, tenga la bondad de decir su nombre.*

MC: Mirta Chamorro.

     Int.: *Mirta Chamorro.*

PA: And, uh, what is your occupation?

     Int.: *¿Cuál es su oficio? ¿De qué se ocupa usted, señora?*

MC: En Colombia vendía loteria.

     Int.: *In Colombia I sold lottery tickets.*

PA: And, uh, where were you born? In Colombia?

     Int.: *¿Donde nació usted? ¿Nació usted en Colombia, señora?*

MC: En Bogotá.

     Int.: *¿Colombia?*

MC: Colombia.

     Int.: *I, uh, I was born in Bogotá, Colombia.*

PA: And are you a citizen of Colombia?

     Int.: *¿Es usted cidadana de Colombia, señora?*

MC: Sí, señora.

     Int.: *Yes, I am.*

PA: Are you a citizen of the United States?

     Int.: *¿Es usted ciudadana de los Estados Unidos?*

MC: No, señor.

     Int.: *No, sir.*

PA: Uh, did you enter the United States, uh, on May the 15th, 1983?

     Int.: *¿Entró usted a Estados Unidos el día 15 de mayo de 1983?*

MC: Sí, señora.

     Int.: *Yes, I did.*

PA: Uh, when you entered did you have any papers or documents that allowed you to enter or gave you permission to enter?

     Int.: *Cuando usted entró, señora, ¿tenía usted documentos o papeles que la autorizaran a entrar legalmente a este país?*

MC: No, señorita.

     Int.: *No, sir.*

PA: Did you know you were entering the country illegally?

Int.: *¿Sabía usted? puede usted contestarle al licenciado. Excuse me, I'm advising her not to answer "yes, Ma'am" or "no, Ma'am" because I'm just the interpreter. Excuse me. Señora, cuando usted conteste, conteste al licenciado porque yo no más como una mani, ma, maquinita le estoy traduciendo. Cuando usted entró a este país, señora, ¿sabía usted que estaba entrando ilegalmente?*

MC: Sí, señorita.

Int.: *Yes, sir.*

PA: And did you pay anybody money in Colombia to make arrangements for you?

Int.: *¿Y le pagó usted a alguien dinero en Colombia para hacer arreglos para su entrada a Estados Unidos, señora?*

MC: Um, nos cobraron noventa y cinco mil.

Int.: *We were charged ninety-five thousand.*

PA: Uh, that would be Colombian pesos?

Int.: *Noventa y cinco mil pesos colombianos, señora?*

MC: Colombianos.

Int.: *Yes, Colombian pesos.*

PA: When you entered the United States, when you actually entered the United States, were you in an aircraft?

Int.: *Cuando usted entró a los Estados Unidos, cuando de hecho entró usted al territorio norteamericano, ¿estaba usted en un avión?*

MC: Sí, una avioneta era.

Int.: *It was a small airplane—a small aircraft.*

PA: Was the girl that just testified before you also in that aircraft?

Int.: *La, la señora o señorita que acaba de atestiguar aquí antes que usted, ¿también estaba en esa avioneta junto con usted?*

MC: Sí, señora.

Int.: *Yes, sir.*

TASK SHEET 26. *ROBERTO QUESADA*

Instructions

Imagine you are in court. The witness, Roberto Quesada (RQ), is on the stand under oath and the prosecuting attorney (PA) is questioning him. The PA and RQ should read their parts with feeling, allowing the interpreter time to do his or her work. The interpreter should be as polite as possible so that the witness feels comfortable and makes a good impression on the court.

SECOND WITNESS: Roberto Quesada Murillo

PA: Sir, would you state your name, please?
      Interpreting _____

RQ: Roberto Quesada Murillo.
      Interpreting _____

PA: Where were you born?
      Interpreting _____

RQ: En Saltillo.
      Interpreting _____

PA: And of what country are you a citizen?
      Interpreting _____

RQ: De México, señor.
      Interpreting _____

PA: I call your attention to the night of March 23rd and the morning of
      March 24th. Were you in the United States at that time?
      Interpreting _____

RQ: ¿El 24 de marzo?
      Interpreting _____

PA: Yes.
      Interpreting _____

RQ: No, señor.
      Interpreting _____

PA: Do you recall entering the United States during the month of March at all?
      Interpreting _____

RQ: No, señor.
      Interpreting _____

PA: When did you last enter this country?
      Interpreting _____

RQ: Esta es la primera vez.
      Interpreting _____

PA: When was that, sir?
      Interpreting _____

RQ: Hum, no recuerdo, como el 22.
      Interpreting _____

PA: Did you have any documents or papers to authorize your entry?
Interpreting _____

RQ: No, señor.
Interpreting _____

PA: Were you inspected by immigration officials when you entered the United States?
Interpreting _____

RQ: ¿Inspeccionado? No entiendo, señor?
Interpreting _____

PA: Did you enter through a port of entry?
Interpreting _____

RQ: No, señor.
Interpreting _____

PA: Did you enter illegally?
Interpreting _____

RQ: Sí, señor.
Interpreting _____

PA: Would you explain for the court the circumstances surrounding that entry?
Interpreting _____

RQ: Sí, señor, Pues entré . . . (pause) ¿Cómo entré?
Interpreting _____

PA: Yes, sir. Did you cross through a fence or . . .?
Interpreting _____

RQ: Sí, por uno.
Interpreting _____

PA: Had you made any arrangements for a ride before you left Mexico?
Interpreting _____

RQ: Sí, señor.
Interpreting _____

PA: How did that come about?
Interpreting _____

RQ: Bueno, pues, es como no traía dinero, busqué un raite.[27]
Interpreting _____

---

27. *un raite:* Mexican version of *a ride.*

TASK SHEET 27. VARIETIES OF LANGUAGE

Instructions

1. Here is the same script with the transcript of the original interpreter. Compare this version with yours.

2. Translate the original Latin American Spanish into Castillian and the American English into British English.

SECOND WITNESS: Roberto Quesada Murillo

PA: Sir, would you state your name, please?

     Int.: *Señor, dé su nombre por favor.*

RQ: Roberto Quesada Murillo.

     Int.: *Roberto Quesada Murillo.*

PA: Where were you born?

     Int.: *¿En donde nació?*

RQ: En Saltillo.

     Int.: *In Saltillo.*

PA: And of what country are you a citizen?

     Int.: *¿De qué país es usted ciudadano?*

RQ: De México, señor.

     Int.: *Of Mexico, sir.*

PA: I call your attention to the night of March 23rd and the morning of March 24th. Were you in the United States at that time?

     Int.: *Le llamo su atención a la noche del 23 de marzo y la mañana del 24 de marzo. ¿Estuvo usted en los Estados Unidos en ese día?*

RQ: ¿El 24 de marzo?

     Int.: *March 24th?*

PA: Yes.

     Int.: *Sí.*

RQ: No, señor.

     Int.: *No, sir.*

PA: Do you recall entering the United States during the month of March at all?

     Int.: *¿Recuerda haber entrado a los Estados Unidos durante el mes de marzo?*

RQ: No, señor.
      Int.: *No, sir.*

PA: When did you last enter this country?
      Int.: *¿Cuando fue la última vez que entró usted a este país?*

RQ: Esta es la primera vez.
      Int.: *This is the first time.*

PA: When was that, sir?
      Int.: *¿Cuando fue esto, señor?*

RQ: Hum, no recuerdo, como el 22.
      Int.: *I don't remember, around the 22nd.*

PA: Did you have any documents or papers to authorize your entry?
      Int.: *¿Tenía sus documentos, o papeles autorizando su entrada?*

RQ: No, señor.
      Int.: *No, sir.*

PA: Were you inspected by immigration officials when you entered the United States?
      Int.: *¿Fue usted inspeccionado por un oficial de inmigración cuando entró usted a los Estados Unidos?*

RQ: ¿Inspeccionado? No entiendo, señor.
      Int.: *Inspected? I don't understand that word, sir.*

PA: Did you enter through a port of entry?
      Int.: *¿Entró usted por la garita?*

RQ: No, señor.
      Int.: *No, sir.*

PA: Did you enter illegally?
      Int.: *¿Entró usted ilegalmente?*

RQ: Sí, señor.
      Int.: *Yes, sir.*

PA: Would you explain for the court the circumstances surrounding that entry?
      Int.: *¿Puede usted explicarle a la corte las circunstancias de por cómo usted entró usted?*

RQ: Sí, señor, Pues entré . . . (pause) ¿Como entré?
      Int.: *Yes, sir. Well I entered . . . Uh, you mean the way I came in?*

PA: Yes, sir. Did you cross through a fence or . . .?
     Int.: *Sí, señor. ¿Cruzó usted por un cerco?*

RQ: Sí, por uno.
     Int.: *Yes, through a fence.*

PA: Had you made any arrangements for a ride before you left Mexico?
     Int.: *¿Había hecho usted, ah, arreglos para obtener un raite antes de salir de Méjico?*

RQ: Sí, señor.
     Int.: *Yes, sir.*

PA: How did that come about?
     Int.: *¿Como fue que sucedió eso?*

RQ: Bueno, pues, es como no traía dinero, busqué un raite.
     Int.: *Well, since I didn't have any money, I asked for a ride.*

TEACHING UNIT 17. COMPARING HEADLINES AND TITLES

Objectives

1. To reinforce the idea that different languages and cultures organize meaning and lexis in different ways.

2. To illustrate how translators transfer meanings, not words. If different cultures and languages organize meaning and lexis in different ways, the translator has to deverbalize the SLT so as to transmit the meaning adequately in the TLT.

3. To reinforce awareness of linguistic contrasts between the two languages when writing headlines: use of capital letters, alliteration, articles, gerunds, word play, and so on.

Tasks

1. Cards are made with a headline in one language on each. The cards are distributed and the students are asked to find their partners—for example, the student who has been given "Una época crucial para el viejo continente. Europa acelera su historia." has to find the student who has "Europe at the Crossroads of History. Seizing the Moment."

2. When they have found their partners, they are asked to compare the titles. They are given photocopies of their article and are asked to analyze the differences in the headlines and draw conclusions.

3. Each pair is then asked to present their headlines and conclusions to the rest of the class. When all the headlines have been looked at, the class will decide if there are any characteristics that can be said to be shared by several examples and if they show anything about Spanish or English language and culture.

Commentary

The material for this exercise is taken from *Leonardo*, the special edition published in 1992 by *The Independent, El País, La Repubblica*, and *Le Monde* to mark Expo '92 and "The Age of Discoveries." The work is based on a comparison of the headlines in the Spanish and English editions.

A detailed analysis of the English and Spanish editions of *Leonardo* would be very interesting. The translation is excellent, on the whole, and yet there are no credits for the translators. Here are some conclusions drawn from looking at the headlines chosen for this exercise.

1. At a formal level the English use of *capital letters* in titles and headlines should be noted.

2. *Alliteration* is a common device used to draw attention in English headlines: 6 "Seeking Secrets of the Stars," 12 "Policing Peace," 14 "Catching the Capitalist Bus," 17 "The Economics of Ecology."

3. *Articles* are more commonly omitted in English headlines than in Spanish. The Leonardo headlines also give examples of words that do not take an article in English but do in Spanish: 1 (tolerance), 2 (history), 3 (peace), 17 (ecology, but the environment), 19 (health), 20 (knowledge and education), 22 (leisure), 23 (play).

4. *Gerunds* are often used in English headlines but very rarely in Spanish. There are no examples of gerunds in the Spanish titles but in the English there are several: 2 "Rejecting History," 6 "Seeking Secrets of the Stars," 9 "Facing the New Facts of Life," 11 "Seizing the Moment," 12 "Policing Peace," 14 "Catching the Capitalist Bus," 18 "Fighting for the Old Values," 21 "Seeking a Religious Dialogue," and 23 "Writing is an Instrument of Memory."

5. English headlines tend to be more eye-catching and frequently resort to *word play, metaphors,* and *cultural references.* In the English version of *Leonardo* there are many: 3 "The Planetary Melting Pot," 4 "The 20th Century Will Be a Clean Finish?," 7 "The Scarred Environment," 9 "Facing the New Facts of Life," 10 "Scientists Seek the Quantum Leap," 11 "Europe at the Crossroads of History," 14 "Catching the Capitalist Bus," 15 "Demographic Pressures when Worlds Collide," 16 "Seville's Brave New World," 19 "A Prescription for Health," 20 "The Chain of Knowledge: A Breakdown in Education." In the Spanish version there are not so many: 7 "Arañazos del hombre," 18 "Nudos en los lazos de familia," 20 "La educación aún en suspenso," 22 "La humanidad se pone en juego."

6. Many comments could be made about specific lexical changes. Here are just a couple. "La noche más hermosa" is the title of an article by Joaquín Estefanía, the editor of *El País.* I believe the title refers to his hopes for a more tolerant future, perhaps a dream. In Spanish *la noche es hermosa* (connotational meaning: *cálida, suave romántica*). In England, the night is usually not beautiful but wet and cold. Hopes and aspirations are associated with the dawn, and the English translator has chosen "The Dawn of Tolerance."

"Un espíritu andaluz" is the title of an article by Rafael Alberti in which he praises the spirit of Andalusia and reaffirms his roots there. The English translation is "An Andaluz Heart." Throughout the text, the expression *the spirit of Andalusia* appears several times. Probably *spirit* has been avoided in the title because the polysemy of spirit might cause misunderstandings out of context. Is the article about an Andaluz *brandy* or an Andaluz *ghost*?

TASK SHEET 28. *LEONARDO*

LEONARDO: LA ERA DE LOS DESCUBRIMIENTOS
LEONARDO: THE AGE OF DISCOVERIES

1. *La noche más hermosa*
    The Dawn of Tolerance

2. *El repudio de la historia*
    Rejecting History

3. *La geopolítica de la amnesia*
    The Planetary Melting Pot

4. *El siglo acaba limpiamente*
    The Twentieth Century Will Be a Clean Finish?

5. *El día 31 de diciembre de 1999*
    The Last Day of 1999

6. El próximo siglo será el de la exploración espacial: *Un viaje pendiente*
    Space Holds the Final Mystery: *Seeking Secrets of the Stars*

7. El desequilibrio ecológico en todo el mundo: *Arañazos del hombre*
    Ecological Imbalance is Growing Worse: *The Scarred Environment*

8. *Un espíritu andaluz*
    An Andaluz Heart

9. La biotecnología modifica la práctica médica: *Indicios para la selva de lo vivo*
    Biotechnology Challenges Medical Ethics: *Facing the New Facts of Life*

10. *Caminos predecibles de la ciencia*
    Scientists Seek the Quantum Leap

11. Una época crucial para el viejo continente: *Europa acelera su historia*
    Europe at the Crossroads: *Seizing the Moment*

12. La estabilidad internacional sigue amenazada: *Cruenta posguerra fría*
    International Stability Could Be Threatened: *Policing Peace*

13. *La Europa del derecho ya existe*
    A Peaceful Revolution in the Law

14. Los economistas reinterpretan el mundo: *Economía de gestos*
    Economists Take on a New Role: *Catching the Capitalist Bus*

15. En el 2.000 habrá 6.200 m de habitantes: *5.000 m de parias*
    Demographic Pressures when Worlds Collide

16. *Calles en una tierra olvidada*
    Seville's Brave New World

17. Medio Ambiente y economía van juntos: *Agujeros en el cielo*
    Global Pollution: *The Economics of Ecology*

18. La familia tradicional resiste los embates: *Nudos en los lazos de familia*
    The Traditional Family Is under Attack: *Fighting for the Old Values*

19. Incógnitas de la medicina de mañana: *Nuevo paradigma de la salud*
    Reshaping of Society's Services: *A Prescription for Health*

20. Sociedades enfermas del mal escolar: *La educación aún en suspenso*
    The Chain of Knowledge: *A Breakdown in Education*

21. *El hombre del futuro busca otras formas de religiosidad*
    Seeking a Religious Dialogue in a World that Lacks Values

22. La sociedad del ocio trata de huir del vacío: *La humanidad se pone en juego*
    Leisure in the Future: *The Human Race Discovers Play*

23. *La palabra futuro está en decadencia y no hay que fiarse de la felicidad*
    Writing Is an Instrument of Memory and without It There Can Be No Thought

24. Encuesta: pesimismo juvenil ante el próximo milenio: *Lo tenemos bastante difícil*
    A Straw Poll of the World's Young: *Few Hopes and Many Fears*

CHAPTER 15

RESTRICTED CODES AND TRANSCODING

TEACHING UNIT 18. STANDARDIZED LANGUAGE

Objective

This is a simple introductory exercise to help the students think about which fields of discourse use standardized language—that is, words and expressions that have become institutionalized and have only one possible translation in the TL.

Tasks

1. The students are given a list of expressions that have a standardized equivalent and asked to decide which field of discourse they belong to.

2. They are asked to find the standardized equivalent in English and look for other standardized expressions from the same fields. They are then asked to consider which other fields of discourse have standardized expressions.

TASK SHEET 29. STANDARDIZED LANGUAGE

1. Look at the following list of expressions and decide which field they belong to. Find the equivalent expression for each one in English.

2. Try to think of other expressions in these fields that only have one possible equivalent in English. Which other discourse fields are likely to use standardized language?

> Recién pintado. Perro peligroso. Prohibido fumar. Dirección única.
>
> Se vende piso. Se alquila torre.
>
> Ambulancia. Bomberos. Policía.
>
> Aduanas. Parlamento. Juzgado.
>
> Alcohólicos Anónimos. Planificación Familiar. Pompas Fúnebres.
>
> Aguafiestas. Estar en números rojos.

Don Quijote. El sueño de una noche de verano. La Guerra de las Galaxias. La lluvia ácida. El efecto invernadero. La úlcera de duodeno. SIDA. La carrera armamentista.

H20. Mecánica cuántica. La segunda ley de termodinámica. Energía transmitida por la onda electromagnética.

EE.UU.	OTAN	ONU	OMS.	
PNB	IVA	FMI	Nivel de vida	Balanza de pagos

TEACHING UNIT 19. RECIPES AND INSTRUCTIONS

Objectives

1. To introduce the students to the use of parallel texts as a source of documentation for translation.
2. To make students aware of conventions in recipes.

Tasks

Recipes cannot be said to be wholly standardized in either language but there are certain conventions that are observed in cookbooks. The students are asked to compare the formal, lexical, and syntactic features of English and Spanish recipes for cooking a Spanish omelette, before translating the Spanish text into English.

TASK SHEET 30. *Tortilla de patatas*

Instructions

1. Compare the English and Spanish recipes. Notice the way they are set out in English and Spanish. What differences do you notice in verb forms, sentence structures, and vocabulary?
2. Translate the Spanish text into English.

   SPANISH OMELETTE

   4 eggs

   2 medium onions

   4 medium potatoes

   salt, pepper, olive oil

   Put plenty of olive oil into a medium-sized frying pan with sloping sides and when very hot add the thinly sliced raw potatoes. Cook 5 to 10 minutes until they are tender but not brown or crisp. Add the sliced onion and continue cooking. When this is tender drain off excess fat and pour the eggs, lightly beaten with a fork, over the potatoes and onions in the pan. Add salt and pepper to taste. Lower heat and continue to cook until nearly set. Then place a lid or large plate over the top of the pan and quickly turn the pan over so the omelette is in the lid. Slide it back into the pan, cooked side uppermost, and leave to cook gently until the other side is cooked. Slide onto a serving plate.

   This is the Spanish tortilla as commonly made in Barcelona. It bears no relationship to the Mexican tortilla and is also distinct from the French omelette. It is often eaten as the main course of the lighter evening meal in Barcelona (where the large meal comes at midday) and it is frequently taken cold on picnics and eaten as an appetizer.

Variations: Add sliced courgettes (zucchini), artichokes, or fresh chopped spinach to the pan when you put in the onions.

TRUITA DE PATATAS (TORTILLA DE PATATAS)

Es la llamada en castellano tortilla española, desde luego ubicua en España, caliente o fría, cortada en cuñas sobre un plato o puesta entre dos rebanadas de pan como bocadillo (!), o hecha cubitos pinchados con un palillo como aperitivo o tapa. No cabe afirmar, pues, que sea un plato exclusivamente catalán, pero típico sí lo es, tanto en Cataluña como en cualquier región del país.

PARA 4 A 6 PERSONAS
(COMO ENTRANTE, ACOMPAÑAMIENTO O PLATO PRINCIPAL)

1/2 kilo de patatas peladas y cortadas en rodajas finas

1/4 a 1/2 litro de aceite de oliva

6 huevos ligeramente batidos

Sal y pimienta

Saltear las patatas a fuego medio en una sartén de 25 a 30 centímetros de diámetro, dosificando el aceite, del cual reservaremos como 1/8 de litro, para que las cubra apenas. Es preciso evitar que las rodajas se peguen entre si: tampoco deben tomar color pardo. Escurrir las patatas, desechar el aceite y echar las patatas en el huevo batido, sazonando con sal y pimienta.

En la misma sartén calentaremos fuertemente el 1/8 de litro de aceite y luego echaremos la mezcla de patatas con huevo, procurando distribuir de manera uniforme las rodajas de patata. Reducir la llama y continuar hasta que el huevo empiece a tomar color, removiendo de vez en cuando la sartén para evitar que se pegue la tortilla.

Cubrir la sartén con una bandeja o tapadera de olla de tamaño apropiado, darle la vuelta con las precauciones que son del caso, y continuar hasta dorar uniformemente la tortilla (Puede voltearse varias veces, y algunos especialistas incluso lo recomiendan a fin de obtener un resultado más homogéneo)

Nota: Muchas tortillas incluyen algo de cebolla picada, que se habrá salteado junto con las patatas.

TEACHING UNIT 20. INSTITUTIONAL REPORTS—THE UNITED NATIONS

Objectives

1. To help the students to distinguish between standardized and nonstandardized language.

2. To see how context influences register: field, mode, and tenor.

Tasks

1. The parallel texts used here are the introductions to two speeches taken from the *Acts of the 39th Session of the General Assembly of the United Nations*: the first is by Raúl Alfonsín and the second is by Ronald Reagan. The first text (Task Sheet 31) is handed out with a questionnaire to establish the context, the author, the field, the mode, and the tenor.

2. When the questions have been answered in groups and discussed in the class as a whole, the students are asked to underline any language that they think is standardized and must have an established equivalent.

3. The students are given Ronald Reagan's speech (Task Sheet 32) and asked to analyze it in the same way. They are then asked to compare the two texts.

4. The Alfonsín speech is translated individually for homework.

Commentary

Much of the business of international organizations and institutions is carried out in formalized, standardized language. When the language is standardized, the students cannot be expected to transcode without a language model in the TL. Parallel texts in the SL and the TL have to be provided at a first level. Later on students should learn to do their own documentation and find models of the field of discourse they are translating.

TASK SHEET 31. Raúl Alfonsín

Instructions

1. Read Alfonsín's speech, transcribed from the *Acts of the 39th Session of the General Assembly of the United Nations* (1985).

2. Analyze the text using the questionnaire on the next page.

3. Underline any language in the text that you consider to be standardized—that is, for which there is a fixed formal equivalent in English.

Se abre la sesión a las 15.55 horas.

Discurso de Su Excelencia el Dr. Raúl Alfonsín, Presidente de la República Argentina.

El Presidente (interpretación del inglés): Esta tarde la Asamblea escuchará un discurso del Presidente de la República Argentina.

El Dr. Raúl Alfonsín, Presidente de la República Argentina, es acompañado al Salón de la Asamblea General.

El Presidente (interpretación del inglés): En nombre de la Asamblea General, tengo el honor de dar la bienvenida a las Naciones Unidas a Su Excelencia el Dr. Raúl Alfonsín, Presidente de la República Argentina, y lo invito a hacer uso de la palabra.

El Presidente Alfonsín: Sr. Presidente: Deseo en primer lugar hacerle llegar mis felicitaciones personales por su elección unánime al alto cargo que ocupa. Nuestra satisfacción es doble: porque sus reconocidas calidades humanas y profesionales representan una contribución invalorable al éxito de los trabajos de la Asamblea General y porque además representa a Zambia, a Africa, continente hermano de la América Latina cuyas esperanzas y reclamos compartimos.

Deseo además testimoniar nuestro agradecimiento al Dr. Jorge Illueca, Jefe de Estado de Panamá y eminente diplomático latinoamericano, quien con tanto acierto presidiera el trigésimo octavo período de sesiones de la Asamblea General y hacia quien los argentinos tenemos motivos muy especiales de agradecimiento.

Asimismo damos la bienvenida a esta Organización a Brunei Darussalam, cuya incorporación pone nuevamente de relieve la universalidad de este foro.

Hace diez meses, cuando Argentina recuperaba su vida democrática, dije ante el Congreso de mi país que la política exterior que desarrollaríamos iba a ser la natural extensión de la política interior. Ambas debían basarse en las mismas aspiraciones y sobre todo en un idéntico sistema de valores. Y puesto que no practicamos dos morales, no tenemos dos políticas.

Questionnaire

1. Dimensions of language user:
   a) Who is the author? *Idiolect*: marked /unmarked?
   b) Where does he come from? *Regional dialect*: marked/unmarked ?
   c) Which social class does he come from? *Class dialect*: marked/unmarked?
   d) When did he write? *Time*: distant/recent?
   e) Why did he write? *Motive*: simple/complex?

2. Dimensions of lanaguage use:
   a) *Mode*: Is the text meant to be spoken/spoken as if not written/not neccessarily to be spoken/read in silence?
   b) Is the *presence of the author* intrusive/unobtrusive?
   c) Is *reader participation* implicit/explicit?
   d) *Tenor*: Is the relationship between writer and reader symmetrical or asymmetrical? Is the style frozen/formal/consultative/ casual/intimate?
   e) What is the *field* of the text?
   f) What is the *topic* of the text?

TASK SHEET 32. RONALD REAGAN

Instructions

1. Read Reagan's speech, transcribed from the *Acts of the 39th Session of the General Assembly of the United Nations* (1985).

2. Analyze the text using the questionnaire in Task Sheet 31.

3. Underline any language in the text that you consider to be standardized—that is, for which there is a fixed formal equivalent in English.

4. Translate Alfonsin's speech (Task Sheet 31) making use of the equivalent standardized expressions you have found in Reagan's speech.

   The meeting was called to order at 10:30 a.m.

   ### Address by Mr. Ronald Reagan, President of the United States of America

   The President: This morning the Assembly will hear an address by the President of the United States of America.

   Mr. Ronald Reagan, President of the United States of America, was escorted into the General Assembly Hall.

   The President: On behalf of the General Assembly, I have the honour to welcome to the United Nations His Excellency Mr. Ronald Reagan, the President of the United States of America, and to invite him to address the Assembly.

   President Reagan: First of all I wish to congratulate you, Mr. Lusaka, on your election as President of the General Assembly. I wish you every success in carrying out the responsibilities of that high international office.

   It is an honour to be here and I thank you all for your gracious invitation. I would speak in support of the two great goals that led to the formation of this Organization—the cause of peace and the cause of human dignity.

   The responsibility of this Assembly—the peaceful resolution of disputes between peoples and nations—can be discharged successfully only if we recognize the great common ground upon which we all stand: our fellowship as members of the human race, our oneness as inhabitants of this planet, our place as representatives of billions of our countrymen whose fondest hope remains the end to war and to the repression of the human spirit. These are the important, central realities that blind us; that permit us to dream of a future without the antagonisms of the past. And, just as shadows can be seen only where there is light, so, too, can we overcome what is wrong only if we remember how much is right; and we will resolve what divides us only if we remember how much more unites us. This chamber has heard enough about the problems and dangers ahead; today let us dare to speak of a future that is bright and hopeful, and can be ours only if we seek it. I believe that future is far nearer than most of us would dare to hope.

TEACHING UNIT 21. WEATHER REPORTS

Objectives

1. To distinguish between standardized and nonstandardized language. Weather reporting has been chosen as a good example of *transcoding* within a restricted code.

2. To make the students aware of the problem of reformulation and collocation (lexical patterning and the likelihood of certain words occurring with other words and the naturalness of the resulting combinations).

3. To extend the students' encyclopedic knowledge of the geography of the United Kingdom.

Tasks

1. The students are asked to find on a map the places named in the weather report (Task Sheet 33).

2. They are asked to use the *BBI Combinatory Dictionary of English* to make collocation lists for meteorological vocabulary.

3. They are asked to analyze the verb forms used in the English text.

4. They are asked to translate the Spanish text (Task Sheet 34).

Commentary

Collocation is not rule based and is not even always meaning based. For example, *carry out, undertake* and *perform* have similar meanings and might be expected to collocate with *visit*. However, English speakers typically *pay a visit* or less typically *make a visit*, but they are unlikely to *perform a visit* (Baker, 1992: 47).

The standardized nature of meteorological language can be seen in successful attempts to produce automatic translation programs for weather reports. The program developed by the Canadian Environment Department to translate weather reports from English to French is the most famous. It took two years to develop with four full-time research workers. TAUM-METEO is "the closest approximation to fully automated high quality translation among currently operational systems" (Tucker, 1987: 30).

The TAUM-METEO methodology is based on a transfer system with two subcomponents: lexical and structural. The system is overtly semantic, with domain-specific markers, such as "atmospheric conditions which consist of a weather condition optionally modified by a locative or temporal specification: but the condition itself cuts across syntactic categories: (1) mainly sunny today (2) a few showers this evening." The transfer is effectively incorporated into the analysis, which covers most operations. Those it does not cover, such as correct placement of French adverbs, are dealt with in the synthesis stage. The equivalents for *analysis* and *synthesis* in the terminology we have been using for the translation process are *comprehension* and *reformulation*.

From the outset, TAUM-METEO was designed to operate in an extremely narrow sublanguage (restricted code). It works with only 1,500 dictionary entries, including several hundred place names, and input texts (SLT) containing no tensed verbs. It has been operating since 1977 and translates about 5 million words a year with a success rate of 80% without post-editing. This success is unique among automatic-translation programs now functioning. Given similar conditions, a rigidly controlled sublanguage, our prose-translation students could do even better. Even with a less rigid control of the sublanguage (parallel texts of weather reports from newspapers in Spanish and English) they can learn to do better than the most efficient machine-translation program in the world.

Traditional dictionaries do not help much with collocation although the *Collins Cobuild Dictionary* does give some information. *The BBI Combinatory Dictionary of English: A Guide to Word Combinations* (Benson, Benson, and Ilson, 1986) is very useful so far as it goes: 70,000 collocations under 14,000 main entries. A full dictionary of collocation in English would be immense.

The same authors recently published a workbook with exercises, *Using the BBI Combinatory Dictionary of English* (1992). The exercises are designed to help students distinguish between collocation and free combination, such as:

Can you give a *concrete* EXAMPLE? _____ (Collocation)

That's a *good* EXAMPLE. _____ (Free combination)

The *BBI* contains the following entry for *example*:

example *n* . (1) to cite, give, provide an—, (2) to set an—for, (3) to make an—of, (4) to follow smb's—, (5) a classic, concrete, extreme, glaring, striking, illustrative, impressive, prime, shining, typical—, (6) (misc) to lead by personal—.

Note: the *BBI* entry contains *concrete example* but not *good example*. So *concrete example* is the collocation, while *good example* is a free combination.

TASK SHEET 33. THE WEATHER

Instructions

1. Identify the different places mentioned in the text below on a map of the United Kingdom.
2. Using the *BBI* and the text, make collocation lists for the following nouns: weather, temperature, wind, rain, sun, sea.
3. Which verb forms are used most frequently in this text?

THE WEATHER: Mainly dry, some sun

A ridge of high pressure will cross the UK from the W, followed by troughs of low pressure moving into NW districts later.

London, E Anglia, SE and E England: Rain in places at first, becoming mainly dry, bright or sunny intervals developing. Wind W, light or moderate. Max temp 19 to 21C (66 to 70F).

Central S, NW, Central N and NE England, Midlands, Channel Islands: Mainly dry, bright or sunny intervals developing. Wind W, light or moderate. Max temp 18 to 20C (64 to 68F).

SW England, S and N Wales: Bright or sunny intervals developing, a little drizzle on coasts. Wind W, light or moderate. Max temp 17 to 19C (63 to 65F).

Lake District, Isle of Man, Borders, Edinburgh and Dundee, Aberdeen, SW and NE Scotland, Glasgow, Central Highlands, Moray Firth: Bright intervals, becoming cloudy, occasional rain later. Wind W, moderate, becoming SW, fresh. Max temp 16 to 18C (61 to 64F).

Argyll, NW Scotland, N Ireland: Cloudy outbreaks of rain by afternoon. Wind W, moderate, becoming SW, fresh. Rather cool. Max 14 to 16C (57 to 61F).

Orkney, Shetland: Cloudy, occasional rain or drizzle. Wind variable, light or moderate. Max temp 13 to 15C (53 to 59F).

Outlook: Rain in N spreading S, followed by brighter showery weather.

SEA PASSAGES

Southern North Sea, Straits of Dover: slight becoming moderate or rough.

English Channel (E): slight becoming rough.

St George's Channel, Irish Sea: moderate, becoming rough or very rough.

TASK SHEET 34. *El tiempo*

Instructions

1. Read the text and use an English-language atlas to find the places mentioned.

2. Translate the text using the knowledge you have gained from Task Sheet 33 about this text type in English.

EL TIEMPO: Predominantemente estable y seco

La práctica totalidad del país seguirá también hoy inmersa en un régimen de altas presiones, situación que nuevamente se va a traducir en el predominio de los cielos poco nubosos o despejados. La mayor inestabilidad se centrará nuevamente en la zona pirenaica y en Baleares, donde se esperan algunos chubascos tormentosos. Los vientos soplarán flojos de dirección variable, excepto en el Estrecho, donde habrá moderado de Levante, y las temperaturas no experimentarán grandes cambios.

CATALUÑA. Nubosidad variable, con riesgo de algún chubasco tormentoso, más probable en la zona pirenaica y proximidades. Vientos moderadamente fuertes del Norte. Máximas de 26º y mínimas de 13º.

ANDALUCIA. Cielos poco nubosos o despejados. Vientos fuertes de Levante en el Estrecho. Temperaturas estacionarias. Máximas de 31º y mínimas de 16º.

BALEARES. Nubosidad abundante en el extremo norte del archipiélago, con algunos chubascos tormentosos. Nubosidad variable en el Sur. Vientos fuertes del Norte. Temperaturas agradables. Máximas de 25º y mínimas de 16º.

CANARIAS. Cielos poco nubosos o despejados. Vientos moderados del Noreste. Temperaturas moderadamente altas. Máximas de 27º y mínimas de 16º.

CANTABRICO. Cielos poco nubosos o despejados, con algunas nieblas matinales en Cantabria y País Vasco. Vientos flojos del Sureste. Temperaturas suaves. Máximas de 18º y mínimas de 11º.

El País

TEACHING UNIT 22. METEOROLOGICAL EXPRESSIONS USED METAPHORICALLY

Objectives

1. To establish the principle that the same expressions may be standardized in one field of discourse but not in another. In the previous exercise, translating weather reports, the meterological expressions were standardized. In this exercise, meteorological expressions are used metaphorically in an economics text.

2. To illustrate the difference between denotative and connotative meaning. In the previous exercise, the vocabulary was concrete and denotative and had to be translated accordingly. We used Delisle's notion of transcoding rather than translating and pointed out that weather forecasts are a text type that can be successfully translated by computers. In this text, the weather expressions are used metaphorically, for their connotative meaning, and they cannot be transcoded.

3. To consider text types and stress the multifunctionality of most texts. Economics texts are not uniformly informative, concrete, objective.

Tasks

1. All language is abstract in that words are signs in a semiotic system, an abstract system of symbolization, but some words are more abstract than others. However, even the most abstract language has its origins in words that were first used to denote some concrete object or action. The students are asked to analyze the text (Task Sheet 35) using the concrete and abstract language model used by Mary Mason (1990: 16) to illustrate the difficulty of reading economics texts. The first part of the exercise is done in pairs and followed by a class discussion based on the results of their analysis.

2. The students are then asked to isolate the topic, main events, and subsidiary details of the text. They are given the *skopos* of the translation: a translation for *The Independent*. As homework they are asked to find an article translated from *The Independent* for *El País* and vice versa.

3. The third step is for the students to isolate words and phrases that are culturally bound to Spain. Examples and metaphors are often used by authors to clarify a difficult text, but what is included and excluded depends on the author's cultural background. In an economics text written by a Western, middle-class academic, these examples and metaphors may be just what makes the text opaque for a student from a developing country. Spain and Britain share European cultural values, and readers of *El País* and *The Independent* have much in common. However, there are some metaphors in the Spanish text that would hinder rather than help the British reader. The first part of the discussion, about culturally

bound expressions, should take place in groups of four; make sure there is one exchange student in each group.

4. Finally, the students are asked to translate the text. This may be a group translation.

Commentary

Modern economics is based on modelling systems made possible by the capacity of language to express abstract ideas (Papps and Henderson, 1977). The fact that there is very little concrete language for the ordinary person to grasp and that there are references to other semiotic systems makes reading economics texts very difficult. Mary Mason compares the experience to dancing on air.

Analysis of Concrete and Abstract Language in *Llueve sobre mojado*.

1. Morphology

The primary parts of speech used in concrete language are words used according to the traditional grammatical description—that is, nouns are naming words, verbs are doing words, and adjectives are describing words. Concrete nouns are "first order nominals referring to entities with spatio-temporal extension: people, places, things" (Lyons, 1977: 446).

In this text, it is doubtful whether any of the nouns fall into this category. *El dólar norteamericano* and *el marco alemán* do not refer to *one greenback* or *ein Mark*, but to another semiotic system, the money system. Other nouns that belong to this system are: *los cambios, el resto de las monedas, mercados financieros* and *el SME*. *El Tratado de Maastricht* does not just refer to the published treaty (a copy of which, at the time of writing, is hard to find), but really to the whole questionable future of the further unification of Europe.

Only the time phrases seem to be clearly denotative, but they can hardly be said to have a spatial entity: *los últimos días, de momento, las próximas semanas, el día 21, unas horas después de que.*

2. Semantics

The most salient feature of this text is that nearly all the nouns are used metaphorically, and the verbs and adjectives that accompany them collocate with the primary use of the noun. Furthermore, there are many examples of personification.

The meteorological language is extensive, starting with the headline, *Llueve sobre mojado*, which is a common metaphor to express superfluity, having more than you need of something (*taking coals to Newcastle*). The other examples of meteorological language are: *La tormenta monetaria ha descargado* (metaphor and personification). The verb has a transitive form, but here it is used intransitively;

economías muy castigadas (metaphor, personification); *muchas nubes y muy pocos claros en el horizonte* (metaphor); *terremoto*: (metaphor); *un pedrisco con daños limitados* (metaphor); *devastadora gota fría* (metaphor).

El desplome del dólar norteamericano y la apreciación del marco alemán shows nominalization of verbs and personification of currencies. This is typical of economic language and refers to another semiotic system, the law of supply and demand. No agent is responsible for bringing down the dollar or raising the mark.

These activities of the dollar and the mark *han puesto en danza los cambios del resto de las monedas financieras y han provocado un importante alarma y revuelo en los mercados financieros* and *las economías que andan maltrechas.* These are further examples of nominalization, metaphor, and personification.

3. Syntax

Nominalization of verbs is a significant feature of this text. When it occurs, the agent is not realized. The majority of the verbs used in the text do have agents, but the agents are, on the whole, metaphors for signs belonging to another semiotic system: the money system or the economics system. We might well agree with Mary Mason that reading this kind of text is like dancing on air.

Most weather metaphors are not culturally bound, and many other metaphors refer to semiotic systems (the money system or the economics system) that are shared by both cultures. However, some of the weather metaphors present problems of cultural transfer. *Llueve sobre mojado* is a fairly common expression in Spanish, and students should know that it cannot be translated literally. They may have difficulty finding a similar saying in English, so they should be directed to the library to look up *rain* and other related words in the *Oxford Dictionary of Proverbs*. A possible translation could be, "It never rains but it pours."

The last two weather expressions are culturally bound: *pedrisco con daños limitados* and *devastadora gota fría*. Nearly every spring in Catalonia there is an item on the news about an unexpected hailstorm in Lerida that has destroyed a part of the soft-fruit crop. Fruit farming in Lerida is a fairly recent venture and, as in orchards in the rest of Spain, the fruit harvest is often quite early. A hailstorm in England is not regarded as a natural catastrophe. *La gota fría* has become quite a bugaboo in Spain. It produces torrential rain when the lower atmosphere is hot and cold air enters the upper atmosphere. It can cause severe flooding, deaths, and destruction. There is no direct equivalent in English. In the translation, it would be better to look for other metaphors of destruction that are more meaningful to the English reader, such as *gale-force winds* or *hurricane*.

TASK SHEET 35. DANCING ON AIR

Instructions

1. Analyze the text following this model:

	CONCRETE LANGUAGE	ABSTRACT LANGUAGE
a) MORPHOLOGY	Primary parts of speech	Changes of word class
b) SEMANTICS	No metaphor, personification, etc.	Metaphor, personification, etc.
	Verbs exhaustively analyzable in terms of the transitivity system	Metaphor needed to categorize verbs
c) SYNTAX	Agents realized	Agents not realized

2. Isolate the topic, main events, and subsidiary details of the text. You are asked to translate this article from *El País* for *The Independent*. Look for articles in either of these two newspapers that have been translated from the other one.

3. Isolate any expressions that may be culturally bound and look for translation solutions.

El País, el 30 de agosto de 1992

Llueve sobre mojado

La crisis monetaria pone en evidencia las enormes dificultades de las economías nacionales para superar la recesión

La tormenta monetaria ha descargado sobre unas economías muy castigadas por la crisis y ha dejado muchas nubes y pocos claros en el horizonte. El desplome del dólar norteamericano y la apreciación del marco alemán en los últimos días han puesto en danza los cambios del resto de las monedas y han provocado un importante revuelo en los mercados financieros. Los bancos centrales y los Gobiernos de numerosos paises, entre ellos el español, han tenido que reconocer lo maltrechas que andan sus economías domésticas y asegurar, individual y colectivamente, que de momento no va a haber un terremoto en el Sistema Monetario Europeo (SME).

La tormenta puede quedarse en eso, en un pedrisco con daños limitados, o tomar forma de devastadora gota fria en las próximas semanas. Pero esto último sólo se sabrá el día 21, unas horas después de que se conozcan los resultados del referéndum francés sobre el Tratado de Maastricht.

TEACHING UNIT 23. JOB OFFERS

Objective

To make the students aware that even standardized language is not eternal but develops with social and cultural change.

Tasks

1. The students are given an example of traditional Spanish and English advertisements for a job (Task Sheet 36). They are asked to compare the format, syntax, and verb forms.

2. They are given an example of modern-style Spanish and English advertisements (Task Sheet 37) and asked to compare them.

3. Then, they are asked to compare the traditional Spanish model and the modern one and try to think of reasons for the changes in the model.

4. Finally, they are asked to translate the traditional Spanish advertisement into English, following the modern model rather than the traditional one.

Commentary

The type of text inserted in the section of job offers in the Spanish press has changed in the last four or five years. It seems to be strongly influenced by American and British models. According to Joaquín Sanmartín,[28] this reflects a change in job-recruitment methods. Until quite recently, the advertisements were designed to cover middle- and lower-grade posts, as it was this section of the workforce that used newspapers to look for a job. Now, top-grade posts are also advertised, and normally the whole process is organized by companies specialized in selecting personnel. These companies include psychologists, economists, lawyers, and technicians, and the advertisements they produce are much closer to the English-language models found in the European press. Lower-grade job offers seem to be following the same model of text type, although they may not be the work of one of the specialized companies.

I discovered this change in text types when I was looking for new texts to use in this exercise. The old examples I had all followed the traditional format:

Se requiere/Se exige/Se pide: followed by a list of the qualifications the candidate should possess.

Se ofrece: followed by a list of job conditions.

---

28. Joaquín Sanmartín is the director of Selector, a company that specializes in finding staff for other companies. Quoted in "Se busca directivo: Los anuncios en prensa constituyen la forma más eficaz para encontrar un buen ejecutivo," *El País*, 1 Nov. 1992.

To my surprise, very few recents ads followed this format. There were a few examples for salesmen or -women and an offer from a magazine for a journalist, which I include below.

Four or five years ago, the differences between the English and Spanish models were quite marked. The Spanish model was characterized by its schematic format, nominalization, and use of the reflexive. The English model was more like a real advertisement, presenting the job as an attractive option. Complete sentences, the auxiliaries *should* and *would,* and the second-person singular were commonly used. In comparison with the rather brusque Spanish—"***Se requiere:** Dominio del inglés, Experiencia empresarial"*—the English version was more encouraging: *You should speak fluent English. Business experience would be an advantage.* Now the Spanish model seems to be following the English one.

TASK SHEET 36. *OFERTAS DE EMPLEO* (**TRADITIONAL**)

Instructions

Compare the traditional Spanish model with the English model: Comment on differences in format, syntax, and verb forms.

TRADITIONAL SPANISH MODEL

IMPORTANTE EDITORIAL DE
PUBLI-CACIONES SEMANALES
precisa:

REPORTERO/A

Se exige:

*Disponibilidad para viajar.

Realización de textos y fotos en temas de actualidad.

Experiencia en el puesto

Se ofrece:

Colaborará como free lance y la retribución será a convenir en entrevista personal con la propia empresa.

Escribir urgentemente carta manuscrita con datos de contacto e historial profesional, indicando en el sobre la Ref.9923 a :

GÜPPO/Anuncios. c/Balmes, 18.

08007 BARCELONA

ENGLISH MODEL

CONSULTANT TRAINEES

Our Client is a leading International Management organization with operations in Europe, America, Australia, and the Far East. Their clients include many of the most prestigious and successful names in world business.

They currently have immediate opportunities for Consultant Trainees for projects in Spain.

You should possess good interpersonal communication skills and speak fluent English. Business experience would be an advantage. Minimum age for these positions is 25.

If you are available immediately or in the near future and are looking for an unusual, exciting and demanding career with outstanding prospects, send your curriculum vitae in English to:

Litchfield Associates N.V. Halverwege 3, 2402 NK Alphen a/d Rijn. Netherlands Fax (31) 172030526

TASK SHEET 37. *OFERTAS DE EMPLEO* (**1992**)

Instructions

1. Compare the 1992 Spanish and English models as you did in Task Sheet 36, looking at format, syntax, and verb forms.
2. Now compare the traditional Spanish model and the 1992 one. Do you notice any changes? Can you think of any reasons for these changes?
3. Translate the traditional Spanish advertisement into English, making any adaptations you think appropriate. Explain which strategies you have used and why.

DIRECTOR DE RECURSOS HUMANOS

Importante compañía multinacional del sector bebidas alcohólicas y licores, desea incorporar a sus oficinas en Madrid un Director de Recursos Humanos para España.

En dependencia del director General se responsabilizará de la elaboración e implantación de las diferentes políticas de personal de la compañía así como de las relaciones laborales, administración general y presentación de la empresa ante instituciones jurídicas.

Buscamos un licenciado en Derecho, con al menos 4 años de experiencia en puesto similar adquirida en empresa multinacional y buenos conocimientos de Derecho Laboral. Deseable buen nivel de inglés.

Es un gran reto profesional que ofrece incorporación inmediata a empresa en expansión, con grandes posibilidades de desarrollo profesional. Atractiva retribución, no descartándose candidaturas por motivos económicos

Rogamos a los interesados envíen CV y fotografía a, Price Waterhouse —SELECCION DE DIRECTIVOS—Paseo de la Castellana, 43, 28046 Madrid, indicando en el sobre la referencia (AFL-1990)

MANAGEMENT CONSULTANCY PRODUCTIVITY IMPROVEMENT

Outstanding career and earnings potential with worldwide market leader.

PRESENTING ANALYSTS

SENIOR OPERATIONS MANAGERS

PROJECT MANAGERS

TRAINERS

Our Client is an international leader in productivity improvement and is currently experiencing exceptional growth with tremendous demand for their services throughout Europe. They can provide exceptional career development and potential for experienced Analysts, Senior Operation Personnel and those with the drive and aptitude to learn. They currently have immediate opportunities for projects in Spain.

You should possess good interpersonal, communication and leadership skills. Fluency in English is essential and other language capabilities are an advantage.

Rewards are outstanding for those who can deliver results!

All applications will be dealt with in strict confidence. Please forward your curriculum vitae to: European Recruitment Manager, 24, The Strand, London, N5, U.K.

Quote the following reference on envelope and CV: ID REF/SEN/EP/2292

TEACHING UNIT 24. BUSINESS LETTERS

Objectives

1. To give students practice with a text type (the formal letter) that may be useful for them professionally, as prose translators.

2. To give students practice in using the correct register for business letters. By following models and parallel texts, they are encouraged to use appropriate formal expressions without overusing unnecessary jargon, to be brief and clear, and to use proper emphasis and reference.

3. Stress is given to formal differences between Spanish and English: the layout, punctuation, capital letters, and treatment of numbers.

Tasks

1. Task Sheet 38 provides exercises in punctuation and register and Task Sheet 39 provides exercises in layout.

2. Task Sheet 40 is an example of a very poor translation into English of a business letter. The mistakes are very basic: syntax, vocabulary, spelling. The students are asked to correct the letter.

3. Task Sheet 41 gives practice in translating letters of complaint. The students are given models of useful language for formal complaints and a parallel text in English, complaining about a mistake in an electricity bill. They are asked to translate a Spanish letter complaining about a mistake in a telephone bill.

4. Task Sheet 42 gives practice in translating letters written in reply to a complaint. The Spanish text is a letter from COOB '92 to spectators who had written complaining about the equestrian event that took place on 7 August 1992. The formal expressions are underlined in the Spanish text. The English equivalents of these expressions are given below with a list of equestrian-sports vocabulary. The students are asked to translate the Spanish letter using the models they have been given.

TASK SHEET 38. PUNCTUATION AND REGISTER (Allen, 1974: 26)

Instructions

A. A business letter should be brief and clear, written in simple English without any unnecessary jargon. Consider the following letter.

> The Middleditch China Co. Ltd.,
> 221–227 London Road,
> Stoke-on-Trent,
> Staffs.

7 May 1973

Dear Sir,

Your esteemed order of the 29 ult is to hand for which we thank you. Enclosed please find our invoice for the following items which we have pleasure in forwarding under separate cover:

> 1 doz. "Oriental" dinner plates, gilt edged
> 1 doz. "East Indies" side plates, plain centres
> 1 doz "Parakeet" fish plates, unglazed
> 2 doz "Gulf Stream" tea plates, rose design, to follow.

Trusting that your good self will derive every satisfaction from our products,

> We remain,
> Yours faithfully,
>
> I. Loftus
> (for the Middleditch China Co. Ltd.)

Mr F. Bridges,
Linden Lea,
Hallaton,
Leicestershire.

B. The letter can quite easily be turned into appropriate, everyday English as below:

> Thank you for your order of 29 August. We are forwarding all the crockery you ordered separately, except for the tea-plates, which are temporarily out of stock. Our invoice is inclosed.
>
> Yours faithfully,
>
> I. Loftus
> (for the Middleditch China Co. Ltd.)

C. Here are three ways to say the same thing. Which do you find the easiest to understand?

> a) Dear Madame, Unhappily, since my personal circumstances have changed, I find myself obliged to cancel the order I left with you on Monday.
>
> b) Dear Madame, A number of personal reasons that are difficult to explain caused me to have to cancel the order I gave you on Monday.
>
> c) Dear Madame, I am sorry but I must cancel the order I gave you on Monday.

Four basic principles

1. *Brevity and clarity*: Even if one cannot always be brief, one should at least control the length and be concise.

2. *Emphasis*: What is the letter about? Why has it been written?

3. *Proper reference*: Always refer to previous correspondence, letter heading, date, order number.

4. *Layout*: The layout of a business letter can vary. In Task Sheet 39 you are given a model of a possible layout.

D. Punctuate the following letter, putting in capital letters where necessary.

> department of education and science mowden hall staindrop road darlington county durham darlington 60155—610/9110—9 september 1981—miss jane ridge 105 grangeside ave inglemire lane hull hu42 yorkshire dear miss ridge i am pleased to inform you that as you have completed to the departments satisfaction a scheduled course of training you are eligible for the status of qualified teacher i have been asked to convey the congratulations of the secretary of state who wishes you many years of happiness in the teaching profession an employing local education authority may ask you to produce this letter as evidence of your eligibility for qualified teacher status yours faithfully department of education and science j blatcher principle secretary

TASK SHEET 39. LAYOUT

Instructions

This is a layout for a business letter. Write out the letter that you have punctuated in Task Sheet 38 following this layout.

A. company letterhead

B. reference of the writer   C. the date

D. name and address of the person to whom the letter is written

E. salutation

F. subject of the letter

G. body of the letter

H. subscription (usually "Yours faithfully,")

DD. an alternative position for D   J. name of the company

K. writer's name with his or her
position in the company below

L. enclosures (if any)

TASK SHEET 40. CORRECTING A LETTER

Instructions

This letter has obviously been written by someone whose English wasn't very good and who didn't have much idea about how to write a business letter. Would you buy a wig from this company? Try to correct the English and see if you can improve the content and style of the letter.

GISELA
MAYER
COLLECTION
WEIN MARKT 2
8940 MEMMINGEN
Memmingen, January

Dear Sirs,

We would like to offer you our new mannequin wig collection 1991. Our collection has a very good styling, and we think that you can work good together with our ideas.

We gave you all the service like your orther partners, and offer you special prices and discounts like other wig companies.

Of course we send you some samples, too, if you would like to see our quality.

We wold be happy to hear from you soon.

Best regards

Gisela Mayer

PS: We are looking for a company our people who are selling our collection in your country.

TASK SHEET 41. LETTERS OF COMPLAINT

Instructions

1. Study (a) the standardized expressions of complaint and (b) the parallel text before you try to translate the Spanish letter.

2. Translate the Spanish letter, taking special care with your treatment of numbers.

a) **Standardized expressions of complaint**

    i)   I'm writing to complain about
                               express my deep concern

    ii) I must draw your attention to the fact that I am in no way responsible.
         I would like to emphasize the importance of the matter.

    iii) I must insist that you put matters right.
                       on your immediate action in this matter.

    I feel that you should XXX as soon as possible.

    It seems to me that the least you can do is XXX without further delay.

    It would appear to me that you have a responsibility to XXX immediately

    I should therefore be grateful if you could XXX

b) **Parallel Text**

37 Briars Lane
Selly Oak
Birmingham B29 6LE
8th April, 1992

Dear Sir,

I'm writing to complain about a mistake in my electricity bill, dated the 4th of April, 1992. The bill was £236 for the first quarter of the year. I must draw your attention to the fact that, during the months of February and March, I was visiting relatives in Australia and the electricity was turned off. It seems obvious to me that I have been overcharged. I must insist that you put matters right without delay. If I do not hear from you immediately, I shall get in touch with the Consumer Advice Bureau.

Yours faithfully,

Córcega, 144, 3–2
08001 Barcelona
10 de agosto, 1992

Núm. Abono: 3026201

Estimado Señor:

Me dirijo a Vd para comentar un error en la factura nº 08–h261–049718 con fecha del 1 de agosto, 1992. Aunque en el apartado de servicio automático el cobro se refiere al periodo del 5 de mayo al 3 de julio de 1992, el IVA se ha calculado al 15%, tasa que no entró en vigor hasta el 1 de agosto, 1992. La cantidad asciende a 7.359,42 pesetas y calculando el IVA al 13% la Compañía Telefónica me debe el 2% de dicha suma, es decir, 147,18 pesetas.

Esperando su respuesta, le saluda atentamente,

TASK SHEET 42. Answering Letters of Complaint

Instructions

Translate the following letter making use of the formal expressions given below.

Estimado Señor:(1)

En relación a su reclamación(2) por la competición de saltos del pasado día 7.8.92 motivado por el hecho de que muchos jinetes se negaron a salir a la pista de obstáculos o regresaron a la cuadra al pasar las primeras vallas, lamento tener que decirle(3) que la razón por la cual el jinete puede decidir si sale a la pista en la tercera manga clasificatoria viene establecida(4) en el nuevo reglamento de la Federación Ecuestre Internacional (art. 637 ap. 2.4.).(5)

En este sentido, el Comité Organizador de los JJ.OO. tiene la obligación de dar cumplimiento a esta normativa,(6) aunque no sea de su agrado,(7) por lo que los espectadores asistentes recibieron una nota informativa, que ahora adjuntamos(8) nuevamente en la que se explicaba tal circunstancia.

En cualquier caso la sonora protesta del público asistente parece que va a dar lugar a una modificación del artículo 637 del nuevo reglamento cuya parte más polémica le adjuntamos con la presente.

Esperando que esta respuesta dé cumplida satisfacción moral a su reclamación y agradeciendo el interés y confianza depositada en el COOB '92 (9) reciba un saludo cordial,

Cordialmente,(10)

Formal expressions

1. Dear Sir

2. In answer to your complaint

3. I regret to inform you

4. are laid down

5. the new Rules of the Equestrian Federation (Art. 637, Section 2.4)

6. the Organizing Committee is obliged to see that this rule is observed

7. whatever its own feelings on the matter may be

8. which we enclose here

9. I would also like to thank you for the interest and trust you have shown in COOB '92.

10. Yours sincerely

Equestrian vocabulary

la competición de saltos = the jumping competition

los jinetes = the riders

la pista = the course

la cuadra = the stables

vallas = fences

Possible Translation

Dear Sir,

In answer to your complaint about the jumping competition of 7 August 1992, provoked by the fact that many riders refused to go out to the course or returned to the stables after clearing the first fences, I regret to inform you that the justifications for the rider's decision as to whether or not to go out for the third qualifying round are laid down in the new Rules of the International Equestrian Federation (Art. 637, Section 2.4).

The Organizing Committee therefore is obliged to see that this rule is observed whatever its own feelings on the matter may be, and the spectators received an explanatory note to that effect, which we enclose here.

In any case, the audible protest of the public may well have given rise to a modification of Article 637 of the new Rules. We also enclose the controversial section. I hope that this reply will provide you at least with moral satisfaction. I would also like to thank you for the interest and trust you have shown in COOB '92.

Sincerely,

TEACHING UNIT 25. TRANSLATING TESTIMONIALS

Objective

To compare the layout, formal expressions, and register of the text type, in this case a professional recommendation.

Task

The students are asked to translate the Spanish letter of recommendation, making use of the layout, formal expressions, and register of the English model.

Commentary

In the previous unit, the main objective is to give practice in translating a text type that may be useful to the students as professional prose translators. In this unit, parallel texts are again used.

TASK SHEET 43. TESTIMONIALS

Instructions

1. Study and compare both letters of recommendation before you try to translate the Spanish letter.

2. Translate the Spanish letter, taking special care with standardized expressions and layout.

> Universidad Autónoma de Barcelona
> Escuela Universitaria de Traductores e Interpretes
> Dirección
>
> 25 May 1987

To Whom It May Concern:

Prof. X was a member of the English-language translation team for the Barcelona Olympic Candidacy and continues to be a member of this same team, which is now the official English-language translation team of the *Comité Organizador Olímpico Barcelona '92* (COOB '92).

Her efficiency and success in this endeavour were instrumental in making it possible for this School of Translators and Interpreters (EUTI) to undertake negotiations to sign a formal agreement with the COOB '92 according to which the EUTI will coordinate translation and Interpreting and the training of translators and interpreters for the 1992 Olympic Games.

Sincerely,
Dr. Sean Golden
Secretary (EUTI)

OFICINA OLIMPICA
Plaça de la Font Màgica, s/n
08004 BARCELONA
Barcelona, el 15 de mayo de 1987

A quien corresponda,

Es un placer certificar que X, profesional de la traducción y de trabajos lingüísticos en general, ha colaborado con la Oficina Olímpica para la promoción de la Candidatura de Barcelona a los Juegos de Barcelona de 1992, y sigue colaborando con el COOB'92, organismo encargado de la preparación y organización de los Juegos a partir de designación oficial.

La Sra. X trabajó intensamente en la versión inglesa del informe final de candidatura, llevando a cabo un trabajo impecable y compartiendo la responsabilidad colectiva, sin duda alguna, de que Barcelona consiguiese la nominación olímpica. Como especialista, en consecuencia, merece toda nuestra confianza y nuestro reconocimiento.

Atentamente,
Alfredo BOSCH
Agregado de prensa (COOB'92)

TEACHING UNIT 26. CONTRACTS—PLAIN ENGLISH

Objectives

1. To distinguish between two translations of a contract. The first follows a traditional model, and the second is in "plain English." The movement toward "plain language" in legal and administrative documents is significant in both English and Spanish.

2. To make the students aware of the restrictions involved in translating contracts, acts of meetings, laws, and regulations. It is important to maintain the coherence and semantic ordering of the texts, because these texts may be used as parallel working documents.

Tasks

1. Task Sheet 44 includes the first part of the "Declarations" in the Preamble to the COOB '92 Sponsors' Contract in (a) the Spanish original, (b) a "traditional" translation, and (c) a "plain English" translation.[29] The students are asked to identify the lexical and syntactic differences between the two models. They are then asked to translate the remaining "Declarations" into "plain English."

2. The same process is followed in the section "Definitions of Stipulations."

Commentary

The concern with "plain English" has a long history. In 1731, the British Parliament passed a Statute of Pleading to this purpose:

> Whereas many and great mischiefs do frequently happen to the subjects of this kingdom, from the procedings in courts of justice being in an unknown language, those who are summoned and impleaded having no knowledge or understanding of what is alleged for or against them in the pleadings of their lawyers and attorneys, who use a character not legible to any but persons practising the law:

> To remedy these great mischiefs, and to protect the lives and fortunes of the subjects of that part of Great Britain called England, more effectually than heretofore, from the peril of being ensnared or brought in danger by forms and proceedings in courts of justice, in an unknown language, be it enacted by the King's most excellent majesty, by and with the advice and consent of the lords spiritual and temporal and commons of Great Britain in parliament assembled, and by the authority of the same, That from after the 25th day of March 1733, all writs, processes . . . shall be in the English tongue and language only, and not in Latin and French, or any other tongue or language

---

29. I am indebted to Richard Jacques for these two translations.

whatsoever, and shall be written in a common legible hand and character, and not in any hand commonly called court hand, and in words at length and not abbreviated.[30]

The "plain language" movement has gained considerable strength in recent years; in some provinces of Canada, a law is not considered to be legally binding unless it is couched in terms that any "normal" person can read and understand. Statutes and bylaws have been rewritten to improve clarity and brevity, for example:

Original

Not to use or permit or suffer to be used the demised premises or any part thereof or any building or erections at any time hereafter erected thereon or on any part thereof as and for all or any of the purposes of a brewery or a club (whether proprietor or members) or a public house or other licensed premises or otherwise for the preparation manufacture supply distribution or sale whether wholesale or retail and whether for consumption on or off the premises of all or any alcoholic liquors of any description and not without the previous consent in writing of the Landlord to carry on or permit upon the demised premises any trade business or occupation other than that of a retail shop for the sale of X.

Revision

Not to make or sell alcoholic drinks in the shop or (without the landlord's written consent) to use it except for the sale of X.[31]

"Plain language" is a concern of the government in Spain, as is shown by seminars such as the one held at the Catalan School of Public Administration in June, 1991.

The main differences in the two translations compared in this exercise are (a) lexical: the deletion or substitution in the revised version of terms such as *Whereas, hereinafter, hereto, these present, in (the year) 1992*, and (b) syntactic: the preference for active rather than passive verbs in the revised version.

TASK SHEET 44. *COOB '92*

Instructions

1. The text below is part of the preamble to the COOB '92 Sponsors' Contract. You are given (a) the Spanish original, (b) a "traditional" English translation, and (c) a "plain English" translation.

---

30. Mark Adler, president of Clarity, used this example in the Escola d'Administració Pública de Catalunya, 12 June 1991.
31. Mark E. Vale, the director of the Plain Language Centre of the Canadian Legal Information Centre, used this example in the Escola d'Administració Pública de Catalunya, 12 June 1991.

2. Which of the two translations do you think is easier to understand?

3. What differences do you notice between the two translations?

---

a) MANIFIESTAN

I. Que el Comité Olímpico Internacional (en lo sucesivo COI) dirige el Movimiento Olímpico y posee todos los derechos relativos a los Juegos Olímpicos y al SIMBOLO OLIMPICO (como será definido en lo sucesivo).

b) DECLARE

I. WHEREAS the International Olympic Committee (herinafter referred to as the "IOC") governs the Olympic Movement and owns all the rights in respect of the Olympic Games and the OLYMPIC SYMBOL as hereinafter described.

c) DECLARE

I. That the Interational Olympic Committee (in future IOC) governs the Olympic Movement and owns all rights in respect of the Olympic Games and of the OLYMPIC SYMBOL (as defined below).

---

a)

II. Que el COI ha confiado la organización de los Juegos de la XXV Olimpíada a la ciudad de Barcelona.

b)

II. AND WHEREAS the IOC has entrusted the organization of the GAMES of the XXV Olympiad to the city of Barcelona,

c)

II. That the IOC has entrusted the organization of the Games of the XXV Olympiad to the city of Barcelona,

---

a)

III. Que la ciudad de Barcelona conjuntamente con el Comité Olímpico Español (en lo sucesivo "COE") ha designado al COOB'92 como la entidad exclusiva en lo relativo a organización y dirección de los Juegos de la XXV Olimpíada.

b)

III. AND WHEREAS the city of Barcelona and the Spanish Olympic Committee (hereinafter referred to as the "COE") has appointed COOB '92 to be the exclusive organizer and manager of the GAMES of the XXV Olympiad,

c)

III. That the city of Barcelona and the Spanish Olympic Committee (in future COE) has appointed COOB '92 as the exclusive entity related to the organization and direction of the Games of the XXV Olympiad,

4. Now translate the rest of the preamble into "plain English."

IV. Que el COOB'92 ha iniciado y desarrollado durante el cuatrienio 1989/1992 un Programa Comercial y de Marketing de sus propiedades y/o derechos Olímpicos, que consiste en el Patrocinio y Suministro Olímpico y otras oportunidades relacionadas con el COOB'92 y con los JUEGOS (como serán definidos en lo sucesivo).

V. Que el COOB'92, tiene autoridad para garantizar al Suministrador de MATERIAL DEPORTIVO OFICIAL, ciertos derechos y oportunidades de marketing relativos a los JUEGOS.

VI. Que el Suministrador de MATERIAL DEPORTIVO OFICIAL reconoce el gran valor de dichos derechos y oportunidades de marketing y desea formalizar un acuerdo con el COOB'92, para beneficiarse de los derechos y oportunidades ofrecidos con respecto al MATERIAL DEPORTIVO OFICIAL (como se definirá en lo sucesivo).

VII. Que es muy importante que los derechos y oportunidades relacionados con los Juegos Olímpicos sean utilizados de un modo que conserve y realce el prestigio del Movimiento Olímpico y promueva los logros de sus objetivos como se establece en la CARTA OLIMPICA (como se definirá en lo sucesivo).

VIII. Que en atención a lo expresado vienen a celebrar el presente Contrato de suministrador de MATERIAL DEPORTIVO OFICIAL, el cual se ajustará a los siguientes:

5. The second part of the contract is the definition of the conditions. As before, you are given the "traditional" and the "plain English" versions.

---

a) **PACTOS**

1. **DEFINICIONES** — A los efectos del presente Contrato las partes convienen en utilizar en este contexto las siguientes:

1.1. "JUEGOS" significará los Juegos de la XXV Olimpiada que se celebrarán en el año 1992, en la ciudad de Barcelona y en su alrededores, (España), e incluirá siempre que sea dirigido bajo la autoridad y/o el control y/o el auspicio oficial del COOB'92 lo siguiente:

i) todas las competiciones preliminares, de clasificación, semifinales y finales en todos los deportes;

ii) inauguración, clausura, premios y otras ceremonias oficiales;

iii) acontecimientos deportivos y deportes de demostración tal como han sido aprobadas por el COI;

iv) acontecimientos preolímpicos tal como han sido definidos por la Regla 45 de la CARTA OLIMPICA.

b) CONDITIONS

1. DEFINITIONS For the purpose of these presents the parties hereto agree to the following definitions:

1.1. By GAMES is meant the GAMES of the XXV Olympiad which shall take place in and around Barcelona, Spain in the year 1992 and which shall include the following items, provided always that the same are carried out under the authority, control and or the official auspices of the COOB '92.

i) All preliminary qualifying trials and heats, semi-final and final rounds in every sport.

ii) The opening, closing, award and other official ceremonies.

iii) Any sport event and exhibition sport approved by the IOC.

iv) Any pre-Olympic event within the meaning of Rule 45 of the Olympic Charter.

c) STIPULATIONS

1. DEFINITIONS For the purpose of this present Contract, the parties agree to use the following in this context:

1.1. GAMES means the Games of the XXV Olympiad to be held in and around Barcelona, Spain in 1992 and shall include the following, provided such are conducted under the authority and/or control and/or official auspices of COOB '92 or the COE:

i) all preliminaries, qualifying competitions, heats, semi-finals and finals in all sports;

ii) opening, closing, medal and other official ceremonies;

iii) sport events and demonstration sports as approved by the IOC;

iv) sport events as defined by Rule 45 of the OLYMPIC CHARTER.

---

a)

1.2. ESPAÑA significará el área geográfica con respecto a la cual el COE es reconocido por el COI.

1.3. CARTA OLIMPICA significará la Carta Olímpica (incluyendo sus textos de aplicación) tal como ha quedado reflejada en la edición de 1987, la cual queda incorporada a este Contrato como Apéndice G.

1.4. SIMBOLO OLIMPICA significará los cinco anillos entrelazados propiedad del COI y/o controlado por el mismo, siendo el símbolo más ampliamente reconocido del Movimiento Olímpico.

b)

1.2. By SPAIN is meant that geographical area in which the COE is recognised by the IOC.

c)

1.2. SPAIN means the geographical area in which the COE is recognised by the IOC.

1.3. By OLYMPIC CHARTER is meant the Olympic Charter (including its by-laws) as reflected in the 1987 printed edition, which is incorporated as Appendix G hereto.

1.3. OLYMPIC CHARTER means the 1987 edition of the Olympic Charter (and its by-laws) included as Appendix G of this Contract.

1.4. By the OLYMPIC SYMBOL is meant the five interlaced rings the property of and or controlled by the IOC, being the most widely known symbol of the OLYMPIC MOVEMENT.

1.4. OLYMPIC SYMBOL means the five interlaced rings owned and /or controlled by the IOC, being the most widely recognised symbol of the Olympic Movement.

---

6. Comment on the lexical and syntactic differences between the traditional and the "plain English" translations.

Now translate the remaining definitions into "plain English."

1.5. CON(S) significará Comité(s) Olímpico(s) Nacional(es) reconocido(s) como tal(es) por el COI según las disposiciones de la CARTA OLIMPICA.

1.6. DENOMINACIONES DE LOS JUEGOS significará cualesquiera o todas las denominaciones que indiquen una utilización del MATERIAL DEPORTIVO OFICIAL en los JUEGOS y que se describen en el Apéndice C del presente Contrato.

1.7. EMBLEMA DE LOS JUEGOS significará la yuxtaposición del SIMBOLO OLIMPICO con el logotipo, que está ilustrado en el Apéndice B del presente Contrato y está exhibido de diversas formas tal como se halla indicado en el Manual de Modelos Gráficos del COOB'92, el cual puede ser completado en todo momento.

1.8. MARCAS DE LOS JUEGOS significará el EMBLEMA de los JUEGOS, DENOMINACIONES de los JUEGOS, o ambos según lo requiera el contexto.

1.9. MATERIAL DEPORTIVO OFICIAL significará los productos y/o servicios del Suministrador de los mismos enumerados en el Apéndice D del presente Contrato, los cuales serán utilizados en los JUEGOS al haber sido homologados por la Federación Internacional correspondiente y escogidos por el COOB'92.

1.10. RECINTOS significará los emplazamientos de cada una de las actividades de los JUEGOS, e incluirá las áreas de competición y sus espacios destinados al aparcamiento, los centros de radio y televisión, las áreas de VIPs, las villas de los atletas y las villas de los medios de comunicación y cualquier otra área que exija acreditación o entrada olímpica para obtener el acceso a la misma y que se encuentran bajo el control del COOB'92.

1.11. Suministrador de MATERIAL DEPORTIVO OFICIAL será las Compañías ALLSTAR Fech-Center Gmb H & Co. KG y ULHMANN Fechsport GmbH & Co. KG.

CHAPTER 16

COHESION AND COHERENCE

Cohesion in a text is provided by a network of lexical, grammatical, and other relationships that provide links in the surface structure of the text. Cohesion can be evaluated objectively, but different languages use cohesive devices (reference, substitution, conjunction, lexical and syntactic cohesion, chunking of information in sentences and paragraphs) differently. Translators have to consider the adjustment of cohesive devices from the SLT to the TLT. These devices reflect rhetorical purpose and control interpretation of the text, so changes may affect both the content and the line of argument. Adjustments will mean advantages and disadvantages that will have to be judged in the light of the *skopos* of the translation and the TLT readers. "The topic of cohesion has always appeared to me the most useful constituent of discourse analysis or text linguistics applicable to translation" (Newmark, 1987: 295).

Coherence in a text is provided by a network of relations that underlie the surface text and organize and create the text. To a certain extent, it is subjective, and each reader will find a greater or lesser degree of coherence depending on his or her extratextual knowledge of the world. Different societies view the world differently; therefore, a network of relations that may be valid in one social context may not make sense in another. This is important for the translator who has to take into account the *skopos* of the text and the TLT reader's knowledge of the world.

> No text is inherently coherent or incoherent. In the end, it all depends on the receiver, and on his ability to interpret the indications present in the discourse so that, finally, he manages to understand it in a way which seems coherent to him—in a way which corresponds with his idea of what it is that makes a series of actions into an integrated whole. (Charolles, 1983: 95)

TEACHING UNIT 27. SYNTACTIC COHESION

Objectives

1. To show the importance of the repetition of syntactic and tachygraphic strategies in providing textual cohesion.

2. To find alternatives for strategies used in the SLT that do not have direct equivalents in the TL.

3. To provide insight into comparative structures in Spanish and English.

4. To show how textual coherence is achieved by the network of relations in the text, but that this coherence would be totally clear only in the context in which the text was written, the days leading up to the Gulf War. If time and place separate the TLT readers from that context, a considerable amount of explicature would be needed to make the text coherent.

Tasks

1. The students are asked to analyze a short text written by a Uraguayan writer, Eduardo Galeano, just before the outbreak of the Gulf War in 1991. They are asked to identify the tachygraphic and syntactic devices that provide cohesion in the text.

2. They are asked to think of how they can preserve this cohesion when translating the text into English.

3. They are asked to list the network of references that provide textual coherence to the text.

4. They are asked to consider which implicatures would have to be explicated to make the text coherent to someone who had been marooned on a desert island from August 1990 to August 1991.

Commentary

Textual cohesion is provided by the repeated use of the question form and the subjunctive in the SLT. The inverted question mark at the front of a question in Spanish is a taquigraphical extra marker that does not exist in English. There is word play between *Para qué* (Why?) and *Para que* (So that), and most of the sentences (which are organized as a list) begin with either one or the other. This play on words is not possible in English, but most of the question words in English begin with *W*, so a cohesive effect can be achieved by starting all the sentences with *W* and trying to reinforce the effect by alliteration in the rest of the text. Word order is more fixed, therefore more repetitive, in English than in Spanish, contributing to greater cohesion. The subjunctive in Spanish has no direct equivalent in modern English and perhaps the conditional would be appropriate here instead. Another play on words that cannot be reproduced is *Si estalla la guerra* at the beginning of the text and *Si estalla el mundo* at the end.

Although others may find different coherence patterns in this text, I recognize three main referential networks: (a) war and violence, (b) human rights, (c) black gold.

a) *guerra, invasión, carnicería, armamentos, guerra fría, arsenal, cuartel, crimen, suicidio, grandes potencias, Sadam, Kuwait, Bush, Panamá, Gorbachov, Lituania, Israel, palestinos, Hitler, judíos, árabes*

b) *derecho, privilegio, destino, humanidad*

c) *árabes, financien, petróleo, dos millones de dólares por minuto, vendido*

The text is based on implicatures, so any reader who did not know the background to the text would need to have it explained. What is it that Bush did to Panama that Saddam cannot do to Kuwait?

TASK SHEET 45. SYNTACTIC COHESION

Instructions

1. This short text is very well put together; it is highly cohesive. Which tachygraphic and syntactic devices are repeated throughout the text to contribute to this cohesion?

2. Suggest ways of keeping cohesion in translating this text into English.

3. Translate the text, trying to preserve the cohesion.

4. Do the extratextual references make one or more lexical networks? List any network of references you see.

5. Imagine you are translating this text for someone who was a castaway on a desert island from August 1990 to August 1991. Which of the references would have to be explained?

> *El País*, 17 de enero de1991.   **Preguntitas**
>
> ¿Y si hoy estalla la guerra?
>
> ¿Para qué?
>
> ¿Para probar que el derecho de invasión es un privilegio de las grandes potencias, y que Sadam no puede hacer a Kuwait lo que Bush hace a Panamá y Gorbachov a Lituania?
>
> ¿Para que Israel pueda seguir haciendo a los palestinos lo que Hitler hizo a los judíos?

¿Para que los árabes financien la carnicería de los árabes?

¿Para que quede claro que el petróleo no se toca?

¿O para que siga siendo imprescindible que el mundo desperdicie en arma-mentos dos millones de dólares por minuto, ahora que se acabó la guerra fría?

¿Y si un día de éstos, estalle o no estalle la guerra, estalla el mundo? ¿El mundo convertido en arsenal y cuartel?

¿Quién ha vendido el destino de la humanidad a un puñado de locos, codi-ciosos y matones?

¿ Quién quedará vivo, para decir que ese crimen de ellos ha sido un suicidio nuestro?

Eduardo Galeano (escritor uruguayo)

Possible Translation

Question Marks

EDUARDO GALEANO

What if war broke out today?

What would it prove?

Would it prove that only the superpowers have invasion rights and that Sad-dam cannot do to Kuwait what Bush did to Panama and Gorbachev to Lithuania?

Would Israel be able to go on doing to the Palestinians what Hitler did to the Jews?

Would the Arabs go on paying for the slaughter of Arabs?

Would everyone understand that oil is out of bounds?

Would the world understand how important it is to go on wasting two million dollars a day on arms now that the Cold War is over?

Whether the war breaks out or not . . .

What would happen if the world, this warehouse for weapons, exploded?

Who has sold the future of mankind to a handful of greedy, murderous mad-men?

Who will be left alive to weep and tell the tale of their crime, which is our sui-cide?

TEACHING UNIT 28. REFERENCE, CONJUNCTIONS, AND PARAGRAPHS

Objectives

1. To make students aware of the importance of reference and repetition in providing cohesion in an English text. Unlike Spanish, the English system makes very few distinctions in terms of number, gender, and verb agreement; therefore, greater attention must be paid to making references clear. Patterns of referential cohesion can be adjusted in the SLT to reflect TL preferences.
2. To make students understand that conjunctions are formal markers that signal the way the writer wants the reader to relate what is going to be said to what has been said before. English tends to use more conjunctions than does Spanish, but adjustments for translation purposes are complicated. Conjunctions reflect the rhetorical purpose of the text and control the interpretation; therefore, adjustments affect both the content and the line of argument.
3. To consider how far argument lines can be altered by adjusting conjunctions and so on. Obviously, this will depend on the *skopos* of the translation.
4. To consider the difference between the "othographic" or "typographical" paragraph and the "structural" paragraph (Hatim, 1990: 120) with the suggestion that the latter should be the focus of the translator.

Tasks

1. The students are asked to list all direct references to Xenophon in the Spanish and English texts and to compare the results.
2. They are asked to do the same with the conjunctions.
3. They are asked to make an outline of the structure of both texts and decide if the "typographical" paragraphs coincide with the "structural" paragraphs. They are asked to compare the results in Spanish and English.
4. They are asked to translate the Spanish text for British secondary-school students.

Commentary

Direct references to Xenophon are much more frequent in the English text (37) than in the Spanish text (11). This provides greater surface cohesion in the English text.

Direct reference to subjects in English		Direct references to subjects in Spanish	
Xenophon	10	Jenofonte	4
Xenophon's	6	su	7
he	13	total	11
his	8		
total	37		

The English version begins with the question of the causes of the subject's exile. The main part of the text is organized around arguing the pros and cons of the different events of his life in relation to this question. And *it* has **15 argumentative conjunctions**: *therefore, nevertheless, moreover, however, rather, but, in short,* and so on. The last part of the text is a brief account of the last thirty years of his life and includes **5 temporal conjunctions.**

The Spanish text gives a brief chronological account of his whole life (employing **5 temporal conjunctions**) and only at the end gets to the main issue: *Entre las incertidumbres de su biografía, la que tiene un mayor interés por su significación es la que corresponde al momento preciso de su destierro.* This last part of the text, which is the second part of a long paragraph, includes **6 argumentative conjunctions**: *sin embargo, desde luego,* and so on.

The English text is organized in **7 "typographical" paragraphs**, which correspond to the "structural" paragraphs.

The Spanish text has only **2 "typographical" paragraphs**, the second of which is very long. In my opinion, this "typographical" paragraph is divided into four "structural" paragraphs: (a) Xenophon with the Ten Thousand, (b) Xenophon fighting on the side of the Spartans, (c) Xenophon as a writer in exile, (d) the most interesting question of all: why and when was he exiled? Adjustment of "typographical" paragraphs to fit "structural" paragraphs is a justifiable translation strategy in this case.

ENGLISH

First typographical paragraph

1. X. 428–354 BC
2. Therefore contemporary with Plato.
3. Wealthy family but difficult times.

Second typographical paragraph

4. Nevertheless wealth reflected in his writing (It is important to note this: his writings, not Socrates's).

Third typographical paragraph

5. 401 left Athens
6. 399? exiled
7. Reasons? Admired the thirty oligarchs, Sparta and Thucydides. Quite possibly oligarchic.
8. Moreover, admiration for Sparta was related to oligarchic tendencies.

SPANISH

First typographical paragraph

1. ¿Nacido Atenas? ¿430 ?
2. No se sabe nada de sus primeros 30 años.
3. Sólo Diógenes describe su amistad con Sócrates. Estos años: Guerra del Peloponeso

Second typographical paragraph

4. 401 con los 10.000
5. Lideró el retorno de los Griegos (*Anabasis*)
6. Luego campaña en Asia Minor (*Helenicas*)

Third structural paragraph?

7. Años con Esparta, hasta tal punto, luchó contra Atenas.

Fourth typographical paragraph

9. However, not very interested in politics.

   Admired the old virtues (military, Sparta) but critical of Sparta in *Hellenica*.

Fifth typographical paragraph

10. Unpopularity related to Socrates (not only some of Socrates's circle oligarchic, but all rich men suspected).

Sixth typographical paragraph

11. In short, while in exile because of oligarchic tendencies, also pro-Sparta

Seventh typographical paragraph

12. Rest of life
13. Left Athens 401 to help Cyrus
13. Led the Ten Thousand back to Greece? (*Anabasis*)
14. Short period as a mercenary in Thrace
15. Fought with Sparta 399–94, however, uncertain whether fought against Athens at Coronea.
15. For the next 30 years, country gentleman.
16. Until return to Athens 365. Exile repealed 368.
17. Until death in Athens.

Fourth structural paragraph?

8. Luego exilio (escritor)
9. Hasta que fue a Corinto
10. En algún momento volvió a Atenas donde murió.

Fifth structural paragraph?

11. Muchas incertidumbres pero momento exacto del exilio más significativo (*KEY SENTENCE*).
12. Despúes de Coronea, regalo de Escilunte, ¿acusado de filolaconismo y traición?
13. Sin embargo, los clásicos lo relacionaron con los 10.000.
14. Desde luego, Ciro enemigo de Atenas, pero, además el momento de la muerte de Sócrates.
15. En tales circunstancias, ¿la relaciónaron con Ciro y más tarde con el filolaconismo?

TASK SHEET 46. Xenophon and *Jenofonte*

Reference and conjunctions are devices used to give a text **cohesion**.

Instructions

1. Compare these parallel texts about Xenophon, taken from the introductions to an English edition of his *Conversations of Socrates* and a Spanish edition of his

Helénicas. List all the **direct references** in the English text to Xenophon, such as *Xenophon, Xenophon's life, he, his view*. Now, do the same for the Spanish text.

2. Now list and identify the **conjunctions** or link words in the English and Spanish texts.

The main relations expressed by conjunctions are:
a) **additive**: and, or, also, in addition, furthermore, moreover, besides, similarly, likewise, by contrast, for instance.
b) **adversative**: but, yet, however, instead, on the other hand, nevertheless, at any rate, as a matter of fact.
c) **causal**: so, consequently, it follows, for, because, under the circumstances, for this reason.
d) **temporal**: then, next, after that, on another occasion, in conclusion, an hour later, finally, at last.
e) **continuatives**: now, of course, well, anyway, surely, after all.

3. Make a brief outline of both texts and compare the organization of the information: ordering, paragraphs, sentences, and so on. Do the "typographical" paragraphs coincide with the "structural" paragraphs?

4. Translate the Spanish text into English, making any adjustments in cohesion that you consider would help a secondary-school reader to understand the text.

Xenophon (Waterfield, 1990)

Xenophon, son of Gryllus, was born in Athens c. 428 BC and died c. 354; he was therefore an exact contemporary of Plato (429–347), the other author whose Socratic writings survive. Xenophon's family was fairly well off, but we must take into account Athens's stormy political history in the last decade of the fifth century, and the fact that the Peloponnesian War, which Athens eventually lost, began in 431 and ended in 404. Under such circumstances, and particularly during the formative years of one's life, wealth does not necessarily imply security.

Nevertheless, many details of Xenophon's life, and the topics on which he wrote, reflect the concerns of the well-to-do. He wrote, among other things, on hunting, horsemanship and cavalry command, estate management, and military history. It is important to note this right from the start, so that when we find these topics peppering Socrates's conversations as reported by Xenophon, we avoid the temptation to think that these were Socrates's interests and experiences rather than Xenophon's.

In 401 Xenophon left Athens, and soon afterwards (possibly in 399) he was formally exiled. What were the reasons for this official disfavour? The last couple of years of the fifth century saw a fervent return to democracy in Athens, following the arbitrary and tyrannical rule of the Thirty Oligarchs in 404–03. Quite possibly, then, Xenophon had, or been suspected of, oligarchic inclinations. The historian Thucydides, whom Xenophon held in great esteem, expressed admiration for the moderate oligarchy of 411, and the young Xenophon, too, may well have been impressed by this form of government. Moreover, Xenophon's life and writings reflect an admiration for Athens's enemy Sparta, and such admiration was often expressed by those in Athens who tended towards oligarchy.

However, it is probably more true to say that Xenophon was not particularly passionate about politics; rather, he commended the traditional virtues wherever he found them and, as a soldier, particularly the military virtues of Sparta. In his view, although Athens's past reveals these virtues, Sparta's present more closely conformed to his ideal. But when Sparta acted viciously, he was prepared to condemn it (*Hellenica*).

The question of Xenophon's unpopularity in Athens cannot be separated from his association with Socrates. The duration and depth of this association can only be guessed, but it was there, and in a town as small as Athens was at the time it would have been well known. Not only were several members of Socrates's circle overt or covert oligarchs, but they were all, without exception, members of the upper classes, which in divided political times are always suspected of seeking dominion in one way or another. And the restored democracy was to put Socrates himself to death in 399.

In short, while there are reasons to think that Xenophon was not especially committed to politics, the charges that led to his formal exile are likely to have been based on suspicions of oligarchic and pro-Spartan tendencies.

The rest of Xenophon's life can be briefly chronicled. On leaving Athens in 401, he joined (apparently not with Socrates's wholehearted approval) Cyrus the Younger's expedition to wrest the Persian throne from his brother Artaxerxes. The attempt failed; Xenophon chronicles the expedition and his own part in leading—if he is to be believed—the Greek mercenary troops back to Greece in *Anabasis*. After a short period as a mercenary in Thrace, from 399 to 394 Xenophon fought for Sparta; however, it is not clear whether he actually fought against Athens in the battle of Coronea in 394. For the next thirty years he lived, with his wife and two sons, the life of a country gentleman under Spartan protection, until he returned to Athens in 365 (his exile had been repealed in 368), where he lived until his death.

Jenofonte (Plácido, 1989)

Jenofonte nació en Atenas, o en un distrito del Atica, hacia el año 430 a.C. De los treinta primeros años de su vida no se sabe prácticamente nada. Sólo Diógenes Laercio que lo incluye en sus *Vidas de filósofos*, cuenta la anécdota de cómo se convirtió en discipulo de Sócrates. La imagen de Jenofonte como filósofo socrático era, según se desprende de esto, bastante predominante en la Antigüedad. Estos tuvieron que ser los años, coincidentes con la guerra del Peloponeso y sus inmediatas secuelas que desembocaron en la condena del maestro, en los que Jenofonte mantuvo contactos con él.

En el año 401 intervino activamente en la expedición de los Diez Mil, formada por soldados mercenarios para apoyar a Ciro el Joven en sus pretensiones de conseguir la realeza persa frente a su hermano Artajerjes. Ciro murió en el intento y Jenofonte regresó al mando de la expedición, lo que sirvió de motivo para la redacción del *Anábasis*. Luego se incorporó a las campañas que en la década de los 90 estaba llevando a cabo Argesilao, rey de Esparta, en Asia Menor. Serán los "Cireos" mencionados en las *Helénicas*. Y continuará su colaboración con los espartanos, hasta el punto de que en la batalla de Coronea, en el año 394, combatió de su lado frente a los tebanos y a sus propios compatriotas atenienses. Luego vivió, desterrado de su ciudad, en una finca donada por los espartanos en Escilunte, en Elide, donde escribió una buena parte de su variada obra, hasta que después de la batalla de Leuctra se trasladó a Corinto, y allí vivió un tiempo indeterminado. En algún momento regresó a Atenas, donde murió posiblemente hacia el año 354. Entre las incertidumbres de su biografía, la que tiene un mayor interés por su significación es la que corresponde al momento preciso de su destierro. La residencia en Escilunte , a continuación de la batalla de Coronea, ha llevado a atribuir el motivo del destierro a su filolaconismo, que había llegado a convertirse en auténtica traición. Sin embargo, las fuentes antiguas relacionan el hecho más bien con la expedición de los Diez Mil. Ciro había actuado, desde luego, en los últimos años de la guerra del Peloponeso, de manera hostil a los atenienses, pero, además, la expedición coincide con los momentos dramáticos de la historia ateniense que llevaron a la condena de Sócrates. En tales circunstancias, ante un sistema democrático a la defensiva, cabe la posibilidad de que la aproximación a Ciro de un individuo cercano a los círculos socráticos se haya interpretado como una forma de traición identificada más tarde con el filolaconismo.

TEACHING UNIT 29. COHESIVE REPETITION AND VARIATION

Objectives

1. To show how English has a preference for lexical repetition and pronominalization, whereas Spanish tries to avoid lexical repetition and overuse of pronouns and prefers to use synonyms, superordinates, general words, or paraphrase.

2. To show how comprehension is aided by following the anaphorical chains related to the main concepts discussed in the texts.

Tasks

1. The students are given parallel texts. The first is an extract from the second chapter of *A Brief History of Time,* by Stephen Hawking, in which he explains how Einstein's theory of relativity altered physicists' concepts of reality (time and space). The second is an extract from *El sentido histórico de la teoría de Einstein,* by José Ortega y Gasset, in which he discusses the same phenomenon. The students are asked to list the network of references to the main concepts being discussed in both texts: (a) references to physics before Einstein, (b) references to the theory of relativity, (c) references to reality (or the universe) and time/space.

2. They are asked to compare the networks and draw conclusions about the different strategies used by both writers.

3. They are asked to consider which adjustments might be made to the cohesive devices in the Spanish (SL) text in order to make it easier for the English-speaking (TL) reader.

Commentary

In the parallel biographical texts in Teaching Unit 28, there were many more direct references to the subject of the biography in the English text than in the Spanish text. It was suggested that this was due to the fact that English grammar does not give so many clues of gender, number, and so on, as does Spanish. Therefore, in English it is more important to establish reference and cohesion clearly in other ways. Lexical repetition and pronominalization are strategies used.

Anaphorical chains used by the writers as cohesive devices are essential for understanding texts of the difficulty in this unit. The translator should consider the *skopos* of the translation and decide if the variety of referential devices used in the Spanish text should be unified in the English translation in order to aid comprehension. However, the author of the Spanish text is Ortega y Gasset, and with a writer of his stature, considerable care should be taken in adjusting the SLT to TLT readers' expectations.

The referential networks show quite clearly the absence of repetition and the variety of references in the Spanish text. Ortega y Gasset was a great writer, and the language he uses is very rich. He avoids repetition whenever possible (*tiempo* is only repeated three times in his text, whereas in Hawking's text *time* is repeated seventeen times). Hawking writes about complicated subjects with great clarity. He does not avoid repetition (*time and space* is repeated six times in one paragraph) and he exemplifies the Anglo-Saxon virtues of sincerity, brevity, and relevance. However, we should not assume that these virtues, enshrined in the co-operative principle, are universal (Grice, 1975). Just as there are Anglo-Saxon readers who dismiss some German academic writing as "chaotic," there are German readers who find English-language publications too "narrow" or conclude that they are not saying very much (Clyne, 1983: 43).

SPANISH TEXT	ENGLISH TEXT

1. References to Physics before Einstein

la mecánica clásica	Newton's law of motion
el clásico edificio de la mecánica	Before 1915
al de Galileo y Newton	The old idea
éstos	
la física de Galileo y Newton	
relativas	

2. References to the theory of relativity

la teoría de Einstein	general relativity (2)
su nombre propio	the theory of relativity (2)
la relatividad	the general thory of relativity (2)
el relativismo de Einstein	this new understanding
la mecánica de Einstein	the notion of a dynamic, expanding
su física	universe
relativista	that revolution
su relativismo	
la física de Einstein	

3. References to reality: space/time

en el espacio y el tiempo	time (3)
duración colocación y movimiento	space
un espacio, un tiempo y un	space and time (8)
movimiento absolutos	space/time
éstos	absolute time (2)
ellos	fixed time (2)
éste	a fixed arena
su existencia	in which
noticias indirectas	dynamic quantities
meras apariencias	universe (5)
valores relativos	a finite time (2)

esos inasequibles absolutos en el espacio
el
tiempo y la realidad
las determinaciones concretas que antes
parecían relativas, libres de la
comparación con el absoluto
las únicas que expresan la realidad
una realidad absoluta
otra realidad
aquélla
una sola realidad
ésta
la que la física positiva
aproximadamente describe
esta realidad
una realidad relativa
esta realidad relativa
la única que hay
la relativa
la realidad verdadera
la realidad absoluta
la realidad es relativa

In the story of the twins paradox, Hawking uses the following referential chain: a pair of twins, one twin (2), the first twin, they, the other, one of the twins, he (3).

TASK SHEET 47. STEPHEN HAWKING

Instructions

In this text, Stephen Hawking explains how Einstein's theory has changed our view of time and space.

Make lists of the referential networks related to the main topics of the text:

1. Pre-1915 theories of physics

2. Einstein's theory

3. The universe: space and time

STEPHEN HAWKING

A Brief History of Time

Another prediction of general relativity is that time should appear to run slower near a massive body like the earth. This is because there is a relation between the energy of light and its frequency (that is the number of waves of light per second); the greater the energy, the higher the frequency. As light travels upward in the earth's gravitational field, it loses energy, and so its frequency goes down (This means that the distance between one wave crest and the next goes up). . . .

Newton's laws of motion put an end to the idea of absolute position in space. The theory of relativity gets rid of absolute time. Consider a pair of twins. Suppose that one twin goes to live on the top of a mountain while the other stays at sea level. The first twin would age faster than the second. Thus, if they met again, one would be older than the other. In this case the difference in ages would be very small, but it would be much larger if one of the twins went for a long trip in a spaceship at the speed of light. When he returned, he would be much younger than if he stayed on Earth. This is known as the twins paradox, but it is a paradox only if one has the idea of absolute time at the back of one's mind. In the theory of relativity there is no unique absolute time, but instead each individual has his own personal measure of time that depends on where he is and how he is moving.

Before 1915, space and time were thought of as a fixed arena in which events took place, but which was not affected by what happened in it. It was natural to think that space and time went on forever.

The situation, however, is quite different in the general theory of relativity. Space and time are now dynamic quantities: when a body moves, or a force acts, it affects the curvature of space and time—and in turn the structure of space-time affects the way in which bodies move and forces act. Space and time not only affect but are affected by everything that happens in the universe. Just as one cannot talk about events in the universe without the notions of space and time, so in general relativity it becomes meaningless to talk about space and time outside the limits of the universe.

In the following decades this new understanding of space and time was to revolutionize our view of the universe. The old idea of an essentially unchanging universe that could have existed, and could continue to exist, forever was replaced by the notion of a dynamic, expanding universe that seemed to have begun a finite time ago, and that might end at a finite time in the future. That revolution forms the subject of the next chapter. And years later, it was also to be the starting point for my work in theoretical physics. Roger Penrose and I showed that Einstein's general theory of relativity implied that the universe must have a beginning and, possibly, an end.

Stephen Hawking, *A Brief History of Time* (1988: 35)

TASK SHEET 48. *ORTEGA Y GASSET*

Instructions

In this text, Ortega y Gasset compares the concept of relativity in space, time, and movement in classical theories (represented by Galileo and Newton) with the concept of relativity in Einstein's theory of relativity.

1. Trace and list all references in the text to (a) the classical theories, (b) Einstein's theory, (c) space and time.

2. Compare the results with the reference system to the same concepts in the text by Stephen Hawking.

3. The text by Ortega y Gasset is going to be included in an undergraduate textbook on the history of science. Summarize the main idea of the text in one sentence.

4. Translate the text into English. Your first priority is to make the text as easy to understand as possible. Pay attention to the way you refer to the key concepts used in the text.

ORTEGA Y GASSET

El sentido histórico de la teoría de Einstein

La mecánica clásica reconoce igualmente la relatividad de todas nuestras determinaciones sobre el movimiento, por lo tanto, de toda posición en el espacio y en el tiempo que sea observable por nosotros. ¿Cómo la teoría de Einstein, que según oímos, trastorna todo el clásico edificio de la mecánica, destaca en su nombre propio, como su mayor característica, la relatividad? Este es el multiforme equívoco que conviene, ante todo deshacer. El relativismo de Einstein es estrictamente inverso al de Galileo y Newton. Para éstos, las determinaciones empíricas de duración, colocación y movimiento son relativas porque creen la existencia de un espacio, un tiempo y un movimiento absolutos. Nosotros no podemos llegar a éstos; a lo sumo, tenemos de ellos noticias indirectas (por ejemplo las fuerzas centrífugas). Pero si se cree en su existencia, todas las determinaciones que efectivamente poseemos quedarán descalificadas como meras apariencias, como valores relativos al punto de comparación que el observador ocupa. Relativismo aquí significa un defecto. La física de Galileo y Newton, diremos es relativa.

Supongamos que, por unas u otras razones, alguien cree forzoso negar la existencia de esos inasequibles absolutos en el espacio, el tiempo y la transferencia. En el mismo instante, las determinaciones concretas, que antes parecían relativas en el mal sentido de la palabra, libres de la comparación con el absoluto, se convierten en las únicas que expresan la realidad. No habrá ya una realidad absoluta (inasequible) y otra relativa en comparación con aquélla. Habrá una sola realidad, y ésta será la que la física positiva aproximadamente describe. Ahora bien: esta realidad es la que el observador percibe desde el lugar que ocupa; por tanto, una realidad relativa. Pero como esta realidad relativa, en el supuesto que hemos tomado, es la única que hay, resultará, a la vez que la relativa, la realidad verdadera, o, lo que es igual, la realidad absoluta. Relativismo aquí no se opone a absolutismo; al contrario, se funde con éste, y lejos de sugerir un defecto de nuestro conocimiento, le otorga una validez absoluta.

Tal es el caso de la mecánica de Einstein. Su física no es relativa, sino relativista, y merced a su relativismo consigue una significación absoluta. Para la física de Einstein, nuestro conocimiento es absoluto; la realidad es relativa.

José Ortega y Gasset, "El sentido histórico de la teoría de Einstein," *Obras completas*, Revista de Occidente, Madrid, 1947, vol. 3, 231–42.

BIBLIOGRAPHY

Allen, B. (1974). *English for the Commerce Student.* London: J.M. Dent and Sons Ltd.

Arntz, R. (1982). "Methoden der Fachsprachlichen Übersetzeraus-bildung im Sprachenpaar Spanisch-Deutsch." In R. Rodríguez, G. Thome, and W. Wilss (eds.), *Fremdsprachenforschung und-lehre. Schwerpunkt Spanisch.* Tübingen: Gunter Narr.

Austin, J.L. (1962). *How to Do Things with Words.* Cambridge, MA: Harvard University Press.

Ayala, F. (1972). *Problemas de la Traducción.* Barcelona: Cuadernos Taurus.

Bachrach, J.A. (1974). "An Experiment in Automatic Dictionary Look-up." *Incorporated Linguist* 13 (2): 47–49.

Baker, M. (1992). *In Other Words: A Coursebook on Translation.* London and New York: Routledge.

Barbizet, J. (1979). "Vouloir dire, intonation et structure des phrases." *Folia Linguistica* 13 (3–4): 237–45.

Barbizet, J., J. Duizabo, and R. Flavigny (1975). "Rôle des lobes frontaux dans le langage." *Revue Neurologie* (Paris): 525–44.

Barbizet, J., M. Pergnier, and D. Seleskovitch (eds.) (1981). *Comprendre le langage.* Paris: Didier Érudition (Coll. Linguistique, 12).

Bar-Hillel, Y. (1967). "Dictionaries and Meaning-Rules." *Foundations of Language* 3/4: 409–14.

Barthes, R. (1975). *S/Z.* Paris: Seuil.

Bassnett-McGuire, S. (1980). *Translation Studies.* London and New York: Methuen.

Bathgate, R.H. (1984). "Teaching Translation Students to Think about Science." *Incorporated Linguist* 23 (4): 228–32.

Bell, R.T. (1991). *Translation and Translating.* London: Longman.

Benson, M., E. Benson, and R. Ilson (eds.) (1986). *The BBI Combinatory Dictionary of English.* Amsterdam/Philadelphia: John Benjamins.

——— (1992). *Using the BBI Combinatory Dictionary of English*. Amsterdam/Philadelphia: John Benjamins.

Berk-Seligson, S. (1988). "The Impact of Politeness in Witness Testimony: The Influence of the Court Interpreter." *Multilingua* 7: 411–39.

The Bible (1611). King James Version.

Bloomfield, L. (1933). *Language*. New York: Holt.

Bowen, D. (1985). *The Intercultural Component in Interpreting and Translation Training: A Historical Survey*. Ann Arbor: UMI Dissertation Information Service.

Brinton, E., et al. (1981). *Translation Strategies*. London: Macmillan.

Brislin, R.W. (1976). *Translation*. New York: Gardner.

Brook, G.L. (1955). *An Introduction to Old English*. Manchester: Manchester University Press.

Brown, G., and G.Yule (1983). *Discourse Analysis*. Cambridge: Cambridge University Press.

Butler, P. (1991). *The Economist Style Guide*. London: The Economist Books Ltd.

Capra, F. (1976). *The Tao of Physics*. Fontana/Collins.

Cary, G.V. (1977). *Mind the Stop!* Harmondsworth: Penguin.

Castellano, L. (1988). "Get Rich—but Slow." In C. Picken (ed.), *ITI Conference 2: Translators and Interpreters Mean Business*, p. 133. London: ASLIB.

Catford, J.C. (1965). *A Linguistic Theory of Translation*. Oxford: Oxford University Press.

Charolles, M. (1983). "Coherence as a Principle in the Interpretation of Discourse." *Text* 3(1): 71–97.

Cicero (1959). *De optimo genere oratorum*. Loeb Classical Library. Translated by H.M. Hubbell. London: Heinemann.

Clyne, M. (1981). "Culture and Discourse Structure." *Journal of Pragmatics* 5: 61–62.

——— (1983). "Linguistics and Written Discourse in Particular Languages: Contrastive Studies: English and German." In R.B. Kaplan, R.L. Jones, and G.R. Tucker (eds.), *Annual Review of Applied Linguistics*, pp. 38–49. Rawley, MA: Newbury House.

Coseriu, E. (1977). *El hombre y su lenguaje*. Madrid: Editorial Gredos.

Coulthard, M. (1985). *An Introduction to Discourse Analysis*. Harlow: Longman.

Crystal, D., and D. Davy (1969). *Investigating English Style*. London: Longman.

De Beaugrande, R. (1978). *Factors in a Theory of Poetic Translating*. Assen: Van Gorcum.

De Beaugrande, R., and Dressler W. (1981). *Introduction to Text-linguistics*. London: Longman.

Delisle, J. (1980). *L'Analyse du discours comme méthode de traduction*. Ottawa: University of Ottawa Press.

——— (1981). "De la théorie à la pédagogie: réflexions méthodologiques." In J. Delisle (ed.), *L'enseignement de l'interprétation et de la traduction: de la théorie à la pédagogie*, pp. 135–151. Ottawa: University of Ottawa Press.

Delisle, J., and J. Woodsworth (eds.) (1993). *Translators through History*. Amsterdam/Paris: John Benjamins/UNESCO. Also published in French: *Les Traducteurs dans l'histoire*. Ottawa/Paris: Les Presses de l'Université d'Ottawa/UNESCO.

De Saussure, F. (1916). *Cours de linguistique générale*. Paris: Payot.

Dios habla al hombre. Madrid: Sociedad Bíblica, 1976.

Dudley-Evans, T., and W. Henderson (eds.) (1990). *The Language of Economics: The Analysis of Economics Discourse*. ELT Document 134, Modern English Publications, in association with the British Council.

Duff, A. (1981). *The Third Language*. Oxford: Pergamon Press.

——— (1989). *Translation*. Oxford: Oxford University Press.

Eco, U. (1977). *Tratado de semiótica general*. Barcelona: Editorial Lumen.

Etkind, E. (1982). *Un art en crise. Essai de poétique de la traduction poétique*. Translated by W. Troubetskoy. Lausanne: L'Âge d'homme.

Fernández Ordoñez, F. (1992). "El galope de la historia." In R. Tamames, *Anuario de El País*, p. 13. Madrid: Ediciones El País.

Fisher, J. "Factors Influencing the Design of Syllabi and Support Materials for Non-native Speakers Studying Economics." In T. Dudley-Evans and W. Henderson (eds.) (1990), *The Language of Economics: The Analysis of Economics Discourse*, p. 86. ELT Document 134, Modern English Publications, in association with the British Council.

Fowler, R. (1977). "Cohesive, Progressive and Localising Aspects of Text Structures." In T.A.van Dijk and J.S. Petöfi (eds.), *Grammars and Descriptions*, pp. 64–84. Berlin: William de Gruyter.

——— (1986). "Power." In T. van Dijk (ed.), *Handbook of Discourse Analysis*. Vol. 4, pp. 61–82. London: Academic Press.

Galisson, R. (1980). *D'hier à aujourdhui, la didactique générale des langues étrangères, du structuralisme au fonctionalisme*. Paris: CLE International.

Galisson, R., and D. Costa (1976). *Dictionnaire de didactique des langues*. Paris: Hachette.

Garcia Yebra, V. (1983). *Teoría y práctica de la traducción*. Madrid: Editorial Gredos.

Gombrich, E.H. (1969). *The Story of Art*. New York: Phaidon.

——— (1977). *Art and Illusion*. London: Phaidon.

——— (1978). *Meditations on a Hobby Horse*. London: Phaidon.

Good News Bible. New York: American Bible Society, 1976.

Gregory, M.J. (1967). "Aspects of Varieties Differentiation." *Journal of Linguistics* 3: 177–98.

Gregory, M., and S. Carrol (1978). *Language and Situation: Language Varieties and their Social Contexts*. London: Routledge & Kegan Paul.

Grellet, F. (1991). *Apprendre à traduire: Typologie d'exercices de traduction*. Nancy: Presses Universitaires de Nancy.

Grice, H.P. (1975). "Logic and conversation." In A.P. Martinque (ed.), *The Philosophy of Language*, pp. 159–70. Oxford: Oxford University Press.

Gumperz, J.J. (1982). *Discourse Strategies*. Cambridge: Cambridge University Press.

Gutt, E.-A. (1991). *Translation and Relevance: Cognition and Context*. Oxford: Basil Blackwell.

Halliday, M.A.K. (1973). *Explorations in the Functions of Language*. London: Edward Arnold.

——— (1985). *An Introduction to Functional Grammar*. London: Edward Arnold.

Halliday, M.A.K., and R. Hasan (1976). *Cohesion in English*. London: Longman.

Hatim, B. (1983). "Discourse/Text Linguistics in the Training of Interpreters." In W. Wilss and G. Thome (eds.), *Translation Theory and Its Implementation in the Training of Translation and Interpreting*. Tübingen: Gunter Narr.

——— (1990). "The Status of the Paragraph in Translation: Negotiating Rhetorical Purpose in Texts." *Nouvelles de la Newsletter* : Nouvelle série IX, 120–40.

——— (1991). "Intertextuality and Idiolect as Intended Meaning; A Concern for Both Translator and Literary Critic Alike: with Special Reference to Arabic." *Parallèles* 12: 77–88.

——— (1992). Seminar: Faculty of Translators and Interpreters, Universidad Autónoma de Barcelona (April).

Hatim, B., and I. Mason (1990). *Discourse Analysis and the Translator*. London: Longman.

Hervey, S., and I. Higgins (1992). *Thinking Translation*. London: Routledge.

Hewson, L., and J. Martin (1991). *Redefining Translation: A Variational Approach*. London: Routledge.

Hoey, C. (1983). *On the Surface of Discourse*. London: George Allen and Unwin.

——— (1984). "The Clustering of Lexical Cohesion in Non-narrative Text." *Trondheim Papers in Applied Linguistics* 4, 154–80.

Hönig, H., and P. Kussmaul (1984). *Strategie der Übersetzung*. Tübingen: Gunter Narr.

House, J. (1977). *A Model for Translation Quality Assessment*. Tübingen: Gunter Narr.

Hurtado Albir, A. (1988). "Hacia un enfoque comunicativo de la traducción." *Actas II Jornadas Internacionales de Didáctica del español como Lengua Extranjera*. Madrid: Ministerio de Cultura.

—— (1990a). "La fidélité au sens, un nouvel horizon pour la traductologie." In M. Lederer (ed.), *Études traductologiques*, pp. 75–86. Paris: Minard.

—— (1990b). *La notion de fidélité en traduction*. Paris: Didier Érudition.

—— (1992). "Didactique de la traduction des textes spécialisés." *Actes de la 3ᵉ journée ERLA-GLAT.* Brest: UBO-ERNST de Bretagne.

—— (1994a). "Un nuevo enfoque de la traducción en la didáctica de las lenguas." *Actas III Congreso Internacional Expolingua*, pp. 67–89. Madrid: Fundación Actilibre.

—— (1994b). *Estudis sobre la traducció.* Castelló: Publicacions de la Universitat Jaume I.

—— (1995). "La didáctica de la traducción. Evolución y estado actual." In P. Fernández and J.M. Bravo (eds.), *Perspectivas de la traducción*, pp. 49–74. Valladolid: Universidad de Valladolid.

Jakobson, R. (1959). *On Translation.* Cambridge, MA: Harvard University Press.

—— (1963). *Essais de linguistique générale.* Paris: les Éditions de Minuit.

—— (1971). "Language in Relation to Other Communication Systems." In R. Jakobson, *Selected Writings.* Vol. 2, pp. 697–710. The Hague: Mouton.

Jacobvits, L. (1970). *Foreign Language Teaching and Foreign Language Learning.* Rowley, MA: Newbury House.

Johnson, S. (1755). *A Dictionary of the English Language.* London: Knapton.

Joseph, J.E., and T.J. Taylor (1990). *Ideologies of Language.* London and New York: Routledge.

Katz, J.J. (1977). *Propositional Structure and Illocutionary Force: A Study of the Contribution of Sentence Meaning to Speech Acts.* New York: Harvester.

Keith, H. (1989). "The Training of Interpreters." In C. Picken (ed.), *The Translsator's Handbook*, pp. 163–74. London: ASLIB.

Keith, H., and I. Mason (eds.) (1989). *Translation in the Modern Languages Degree.* London: CILT.

Kelly, L.G. (1979). *The True Interpreter.* Oxford: Blackwell.

Kristeva, J. (1970). *Le texte du roman.* The Hague and Paris: Mouton.

Ladmiral, J.R. (1979). *Traduire, théorèmes pour la traduction.* Paris: Petite Bibliothèque Payot.

La Forge, P.G. (1979). "Reflection in the Context of Community Language Learning." *English Language Training Journal* 33 (4): 247–54.

Lakoff, G., and M. Johnson (1980). *Metaphors We Live By.* Chicago: University of Chicago Press.

Lakoff, R. (1971). "If's, And's and But's about Conjunctions." In C. Filmore and D.T. Langendoen, *Studies in Linguistic Semantics*, pp. 115–50. New York: Holt, Rinehart and Winston.

Larsen, M.L. (1984). *Meaning-based Translation: A Guide to Cross-Language Equivalence*. Larham: University Press of America.

Lavault, E. (1985). *Fonctions de la traduction en didactique des langues*. Paris: Didier Érudition.

Lederer, M. (1973). "La traduction: transcoder ou réexprimer." *Études de linguistique appliquée* 12: 8–25.

——— (1976). "Synecdoque et traduction." *Études de linguistique appliquée* 24: 13–41.

——— (1981). *La traduction simultanée*. Paris: Minard.

——— (1986). "La traduction simultanée, un poste d'observation du langage." In D. Seleskovitch and M. Lederer (eds.), *Interpréter pour traduire*, pp. 245–55. Paris: Didier.

Lederer, M., M. Pergnier, and D. Seleskovitch (eds.) (1978). "Vouloir dire, intonation et structure des phrases." Paper presented to 11th Congress of Societas Linguistica Europaea. The Hague: Mouton.

Leech, G. (1974). *Semantics: The Study of Meaning*. Harmondsworth: Penguin.

Leech, G., and J. Svartvik (1975). *A Communicative Grammar of English*. Harlow: Longman.

Lehrer, A. (1974). *Semantic Fields and Lexical Structure*. Amsterdam and London: North Holland.

Lodge, D. (1988). *Nice Work*. Harmondsworth: Penguin.

Lorenzo, E. (1971). *El español de hoy, lengua en ebullición*. Madrid: Editorial Gredos.

Lyons, J. (1977). *Semantics*. Cambridge: Cambridge University Press.

——— (1989). *Introduction to Theoretical Linguistics*. Cambridge: Cambridge University Press.

Mackin, R. (1981). "The Treatment of Collocation and Idioms in Learners' Dictionaries." *Applied Linguistics* 2 (3): 223–35.

Malblanc, A. (1961). *Pour une stylistique comparée du français et de l'allemand*. Paris: Didier.

Malinowski, B. (1972). "The Problem of Meaning in Primitive Languages." In C.K. Ogden and I.A. Richards, *The Meaning of Meaning*. 10th ed., pp. 296–336. London: Kegan Paul.

——— (1935). *Coral Gardens and their Magic*. Vol. 2. London: Allen and Unwin.

Mason, I. (1982). "The Role of Translation Theory in the Translation Class." *Quinquereme* 5, 1: 18–33.

Mason, M. (1990). "Dancing on Air." T. Dudley-Evans and W. Henderson (eds.), *The Language of Economics: The Analysis of Economics Discourse*, pp. 16–28. ELT Document 134, Modern English Publications, in association with the British Council.

McCloskey, D.N. (1986). *The Rhetoric of Economics*. Brighton: Wheatsheaf Books Ltd.

———— (1988). "Story Telling in Economics." Project on the Rhetoric of Inquiry. Mimeo. Iowa City: University of Iowa.

Merino, J., and P. Sheerin (1989). *Manual de traducción inversa español-inglés*. Madrid: Editorial Anglo-Didáctica.

Milton, J. (1953). *El paradís perdut*. Translation and notes by J.M. Boix i Selva. Barcelona: Editorial Alpha.

Mounin, G. (1955). *Les belles infidèles*. Paris: Cahiers du Sud.

———— (1963). *Les problèmes théoriques de la traduction*. Paris: Gallimard.

Neubert, A. (1985). *Text and Translation*. Leipzig: VEB Verlag Enzyklopädia.

Neunzig, W., et al. (1985). *Informe del proyecto global en la formación de traductores e interpretes*. Barcelona: Universidad Autónoma de Barcelona.

Newmark, P. (1969). "Some Notes on Translation and Translators." *The Incorporated Linguist* (October): 79–85.

———— (1981). *Approaches to Translation*. Oxford: Pergamon Press.

———— (1987). "The Use of Systemic Linguistics in Translation Analysis and Criticism." In R. Steele and T. Threadgold (eds.), *Language Topics: Essays in Honour of Michael Halliday*. Vol. 1, pp. 293–303. Amsterdam: John Benjamin.

———— (1988). *A Textbook of Translation*. London: Prentice Hall.

———— (1991). *About Translation*. Multilingual Matters 74. Cleveland, Philadelphia, Adelaide: Multilingual Matters Ltd.

Nida, E.A. (1964). *Towards a Science of Translating: With Special Reference to Principles and Procedures Involved in Bible Translating*. Leiden: Brill.

———— (1975a). *Exploring Semantic Structures*. Munich: Willheim Fink.

———— (1975b). *The Componential Analysis of Meaning*. The Hague: Mouton.

———— (1992). Seminar. Faculty of Translators and Interpreters, Universidad Autónoma de Barcelona (November).

Nida, E.A., and W.D. Reyburn (1981). *Meaning across Cultures*. New York: Orbis.

Nida, E.A., and C.R. Taber (1969). *The Theory and Practice of Translation*. Leiden: Brill.

Nirenburg, S. (ed.) (1987). *Machine Translation. Theoretical and Methodological Issues*. Cambridge: Cambridge University Press.

Nord, C. (1988). *Textanalyse und Übersetzen*. Heidelberg: Julius Groos.

———— (1991). *Text Analysis in Translation*. Amsterdam: Editions Rodopi B.V.

Ortega y Gasset, J. (1983). "Miseria y esplendor de la Traducción." In *Obras Completas*. Vol. 5, pp. 431–53. Madrid: Alianza.

Orwell, G. (1984). "Politics and the English Language." In *The Penguin Essays of George Orwell*, pp. 354–65. Harmondsworth: Penguin Books.

Papps, I., and W. Henderson (1977). *Models and Economic Theory.* Philadelphia: W.B. Saunders Co.

Payne, J. (1987). "Revision as a Teaching Method on Translation Courses." In H. Keith and I. Mason (eds.), *Translation in the Modern Languages Degree,* pp. 43–51. London: CILT.

Paz, O. (1990). *Traducción: literatura y literalidad.* Barcelona: Tusquets.

Picken, C. (ed.) (1989). *The Translator's Handbook.* London: ASLIB.

Pierce, C. (1931–58). *Collected Papers.* Edited by C. Hartshone. Cambridge, MA: Harvard University Press.

Plácido, Domingo (1989). "Introducción." In *HELENICAS de Jenofonte.* Translated by Domingo Plácido. Madrid: Alianza.

Pratt, C. (1980). *El anglicismo en el español peninsular contemporaneo.* Madrid: Editorial Gredos.

Pym, A. (1992). "In Search of a New Rationale for the Prose Translation Class at University Level." *Interface* 6 (2): 73–82.

Quirk, R., and S. Greenbaum (1973). *A University Grammar of English.* Harlow: Longman.

Rabadan, R. (1991). *Traducción y equivalencia.* León: Universidad de León.

Reiss, K. (1971). *Möglichkeiten und Grenzen der Übersetzungskritik.* Munich: Max Heuber.

——— (1976). *Texttyp und Übersetzungsmethode. Der Operative Text.* Kronberg: Scriptor.

——— (1981). "Type, Kind and Individuality of Text: Decision Making in Translation." In I. Even-Zohar and G. Toury (eds.), "Translation theory and inter-cultural relations." Special issue of *Poetics Today* 2 (4): 121–31.

Reiss, K., and H.J. Vermeer (1984). *Grundlagen einer allgemeinen Translationtheorie.* Tübingen: Gunter Narr.

Rivers, W.M. (1972). "Contrastive Linguistics in Textbook and Classroom." In W.M. Rivers, *Speaking in Many Tongues: Essays in Foreign Language Teaching,* pp. 64–72. Rowley, MA: Newbury House.

Rivers, W.M., and M. Temperley (1978). *A Practical Guide to the Teaching of English as a Foreign Language.* New York: Oxford University Press.

Sapir, E. (1921). *Language.* New York: Harcourt Brace (reprint, Harvest Books, 1949).

Searle, J.R. (1969). *Speech Acts.* Cambridge: Cambridge University Press.

Seleskovitch, D. (1968). *L'interprète dans les conférences internationales. Problèmes de langage et de communication.* Paris: Minard.

——— (1975). *Langage, langues et mémoires. Étude de la prise de notes en consécutive.* Paris: Minard.

———— (1976). "Traduire: de l'expérience aux conceptions." *Études de linguistique appliquée* 24: 64–91.

———— (1980). "Préface." In J. Delisle, *L'Analyse du discours comme méthode de traduction*. Ottawa: University of Ottawa Press.

Seleskovitch, D., and M. Lederer (1986). *Interpréter pour traduire*. Paris: Didier.

Sinclair, J. (1986). "Fictional Worlds." In M. Coulthard (ed.), *Talking about Text*, pp. 43–60. Discourse Analysis Monograph 13. Birmingham: English Language Research.

———— (1987). "Introduction," In J. Sinclair (ed.), *Collins Cobuild Dictionary*. London: Collins.

Skinner, B.F. (1957). *Verbal Behaviour*. Englewood Cliffs: Prentice Hall.

Snell-Hornby, M. (1988). *Translation Studies: An Integrated Approach*. Amsterdam and Philadelphia: John Benjamins.

Sperber, D., and D. Wilson (1986). *Relevance: Communication and Cognition*. Oxford: Basil Blackwell.

Steiner, G. (1975). *After Babel: Aspects of Language and Translation*. Oxford: Oxford University Press.

Steiner, T.R. (1975). *English Translation Theory, 1650–1800*. Assen: Van Gorcum.

Stubbs, M. (1983). *Discourse Analysis: The Sociolinguistic Analysis of Natural Language*. Oxford: Basil Blackwell.

Swan, M. (1980). *Practical English Usage*. Oxford: Oxford University Press.

Sweet, H. (1964). *The Practical Study of Languages*. Oxford: Oxford University Press. (First published 1899.)

Tamames, R. (1970). *Estructura económica internacional*. Madrid: Alianza.

———— (1980). *Estructura económica internacional*. 6th ed. Madrid: Alianza.

———— (1991). *Un nuevo orden mundial*. Madrid: Espasa-Calpe.

Tamames, R. (ed.) (1987). *Anuario de El País*. Madrid: Ediciones El País.

———— (1992). *Anuario de El País*. Madrid: Ediciones El País.

Thomson, G. (1982). "An Introduction to Implicature for Translators." *Notes on Translation* 1. Special edition.

Tucker, A. (1987). "Current Strategies in Machine Translation." In S. Nirenberg (ed.), *Machine Translation. Theoretical and Methodological Issues*, pp. 22–41. Cambridge: Cambridge University Press.

Tytler, A.F. (1907). *Essay on the Principles of Translation*. Reprint. London: Dent.

van Dijk, T.A. (1972). *Some Aspects of Text Grammars*. The Hague: Mouton.

———— (1980). *Text and Context*. The Hague: Mouton.

Vázquez Ayora, G. (1977). *Introducción a la traductología*. Washington, DC: Georgetown University Press.

Venuti, L. (1992). *Rethinking Translation*. London: Routledge.

Vermeer, H.J. (1983). *Aufsätze zur Translationstheorie*. Heidelberg: Julius Groos.

Vide, C., M. Martí, and S. Serrano (1992). "Pensando la mente." *La Vanguardia* 14 November.

Vinay, J.-P. and J. Darbelnet (1958). *Stylistique comparée du français et de l'anglais: Méthode de traduction*. Paris: Didier.

Waterfield, Robin (1990). "Introduction." *Xenophon: Conversations of Socrates*. Translated by Hugh Tredennick and Robin Waterfield. Penguin Classics.

Weymouth, A.G. (1984). "A Learner-Centred Approach to Translation at the Post 'A' Level Stage." *The Incorporated Linguist* 23(3).

Whorf, B.L. (1958). *Language, Thought and Reality*. Edited by J.B. Carrol. Cambridge, MA: MIT Press.

Widdowson, H.G. (1973). "Directions in the Teaching of Discourse." In S.P. Corder and E. Roulet (eds.), *Theoretical Linguistic Models in Applied Linguistics*. Paris: Didier.

——— (1974). "The Deep Structures of Discourse and Translation." In S.P. Corder and E. Roulet (eds.), *Linguistic Insights in Applied Linguistics*. Paris: Didier.

——— (1979). *Explorations in Applied Linguistics*. Oxford: Oxford University Press.

Wilss, W. (1982). *The Science of Translation: Problems and Methods*. Tübingen: Gunter Narr.

Zabaleascoa, Patrick (1993). "Developing Translation Studies to Better Account for Audiovisual Texts and Other New Forms of Text Production." Ph.D. dissertation. Universitat Autónoma de Barcelona.

APPENDIX

SELECTED STRUCTURAL CONTRASTS
AND GUIDED BIBLIOGRAPHY

1. PREPOSITIONS

The correct use of prepositions is a recurrent problem when translating from Spanish to English, and it seems to be an area in which translation interference from the SL is difficult to avoid.

> The relationship expressed by prepositions seems to be clustered in bundles, with similar bundles across language barriers the exception rather than the rule. To aggravate the situation, since the meanings are usually abstract relationships, a student relies heavily on translation to learn how to use prepositions. Nowhere is the student's desire to find a one-to-one correspondence between native and target language more thoroughly frustrated. (Stockwell et al., 1965: 207)

Prepositional meaning is a lexical problem, but incorrect use of prepositions also occasions grammatical problems of co-occurrence with other forms. However, grammatical descriptions are so complex as to provide little aid, and each case has to be learned separately according to the context. Prepositional verbs, prepositional phrases, and phrasal verbs have to be treated lexically, as words to be learned individually.

Bibliography: Prepositions and prepositional phrases (place relations, time relations, other relations as adjunct, as disjunct, as complementation of verb or adjective)

Duff, A. (1981). *The Third Language*. London: Pergamon. See pp. 39–41, 55, 72–73, 97.

García Yebra, V. (1983). *En torno a la traducción*. Madrid: Gredos. See pp. 44, 121–22.

Luque Durán, O.D. (1973). *Las preposiciones*. Madrid: SGEL.

Mott, B., and M.P. García Fernández (1992). *La composición escrita en inglés.* Barcelona: Publicacions Universitat de Barcelona. See pp. 169–89.

Pottier, B. (1968). "Espacio y tiempo en el sistema de las preposiciones." *Lingüística moderna y filología hispánica.* Madrid: Gredos.

Quirk, R., and S. Greenbaum (1980). *A University Grammar of English.* London: Longman. See pp. 143–65.

Rivas, D.J. (1981). *Prepositions in Spanish and English.* Montevideo: Géminis.

Stockwell, R., et al. (1965). *The Grammatical Structures of English.* Chicago: University of Chicago Press. See pp. 207–14, 222–30, 288–89.

2. Determiners

This is another area that causes problems, but here the two languages can be contrasted to some purpose. The students should be shown the relationship between countable and uncountable nouns in English and the use of the article so as to avoid mistakes with nouns like *job* and *work*. Vázquez Ayora (1977: 4.2.3.) suggests that the Spanish tendency to intellectualize or conceptualize explains the use of the definite article in Spanish to generalize, whereas in English the zero morpheme or the indefinite article is used.

> El poeta debe poseer talento.   A poet has to have talent.
>
> El talento no se puede comprar.   Talent cannot be bought.

The English preference for the possessive pronoun where Spanish uses the definite article should be stressed. Almost any English text will provide examples.

> A girl went from table to table ridding herself of <u>her</u> clothes. She began with <u>her</u> gloves. . . . Then she presented <u>her</u> back to Carter and told him to unhook <u>her</u> back lace corsets. Carter fumbled in vain at the catches, blushing all the time, while the girl laughed and wriggled against <u>his</u> fingers. (Graham Greene, *Our Man in Havana* [Harmondsworth: Penguin, 1983], p. 200)

The demonstratives *este* and *ese* often cause problems because students are usually taught *este* is *this* and *ese* is *that*. However the deictic use of *this* is very common in English and *ese* should often be translated as *this* if it is referring to something that has been introduced earlier in the text. For example, in an article about letter bombs sent to the Queen of England (in *Hola*), a new paragraph begins: *Esas misivas*, but the English translation should be *These letters*. There is a very good section in Delisle (1980: 195) on the use of the deictic *this* in English. *This* is certainly very widely used to link ideas between sentences and paragraphs and also in situations where an adverb or pronoun is used in Spanish.

> Aquí Radio Barcelona.   This is the BBC World Service.
>
> Había insistido en ello.   He insisted on this.

Bibliography: Determiners

Abad Nebot, F. (1977). *El artículo. Sistema y usos*. Madrid: SGEL.

Delisle, J. (1980). *L'Analyse du discours comme méthode de traduction*. Ottawa: University of Ottawa Press. See pp. 195–204.

Klein, V. (1976). "Same versus Different Cross-linguistically: The Articles in Spanish and English." In *Papers from the 12th Regional Meeting*. Chicago Linguistic Society.

Mott, B., and M.P. García Fernández (1992). *La composición escrita in inglés*. Barcelona: Universitat de Barcelona. See pp. 67–79.

Quirk, R., and S. Greenbaum (1980). *A University Grammar of English*. London: Longman. See pp. 59–113, 375–405.

Sommerstein, A.H. (1972). "On the So-called Definite Article in English." *Linguistic Enquiry* 3: 2.

Stockwell, R., et al. (1965). *The Grammatical Structures of Spanish and English*. Chicago: University of Chicago Press. See pp. 65–104.

Vázquez Ayora, G. (1977). *Introducción a la traductología*. Washington, DC: Georgetown University Press. See sections 4.2.3.–4.

3. PRONOUNS

Confusion of reference due to careless use of pronouns is one of the dangers of writing in English that is not confined to the non-native speaker.

> How far the pupil will go is not the concern of the teacher and master. Hardly has he shown him the right way than he must let him go on alone. There is only one thing more he can do to help him endure his loneliness: *he* turns *him* away further from *himself*, by exhorting *him* to go further than *he himself* has done. (Herrigel, *Zen in the Art of Archery* [London: Routledge, 1977], quoted in Duff, 1981: 34; emphasis in Duff)

The students are warned to be especially careful whenever they use *it, they, them, that,* or *which*. However ungainly repetition is considered in Spanish, they should not avoid repetition for aesthetic reasons when translating into English. Clarity of reference should have priority. Part of the problem is that the students are used to the greater precision of Spanish pronouns. There are fifteen Spanish forms for the English pronoun *you*. *Su* is an exception in Spanish because it has four possible translations in English: *his, her, its,* or *your*.

The distinction between *whose* and *of which* does not usually pose difficulties. The same distinction between the Saxon genitive and *of* is also understood, but students should be reminded that confusion of reference may arise from use of the Saxon genitive.

It is primarily the director's fault, who clearly has . . .

It is primarily the fault of the director, who . . .

The more basic uses of the pronoun in English are fairly easily assimilated by *inversa* students, for example *lo*, which is often omitted in English.

Mi madre me lo dijo.	My mother told me.

Lo + adjective does occasionally cause problems, although it is really a problem of nominalization.

Lo interesante del caso . . .	What is interesting about the case . . .

Bibliography: Pronouns (personal, possessive, demonstrative, relative)

Brinton, E., et al. (1981). *Translation Strategies*. London: Macmillan Press. See p. 179.

Duff, A. (1981). *The Third Language*. Oxford: Pergamon. See p. 38.

Huddleston, R. (1969). "Some Observations on Tense and Deixis in English." In *Language 45*, 4. See pp. 777–806.

Quirk, R., and S. Greenbaum (1980). *A University Grammar of English*. London: Longman. See pp. 100–14.

Stockwell, R., et al. (1965). *The Grammatical Structures of English and Spanish*. Chicago: University of Chicago Press. See pp. 51–3.

Vázquez Ayora, G. (1977). *Introducción a la Traductología*. Washington, DC: Georgetown University Press. See section 4.2.2.

4. ADJECTIVES

Word order in the noun phrase can cause problems. However, mistakes often arise from having learned the differences too well, which leads to overconfident use of premodification and nouns used as adjectives. For example:

The UN Charter spirit

los diarios hablaban lacónicamente de millones de toneladas de café arrojadas al mar, de trigo quemado, cerdos quemados, naranjas rociadas con keroseno para facilitar las condiciones del mercado.	the newspapers spoke laconically about millions of tons of coffee thrown into the sea, about *burnt wheat* and *cremated pigs*, about oranges sprinkled with kerosene in order to ease market conditions.

Special attention should be paid to the distinction in meaning between adjectival premodification and postmodification in Spanish. For example, *mismo* is particularly tricky.

Que la misma noche que Jesús fue traicionado . . .

The same night he was betrayed . . .

Llegó hasta el mismísimo dormitorio de la soberana.

He got as far as the Queen's very own bedroom.

La reina misma abrió la puerta.

The Queen herself opened the door.

Bibliography: Adjectives (word order and position of adjectives)

Bolinger, D. (1967). "Adjectives in English: Attribution and Prediction." *Lingua 18*: 1–34.

Brinton, E., et al. (1981). *Translation Strategies*. London: Macmillan Press. See pp. 176–9.

Crystal, D. (1971). *Linguistics*. Harmondsworth: Penguin.

Gooch, A. (1967). *Diminutive, Argumentative and Perjorative Suffixes in Modern Spanish*. London: Pergamon.

Mott, B., and M.P. García Fernández (1992). *La composición escrita en inglés*. Barcelona: Universitat de Barcelona. See pp. 83–101.

Quirk, R., and S. Greenbaum (1980). *A University Grammar of English*. London: Longman. See pp. 59–113.

5. NOUNS

Vázquez Ayora (1977: 4.2.6.) warns translators into Spanish of the dangers of *el abuso del sustantivo* when translating from English. *El abuso del verbo* in English is not really a problem in *inversa*. On the contrary, the students tend to use nouns and adjectives with greater flair and precision than they do verbs, and they have to be encouraged to develop the use of a greater variety of verbs expressing opinion, feeling, and movement, and of strong verbs with high semantic content. Grammatical nominalization of other parts of speech is easier in Spanish than in English, and this may cause problems.

el otro	the other one
lo mío	mine
la del pelo largo	the one with long hair

English can only nominalize adjectives to refer to a group of people belonging to a certain category.

¡El pobre!	The poor thing!
Los pobres	The poor
Lo malo es . . .	Unfortunately . . .

Furthermore, in the case of *the poor, the sick, the lonely,* and so on, the adjective is not fully nominalized, as it cannot take the plural morpheme. Mistakes are also made with nouns that are singular or uncountable in one language and plural in the other. Even quite advanced students still err with *news* and *people,* particularly when they are combined with the problem of agreement in the noun phrase.

This sort of news

These kinds of people

This type of advice

Bibliography: Noun phrases (word order and position of adjectives, articles, possessives, use and positions of adverbs, countables and uncountables, explicit subject and repetition of the NP, anaphoric NP)

Bach, E. (1968). "Nouns and Noun Phrases." In E. Bach and R. Harms, *Universals in Linguistic Theory.* New York: Holt, Rinehart and Winston. See pp. 91–124.

McArthur, T. (1975). *An Introduction to English Word Formation.* Harlow: Longman.

——— (1972). *Using English Prefixes and Suffixes.* London: Collins.

——— (1972). *Using Compound Words.* London: Collins.

Mott, B., and M.P. García Fernández (1992). *La composición escrita en inglés.* Barcelona: Universitat de Barcelona. See pp. 67–79.

Quirk, R., and S. Greenbaum (1980). *A University Grammar of English.* London: Longman. See pp. 59–113, 375–405.

Stockwell, R., et al. (1965). *The Grammatical Structures of Spanish and English.* Chicago: University of Chicago Press. See pp. 65–104.

Vázquez Ayora, G. (1977). *Introducción a la traductología.* Washington, DC: Georgetown University Press. See sections 4.2.3–4.

6. VERBS

a) Tense

Stockwell gives a form-to-form comparison of English and Spanish verb forms, but then goes on to say, "The preceding examples illustrate a basic fact of language comparison: differences between languages cannot be accurately and clearly established through translation alone" (Stockwell et al., 1965: 130).

It is essential for students to learn how to use the English tense system in context in a monolingual situation. If they make mistakes when translating due to interference from the SL, they must go back to an intermediate cognitive stage and work out the time references in the TL. The examples given by Brinton et al. (1981: 202) show how important context is in deciding which tense to use in English.

SPANISH	ENGLISH

SPANISH

Present tense

En un clima de tensión que se agrava cada minuto viven los 18.000 habitantes.

Y nada sale en la prensa de toda la Unión Soviética sin que él lo lea.

Regalan primero el álbum y luego venden cromos.

Llevo tres días intentando hablarle.

ENGLISH

Present continuous

The 18,000 inhabitants are living in an atmosphere of constantly mounting tension.

Present perfect

Nothing is published in all the Soviet press unless he has read it.

Present simple

First they give away the album and then they sell the stamps.

Present perfect continuous

I have been trying to talk to him for three days.

Imperfect tense

Conforme me alejaba de las últimas calles del pueblo y entraba en las más concurridas, que conducían a la plaza, me sentía alegre.

Un incidente estuvo a un paso de originar un estallido cuando se pagaban salarios atrasados.

visitaba Madrid con bastante frecuencia

de noche soñaba

En los años que llevaba de vivir en México . . .

Past simple

As I left behind the outskirts of the village and reached the busy streets which led to the square, I felt my spirits rise.

Past continuous

A disagreement almost caused an outbreak of violence when overdue wages were being paid.

"Used to" past

I used to visit Madrid quite frequently.

"Would" past

At night I would dream.

Past perfect continuous

In all the years I had been living in Mexico . . .

The grammatical context is essential in order to establish the translation equivalents of some words. For example, Spanish students often have difficulty distinguishing *bored* and *boring*, *dead* and *killed* unless the *ser/estar* contrast is pointed out to them.

Juan <u>está</u> aburrido.	John is <u>bored</u>.
Juan <u>es</u> aburrido.	John is <u>boring</u>.
<u>Estaba</u> muerto a las nueve.	He was <u>dead</u> at nine.
<u>Fue</u> muerto a las nueve.	He was <u>killed</u> at nine.

The most common mistakes of verb tense made by students are those in which English makes a distinction between the present perfect and the past simple or requires a continuous tense. These points have to be revised in the translation class or referred to the language teacher.

b) Mood and Modals

The use of the English modals *(can, could, be able to, may, might, should, ought to, must and need)* is quite difficult for Spanish prose translators. Often, the choice of modal depends on subtle psychological factors. Extensive reading in English and student exchanges are the best ways of developing sensitivity to these factors. The Spanish subjunctive forces them to look for alternatives as it cannot be "transcoded" into English. In most cases, there are several possibilities open to them. Depending on the context, *hablara* might be translated by *might speak, would speak, speak, spoke, were speaking, to speak, speaking*.

c) Voice

The English passive is usually assimilated fairly well by the students, once they are aware of its importance in formal and technical texts. In the *directa* class they have already been warned against *el abuso del pasivo* in Spanish. Care must be taken with cohesion when using the other impersonal voices in English. Spanish students, like their English counterparts, sometimes begin with *one* and then change to *you* and back again, all in the same paragraph.

It is useful to emphasize alternatives to the passive for translating the Spanish reflexive.

La policia se ha lanzado a la búsqueda de . . .

The police have launched a search for . . .

Se fríe la cebolla, se añade el tomate. . .

Fry the onion and add the tomato . . .

Attention should be paid to the ambiguity inherent in verbs like *se engañan* and *se felicitaban*. The context should clarify whether the translations is *They deceive/congratulate themselves* or *They deceive/congratulate each other.*

Los más fuertes se atribuyen mutuamente la responsabilidad.

The strongest blame each other.

Bibliography: Verb phrases (tense, gerund and infinitive, mood and modals, voice, phrasal verbs, adverbs, word order)

Bolinger, D. (1971). *The Phrasal Verb in English.* Cambridge, MA: Harvard University Press.

Brinton, E., et al. (1981). *Translation Strategies.* London: Macmillan.

Fente Gómez, R. (1971). *Estilística del verbo en inglés y en español.* Madrid: SGEL.

Grady, M. (1970). *Syntax and Semantics of the English Verb Phrase.* The Hague: Mouton.

McCoard, R.W. (1978). *The English Perfect Tense: Choice and Pragmatic Differences.* Amsterdam: North Holland.

Molho, M. (1975). *Sistemática del verbo español.* Madrid: Gredos.

Mott, B., and M.P. García Hernández (1992). *La composición escrita en inglés.* Barcelona: Universitat de Barcelona. See pp. 103–53.

Navas Ruiz, R. (1977). *Ser y estar, el sistema atributivo del español.* Salamanca: Almar.

Newmeyer, F.J. (1975). *English Aspectual Verbs.* The Hague: Mouton.

Palmer, F.R. (1974). *The English Verb.* London: Longman.

——— (1979). *Modality and the English Verb.* London: Longman.

Quereda Rodríguez-Navarro, L. (1975). *Metodología de los verbos compuestos ingleses.* Madrid: SGEL.

Quirk, R., and S. Greenbaum (1980). *A University Grammar of English.* London: Longman. See pp. 26–58, 347–74.

Roldán, M. (1974). "Towards a semantic characterisation of *ser* and *estar.*" *Hispania* 57: 68–75.

Sroka, K.A. (1972). *The Syntax of English Phrasal Verbs.* The Hague: Mouton.

Stockwell, R., et al. (1965). *The Grammatical Structures of English and Spanish.* Chicago: University of Chicago Press. See pp. 105–217.

Vázquez Ayora, G. (1977). *Introducción a la traductología.* Washington, DC: Georgetown University Press.

7. ADVERBS

> Adverb placement in English is somewhat elastic; it is even more so in Spanish. Charting and comparing the patterns and contrasts is an extremely complex task, involving not only adverb, but verb and noun, classification. This task has not yet been accomplished and is not attempted in the present study. (Stockwell et al., 1965: 202)

Further research has been carried out on the use of adverbs in English since that was written, but the results show even greater complexity (e.g., Greenbaum, 1969). Certainly, the position of adverbs is difficult in prose translation, although Spanish and English do have many features in common.

Vázquez Ayora points out the dangers in *directa* of translating all the *-ly adverbs* in English by *-mente adverbs* in Spanish, because Spanish often prefers *prepositional phrases*. The opposite is not a serious problem in *inversa*.

Some basic guidelines can be of use to students. The difference should be understood between style or attitudinal disjuncts and manner adjuncts. The adverbial in the SLT should be classified accordingly so the distinction will be made between disjuncts and adjuncts. A general rule could be to put speech disjuncts at the beginning of the sentence.

Frankly, I was speaking under pressure.   (attitudinal disjunct)

I was speaking frankly under pressure.   (manner adjunct)

In written English (which cannot rely on prosodic elements to clarify ambiguity), adjuncts of manner in transitive sentences usually come after the subject-verb-object, while Spanish prefers to keep the adverb close to the verb.

Habla   bien   el español.   He speaks English well.
V   Adv.   O   S   V   O   Adv.

Another favourite position of the adverb in English, which is impossible in Spanish, is between the auxiliary and the verb (aux.-adverb-verb).

I've already been.   He's always eating.   I had completely forgotten.

Adverb-subject-verb in English is restricted to the verbs *come, go,* and *be,* and the adverbs *here, there, now, then.*

Here he comes.   There I was.

The negative precedes the verb in Spanish, but follows the auxiliary and the verb *to be* in English. Occasionally, the double negative in Spanish may cause problems.

No le dije nada.   I didn't tell him anything.

Some of the more mobile adverbs should be discussed in detail when problems arise in a translation as should subject-verb inversion after a negative or limiting adverb.

Only is often misplaced. The rule is that *only* should be placed near to the word it qualifies.

> He was <u>only</u> joking.   <u>Only</u> he was joking.
>
> At the beginning of a sentence inversion is necessary.
>
> <u>Only</u> at this stage could man . . .

Not only . . . but also has to be used with care. If there is one verb followed by two dependent clauses, *not only* follows the verb, but if there are two verbs *not only* must precede the first verb. In the second example, below, the word order should be *not only represent*.

> The concept of stimulus control *replaces* the notion of referent with respect *not only* to responses which occur in isolation . . . but also to those complex responses called sentences. (B.F. Skinner, *About Behaviourism,* quoted in Duff, 1981: 69; emphasis in Duff)

> The three categories of human sounds—noise, music and speech—*represent not only* spheres of differentiation in our perception of sonic events but also point to different groups of specialists who deal with unique aspects of the world of sound. ("Soundscapes," *UNESCO Courier,* 1976, quoted in Duff, 1981: 69; emphasis in Duff)

The Spanish expressions *cada vez más* and *cuanto más* are usually translated by the comparative form of the adverb in English.

> iban espaciándose cad vez más.
>
> were getting less and less frequent.
>
> Cuanto más se ven empujados . . . más arriesgan.
>
> The more they feel under pressure . . . the more they are willing to risk.

As can be seen from the length of this section, the subject is very complex and has to be studied in the context of the sentence as a whole.

Bibliography: Adverbs

Duff, A. (1981). *The Third Language.* London: Pergamon. See pp. 69–74.

Foster, B. (1970). *The Changing English Language.* Harmondsworth: Penguin.

Greenbaum, S. (1969). *Studies in Adverbial Usage.* London: Longman.

——— (1970). *Verb Intensifier Collocations in English: An Experimental Approach.* The Hague: Mouton.

Mott, B., and M.P. García Fernández (1992). *La composición escrita en inglés.* Barcelona: Universitat de Barcelona. See pp. 157–66.

Schibsbye, K. (1970). *A Modern English Grammar.* Oxford: Oxford University Press.

Stannard Allen, W. (1974). *Living English Structure.* London: Longman.

Vázquez Ayora, G. (1977). *Introducción a la traductología.* Washington, DC: Georgetown University Press.

8. CONJUNCTIONS

If a text is conceived as a map that represents the cognitive concepts, or world vision, of the writer, conjunctions, connectors, or link words can be seen as signposts that signal the way the writer wants the reader to relate what is said to what has been said before and to what is going to be said. Correct meaning and emphasis depend not only on word order, but also on balance, and this balance is to a great extent determined by conjunctions. Textual cohesion is reinforced by conjunctions.

Conjunctions reflect the rhetorical purpose of the writer and help the reader to interpret the text. Argument lines often follow different patterns in Spanish and English. English texts tend to use more argumentative conjunctions than Spanish texts, that is, there are more sign posts in English to indicate the direction of the text. There are no fixed rules for the position of conjunctions in the sentence. However, in English texts the signposts tend to be more visible. For example, conjunctions in initial position are more frequent in English than in Spanish (see Teaching Unit 28).

Bibliography: Conjunctions (connectors of time, place, logic, enumeration, addition, transition, summation, apposition, inference, reformulation, contrast, concession, co-ordination, subordination, ellipses)

Duff, A. (1981). *The Third Language*. London: Pergamon. See pp. 69–74.

García Yebra, V. (1983). *En torno a la traducción*. Madrid: Gredos. See pp. 44, 121–22.

Gleitman, L.R. (1965). "Coordinating Conjunctions in English." *Language* 41: 260–93.

Lakoff, R. (1971). "If's, And's and But's about Conjunctions." In C. Filmore and D.T. Langendoen, *Studies in Linguistic Semantics*. New York: Holt, Rinehart and Winston. See pp. 115–50.

Mott, B., and M.P. García Fernández (1992). *La composición escrita en inglés*. Barcelona: Universitat de Barcelona. See pp. 30–7.

Osgood, C.E. (1979). "From Yang and Yin to and and but." *Language* 49 (2): 380–412.

Quirk, R., and S. Greenbaum (1980). *A University Grammar of English*. London: Longman. See pp. 246–94.

Sinclair, J., et al. (1980). *Skills for Learning: Development*. London: Nelson.

9. SENTENCES AND PUNCTUATION

Many of the problems of word order in the sentence have been discussed in preceding sections. Word order is more rigid in English than in Spanish. The English preference for the subject-verb-object sequence makes it difficult to translate Spanish inverted word order to mark emphasis at the beginning of the sentence.

> No puede dejar de causar desasosiego la lectura de las razones . . .
>
> Más allá de los argumentos concretos . . .
>
> Precisamente por la importancia decisiva que . . .
>
> Lo más probable era . . .
>
> Basta leer . . .
>
> (*El País*, 16 Apr. 1987)

Emphasis at the beginning of the sentence in English can be marked by using *that* followed by inverted word order. However the structure is rather archaic and cannot be used too frequently.

> That Kipling's work is often flawed no admirer would deny, and Wilson's conclusion is that the flaw is due to fear of self-knowledge. (*The Listener*, 17 Nov. 1977)

The relater *que* is compulsory in Spanish whereas in English *that* is often omitted. If it is never omitted, the resulting style is unwieldy in English. English texts that are translations tend to maintain all the *thats*.

> Espero que venga.   I hope (that) he comes.

Punctuation rules in the two languages also differ. English is more generous with commas and prefers a period instead of a colon or a semi-colon, so sentences are usually longer in Spanish. This is due to the Spanish tendency toward articulation and subordination, as opposed to that of English toward juxtaposition and co-ordination.

> Lean el texto antes de traducirlo.   Read the text and translate it.

In Spanish, it is very common to begin a sentence or follow a semi-colon with *y* or *pero*. In English, *and* or *but* are not normally used in initial position if the text is formal.

Un tercer paso lo constituye la integración de la producción agrícola y artesana en la economía socialista, *a través de* la formación de cooperativas que resuelvan o por lo menos amortigüen la falta de economías de escala en sectores tan fragmentados; *y que al propio tiempo* vayan imprimiendo una mentalidad de organización *y* planeamiento, y solidaridad con los demás sectores del sistema.

The third stage is to integrate agricultural and craft production into the socialist economy. *This is achieved* in these greatly fragmented sectors by forming co-operatives that, at least in part, make up for the absence of economies of scale. *At the same time,* these co-operatives help to create a receptive attitude toward organization and planning, *as well as* solidarity with other sectors of the economy.

Tamames (1980)

The rules for the use of capital letters are different in Spanish and English, but the differences are quite straightforward and do not cause undue interference. More capitals are used in English, for example, days of the week, months of the year, titles and headlines.

Bibliography: Sentences (focus, theme, emphasis)

Contreras, H. (1976). *A Theory of Word Order with Special Reference to Spanish*. Amsterdam: North Holland.

Danes, F. (ed.) (1974). *Papers on Functional Sentence Perspective*. The Hague: Mouton.

Firbas, J. (1966). "Non-thematic Subjects in Contemporary English." *Travaux linguistiques de Prague* 2: 239–56.

Halliday, M.A.K. (1967, 1968). "Notes on Transitivity and Theme in English." *Journal of linguistics* 3: 37–81, 199–244; 4: 179–215.

Huddleston, R.D. (1971). *The Sentence in Written English: A Syntactic Study Based on an Analysis of Scientific Texts*. Cambridge: Cambridge University Press.

Hudson, R.A. (1971). *English Complex Sentences*. Amsterdam: North Holland.

Mott, B., and M.P. García Fernández (1992). *La composición escrita en inglés*. Barcelona: Universitat de Barcelona. See pp. 195–222.

Palková, Z., and B. Palek (1977). "Functional Sentence Perspective and Text Linguistics." In W.U. Dressler (ed.), *Current Trends in Text Linguistics*. Berlin: De Gruyber.

Quirk, R., and S. Greenbaum (1980). *A University Grammar of English*. London: Longman. See pp. 166–206, 309–46, 406–29.

Bibliography: Composition Norms (punctuation, capital letters, etc.)

Butler, P. (ed.) (1991). *The Economist Style Guide*. London: The Economist Books.

Cary, C.V. (1977). *Mind the Stop!* Harmondsworth: Penguin.

Delisle, J. (1980). *L'Analyse du discours comme méthode de traduction*. Ottawa: University of Ottawa Press.

Duff, A. (1981). *The Third Language*. Oxford: Pergamon.

Mott, B., and M.P. García Fernández (1992). *La composición escrita en inglés*. Barcelona: Universitat de Barcelona. See pp. 225–40.

Quirk, R., and S. Greenbaum (1980). *A University Grammar of English*. London: Longman. See app. 2: 11, app. 3: 2, 6, apps. 4–6.

Swan, M. (1980). *Practical English Usage*. Oxford: Oxford University Press.

10. PROSE

Certain contrastive generalizations have been made about Spanish and English prose (e.g., Vázquez Ayora, 1977; García Yebra, 1983). Some of these differences have already been mentioned and others require a more profound study than is possible here. The main ones are:

ENGLISH	SPANISH
nominal predominance	verbal predominance
synthesis	analysis
visual presentation	abstract presentation
repetition	variation

Different languages express reality differently, and this may affect the organization of paragraphs, techniques of description, persuasion, negation, and so on. However, depending on the *skopos* of the translation, there are limits to the extent to which a translator can adjust the SLT to the TL's preferences.

> For the conference translator there is a further and very significant reason for keeping the original order whenever possible. Documents are frequently discussed sentence by sentence. It may be impossible to locate a phrase or passage if it has been turned upside down in the translation. (Fuller, 1973: 66)

It is the translator's duty to transmit the meaning of the SLT. Therefore, if confusion of reference occurs easily in English through lack of gender case endings, the translator should be reconciled to using repetition and redesignation techniques. For example, the use of the deictic *this* is based on the visual presentation of English.

The fascination of translating and teaching translating is that translation reflects so many of the imponderables about thought, language, society, and culture. There is no such thing as a final, authorized translation. Each generation has to write its own history books and its own translations. However, it is difficult to disagree with Edmond Becke's conclusions in his preface to the translation of Erasmus's *Colloquia* in 1519.

> For some heretofor submytting themself to servytude, have lytle respect to the observance of the thyng which in translatyng is of all other most necessary and requisite, that is to saye, to render the sense and the very meanyng of the author, not so religiously addicte to translate worde for worde for so the sense of the author is sometimes corrupted and depraved, and neyther the grace of one tongue nor yet of the other is truly observed or aptlie expressed. (Quoted in Kelly, 1979: 45–6)

Bibliography: Paragraph (organization, repetition, redesignation, anaphoric and cataphoric reference)

Chernov, G.V. (1980). "Verbal Redundancy as a Key to Reliable Comprehension of a Verbal Message (Objective and Subjective Factors)." In Barbizet et al., *Actes du Colloque international et multidisciplinaire sur la compréhension du langage*. Paris: Didier.

Clark, E.V. (1977). "From Gesture to Word: On the Natural History of Deixis and Language Acquisition." In J.S. Bruner and A. Garton (eds.), *Human Growth and Development*. London: Oxford University Press.

Crothers, E.J. (1979). *Paragraph Structure Inference*. Norwood: Ablex.

Delisle, J. (1980). *L'Analyse du discours comme méthode de traduction*. Ottawa: University of Ottawa Press. See pp. 188–223.

Duff, A. (1981). *The Third Language*. London: Pergamon. See pp. 42–74.

Halliday, M.A.K., and R. Hasan (1976). *Coherence in English*. London: Longman.

Russell, P. (1981). "The importance of précis writing in a translator training program." In J. Delisle (ed.), *L'Enseignement de l'interprétation et de la traduction*. Ottawa: University of Ottawa Press.

Bibliography: Prose (nominal predominance/verbal predominance, synthesis/analysis, visual/abstract presentation, repetition/variation)

Anderson, J.R., and R. Hastie (1974). "Individuation and Reference in Memory: Proper Names and Definite Descriptions." *Cognitive Psychology* 6 (4).

Crystal, D., and D. Davy (1983). *Investigating English Style*. London: Longman.

Dressler, W.U. (ed.). *Current Trends in Textlinguistics*. Berlin: De Gruyber.

Flamand, J. (1981). "Place de la rédaction dans un programme de formation de traducteurs professionnels." In J. Delisle (ed.), *L'Enseignement de l'interprétation et de la traduction*. Ottawa: University of Ottawa Press. See pp. 249–54.

Fowler, R. (1977). "Cohesive, Progressive and Localizing Aspects of Text Structures." In T.A. van Dijk, *Grammars and Descriptions*. Berlin: De Gräter. See pp. 61–84.

Lee, D. (1992). *Competing Discourses: Perspectives and Ideology in Language*. London and New York: Longman.

Toolan, M. (ed.) (1992). *Language, Text and Context*. London: Routledge.

The paper used in this publication meets the minimum requirements
of American National Standard for Information Sciences -
Permanence of Paper for Printed Library Materials, ANSI Z39.48-1992.

• Cap-Saint-Ignace
• Sainte-Marie (Beauce)
Québec, Canada
1996

«L'IMPRIMEUR»